WESTERN WARFARE, 1775–1882

Western Warfare, 1775–1882

Jeremy Black

Indiana University Press
Bloomington & Indianapolis

This book is a publication of

Indiana University Press
601 North Morton Street
Bloomington, IN 4704-3793 USA

http://iupress.indiana.edu

Telephone orders   800-842-6796
Fax orders   812-855-7931
Orders by e-mail   iuporder@indiana.edu

Published simultaneously outside North America by Acumen Publishing Limited

Library of Congress Cataloging-in-Publication Data

Black, Jeremy.
    Western warfare, 1775–1882 / by Jeremy Black.
        p. cm.
    Includes bibliographical references and index.
        ISBN 0-253-33962-6 (cl : alk. paper) — ISBN 0-253-21472-6 (pa : alk. paper)
            1. Military art and science—History—19th century. 2. Military art and
    science—History—18th century. I. Title.

    U41 .B58 2001
    355'.009034—dc21   2001016871

1   2   3   4   5   06   05   04   03   02   01

Designed and typeset by Kate Williams, Abergavenny.
Printed and bound by Biddles Ltd., Guildford and King's Lynn.

For Robert Smith
A Friend and a Patron of Learning

Contents

Preface

This short book is an attempt to take forward my *European Warfare, 1660–1815* (1994). It reflects the features of the earlier book, specifically the focus on the global dimension and the importance of locating military capability and conflict within their political and social contexts. In addition, war is treated not only as a feature of international relations, but also with due weight devoted to civil conflict. In contrast to the earlier book, which placed an emphasis on continuities, the stress here is instead on change. This contributes to, and stems from, a wider view, seen for example in my *Eighteenth-Century Europe* (second edition, 1999), in which I stress a late onset for "modernity" and am less inclined than many others to emphasize the role, impact and consequences of earlier change.

In this book, European has been broadened to Western warfare, in order to give due weight to the importance of developments in the independent states that overthrew European imperial rule in the "New World", both in the USA and in the frequently overlooked, or at least underrated, warfare in Latin America. This has led to a degree of factual narrative, including naming of battles, that is necessary in order to underline the misleading nature of the "canonical" account of military history, with its focus on a relatively narrow range of conflicts and battles. There is an ethical issue – the need not to write out of history, by focusing elsewhere, the many who fought and suffered – but also a powerful intellectual reason for focusing on the weaknesses of the stereotypical account. Furthermore, this approach serves as a powerful reminder of how much has not been tackled in a subject that is frequently presented as, in some fashion, "done".

A closely related viewpoint promoted throughout the book is a caution against unitary models of military modernity; indeed a questioning of the idea of "modernity" itself. In addition, there are warnings against the technological determinism and linear conceptions of developments in military science that still characterize so much of military history, at least as written in the West.

In this study, Western warfare is seen not only in terms of conflict within the West, but also in conflicts that have involved Western peoples. The latter were largely responsible for the shift in power towards Western powers in this period. This shift took various forms. The driving back of the Turks in the Balkans was very different in its causes and consequences from European expansion in Australasia. The common theme was the ability of Western powers to deploy strength effectively. European rule in the Americas was overthrown by Europeans, not Native Americans (Amerindians), while throughout the nineteenth century European military imperialism continued generally to carry all before it in Asia and Africa. Furthermore, only a global perspective, even in this era of Western imperial dynamism, can provide a reliable assessment of what constitutes military capability.

I have been held to a tighter word limit than in *European Warfare, 1660–1815*. As a result, quotations, references and bibliography have been kept to a minimum, and, in light of the intended readership, material not written in English has been omitted. Unless otherwise stated, place of publication is London.

This book reflects the fruits of over two decades teaching military history. I am fortunate that successive generations of students have let me try out ideas on them. In addition, I benefited, while writing this book, from being invited to give papers at the Anglo–American Conference, the University of Illinois, the University of Virginia Summer School at Oxford, the United States Naval Postgraduate School at Monterey and the United States naval Department of Continuing Education at Annapolis and Washington. I would like to thank Steven Gerrard for commissioning the book and proving a supportive editor, Gerry Bryant and Bruce Vandervort for commenting on an earlier draft, John Beeler and Larry Sondhaus for their comments on the naval chapter, Ron Fritze for taking me to the battlefield of San Jacinto and Stan Carpenter for taking me to see those of Bull Run and Antietam.

Jeremy Black

Introduction

Modernity, change and revolution are all important issues and analytical devices in military history. The explanation of change is intertwined with the issue of military capability, for change is seen as providing an account of shifts in capability. Thus, the relationship between change and non-change is used to explain success and failure. A prime example is the argument that Westernization in military practice was the key to capability over the past half-millennium and that those states that failed to Westernize were likely to fail. Military capability, more than many other organized human activity, can be a life or death issue for a state, so gaining a military edge over or at least keeping up with rivals (i.e. changing) can be seen as absolutely critical. Military capability entails arms, training, size of forces, logistical infrastructure, tactical doctrine, morale, and so on. There is also economic potential (and realization), geographical advantages, administrative efficiency and integrity, governmental quality and the measure of support it has in the country, and so on. War tests the resilience and cohesion of entire societies. Relative, rather than absolute, capability is the key factor in conflict, and this was set by the task demanded of the military. Thus, for example, after 1815 the British army was largely designed to hold down an overseas empire, while the Prussians confined themselves to the prospect of war in Europe.

A narrative of change dominates military history, particularly, but not exclusively, as the present day is approached. This is due both to a perception that the tempo and impact of military change increased, and to the weight of scholarly attention on more recent military history. This ensures that, within a general narrative of change, there is debate about which particular changes were most important, about why they were crucial, and about their interrelationship.

Much of this book is devoted to just such a discussion, but it is important to put changes in their context. It is also necessary to note that there was no simple dichotomy of change and continuity, and no inevitable relationship between a failure to adopt particular changes and defeat. Both of these points emerge more clearly if a global dimension is adopted. Such an approach by an individual scholar faces many difficulties, not least problems of linguistic limitations, but rather than, therefore, assuming that a book on Western warfare can assert its superiority and neglect the rest of the world, this study is, in part, based on the idea that an assessment of capability requires the wider context. This is doubly so because much of the importance of Western warfare in world history rests on its role in facilitating Western imperialism.

The notion of modernity is possibly ambiguous. It can entail the judgement of who was the most up-to-date state, or leader of change as believed at the time (for example the French in 1763–1815 or the Germans in 1866–1914), or, as in this book, can focus on historians identifying aspects of warfare and armed forces in the past that can be proposed as marking the path to the modern world.

Any period of study invites the accusation of artificiality. Yet there is a coherence in this period. It centres on the French Revolutionary and Napoleonic Wars. The strength and success of the French military system in part reflected French military developments in the late eighteenth century. Furthermore, the French Revolutionary Wars can be discussed in relation to the War of American Independence, which broke out in 1775.

The experience and image of the Napoleonic Wars dominated subsequent Western military history. Aside from the continuing impact of military practices and doctrines developed during these wars, and the particular role of veterans, there was also a lasting attention created thanks to their analysis by the foremost military theorists of the century, Jomini and Clausewitz. The latter, for example, wrote a study of Napoleon I's invasion of Russia in 1812. Furthermore, Moltke, the architect of successive Prussian successes in 1864–71, sought to emulate Napoleon's combination of mobility and firepower, and his strategy of fixing opponents' forces and then enveloping them. Moltke himself drew on the improvements in Prussian military organization created in response to defeat by Napoleon in 1806, especially the creation by Gerhard von Scharnhorst of a General Staff system.[1] This proved superior to Napoleon's reliance on his own brilliance and his failure to develop a good working staff system that could act not only as a substitute for the strengths and deficiencies of an individual but also provide a method of command and control that was superior to his own. Scharnhorst's system looked forward to that used by Moltke and by subsequent emulators of Prussian success.

In contrast, the influence of Napoleon and, more generally, a reluctance to accept the disciplines of general staff control and a preference for traditional methods of control, ensured that most other armies failed to develop a comparable system in this period. The French under Napoleon III (President 1848–52 and then Emperor 1852–70) were especially conspicuous in this respect. This failure helped ensure both repeated failures to make effective operational use of forces in the wars of the years 1854–71 and, in particular, deficiencies in planning and a lack of success in getting army corps to cooperate to a strategic end, as with the French in 1870, and a failure on the battlefield to maintain control over the development of the battle, as with the French at Solferino in 1859.

The principal victors over Napoleon I were Britain and Russia. Consideration of their military activity also helps provide continuity. Both were involved in conflict with non-Western powers, and the period of this study closes shortly after a Russian advance to within six miles of Constantinople in 1878 that altered power relations in the Balkans, and after the British had defeated both the Zulus (1879) and Egypt (1882), two of the dynamic non-Western forces of the century. Mention of these conflicts is deliberately stressed in order to emphasize the variety of Western warfare and the danger of assuming that any one model prevailed, or would serve. The Russians in Asia, the British in India and the French in Africa all demonstrated great flexibility in successfully adapting to campaign in very different terrain and climate against opponents with very different military traditions to those found in Europe.

This study throws doubt on the notion of a linear continuum of "progress" towards warfare in the modern world. Instead, a more complex dynamic is proposed. This stresses the imbalance of previous treatment of wars in this period, which largely ignores important cases of warfare either in terms of location (Latin America) or type (insurgency and counterinsurgency).

CHAPTER ONE

Western Warfare in its Global Context, 1775–1815

In the 40 years before 1775, much extra-European military activity by the Western powers had been at the expense of other Western powers, rather than of non-Western powers. This was particularly so in North America and West Africa, but also true to a considerable extent in India, although the important British conquest of Bengal had been against the Indians and dated from 1757 to 1765. In one part of the world, in this period, there had even been an important defeat for the Europeans. The Austrians had been unsuccessful in their war with Turkey in 1737–39 and had had to cede back to Turkey, Belgrade, northern Serbia and Little (Western) Wallachia, all of which had been gained in 1718. When combined with the Russian return to Persia in 1732 of lands occupied in 1723, this suggested that far from there being a remorseless process of Western advance, it had in fact come up against barriers, if only temporarily. This could be taken further with the failure to revise the Treaty of Nerchinsk of 1689, by which Russia had accepted its exclusion by China from the Amur Valley.

Such an arrival at limits did not preclude further advances at the expense of less powerful peoples, as with the Russian advance into the Aleutian Isles, but it appeared to suggest that the West did not necessarily always have an unbeatable advantage on land over powerful non-Western states, although failing ambition (for whatever reason) might also have played a part. This apparently excluded European powers for a time from the bulk of south-west, south and east Asia, areas that contained much of the world's population and economic activity.

In 1775–1815, the pace of Western expansion revived, although far from evenly. The most important gains were made by the Russians, the British and the Americans. Russia had been successful at the expense of the Turks in 1768–74 and again in the war of 1787–92. The Turks had hoped to challenge Russia's occupation of the Crimea in 1783, and, by declaring war, gained the

1

initiative, but a Turkish force that landed near Kinburn was defeated after hard fighting. In 1788, the Russians moved on to the attack, focusing on the powerful fortress of Ochakov, which overlooked the entrance to the Bug and the Dnieper. Catherine II's favourite and former lover, Prince Gregory Potemkin, led the besieging army, and bitter naval engagements took place offshore as the Russians struggled to create an effective blockade. After lengthy bombardment, Ochakov was successfully stormed. In 1789, the main Russian army under Potemkin advanced to the Dniester; in 1790 the forts in the Danube delta, such as Izmail, were captured; and in 1791 the Russians advanced south of the Danube. The Turks accepted terms that left Russia firmly established on the Black Sea, a goal that had eluded Peter the Great.

When war was resumed in 1806–12, the deficiencies of the Russian army, which included inadequately developed support services, did not prevent it from being an effective force. In 1806–12, the Russians occupied Moldavia and Wallachia, operated south of the Danube and, as a result of Kutuzov's victory at Ruschuk (4 July 1811), gained Bessarabia at the Treaty of Bucharest. Similarly, the Austrians developed tactical formations to counter Turkish cavalry superiority, especially infantry squares arranged in supporting checkerboard pattern, helping them to defeat the Turks in 1789.

Superior resources, skilful generalship, and firepower also helped give Russia victory against a very different kind of opponent, the Nogais of the Kuban, to the east of the Black Sea. When, in 1783, they resisted incorporation into the expanding Russian state, 3,000 were killed at the battle of Urai-Ilgasi, in August, by a small, disciplined force under Count Alexander Suvorov; and, on 2 October, in another battle at the confluence of the Kuban and the River Laba, Suvorov again inflicted heavy casualties. The Russians also made gains in the Caucasus. In 1783, Erekle II, ruler of Kart'li-Kakhet'I, the principal Georgian state, placed himself under Russian protection, and Russian troops entered Tiblisi. In 1784, a military road through the Dariel Pass, linking Russia and eastern Georgia, was completed. However, the Russians were initially unable to maintain their presence in Georgia; war with Turkey led to the withdrawal of Russian troops in 1787, and Catherine II refused to send them back in 1791 when Erekle was threatened by Persian attack. In 1795, Persian cavalry overran Georgia and sacked Tiblisi. Nevertheless, the Russians captured Derbent in 1796 and annexed much of Georgia in 1801. A Georgian revolt in 1812 was unsuccessful.

The towns of the Caucasus provided centres of control, but the ability of Western forces to force battle on nomadic and semi-nomadic peoples, such as the Nogais, was not always sufficient to guarantee their defeat, for such peoples tended only to risk battle when they had the advantage, and they frequently ambushed extended Russian columns. In Alaska, the Russians found the Tlingits tenacious foes, partly because they had acquired firearms from American and British traders and partly because in this situation the Russians derived little advantage from the naval power they had earlier used in the Aleutian Isles. The European imperial threat was often greatest to non-Western states and peoples when they were vulnerable to superior Western naval power. In 1802, the Tlingits destroyed the Russian base of New Archangel on Sitka.

In the Far East, there was no European military pressure on China, Japan or Siam in the eighteenth century, which represented a total failure to follow up earlier bold, and unrealistic, plans of conquest. Major wars, such as that between Burma and Siam in the 1780s, were waged without reference to European powers. In addition, assertive Asian powers pressed on Western interests; for example, the Bugis besieged Dutch-held Malacca in 1784, and Haidar Ali and Tipu, successive Sultans of Mysore, threatened British interests in southern India from the 1760s to the 1780s.

However, there were areas of Western advance, as well as a willingness to turn to Westerners for military expertise in struggles between non-Western powers. In addition, attacks by assertive Asian powers were less successful than in the past. For example, although concern over the contrast between their weak defences in Malacca and the military strength of the Bugis helped encourage the Dutch to adopt a hesitant role in the Malay world, the siege of Malacca was repelled in 1784.

In India, the British experienced serious checks from the Marathas of Maharastra (West India), as well as from Mysore. In 1778, the British sent an army from Bombay towards the Maratha capital. It was not up to the task, and, in the difficult terrain of the Ghats, the British failed to master the crucial problems of mobility, logistics and terrain, advancing less than a mile a day. When they turned back, they were surrounded by a far larger and more mobile Maratha force. On 12 January 1779, the British commander, Lieutenant-Colonel William Cockburn, recorded, "we remained under a severe cannonade, having the whole flower of the Maratha horse ready to charge whenever an opportunity offered, but our well served artillery and the steadiness of the infantry prevented them". By the following night, however, the army was badly affected by failing morale; desertions sapped its strength and ammunition supplies were falling. The British signed a convention at Wagdaon, agreeing to withdraw to Bombay. A well trained force could only achieve so much, especially if on difficult terrain in the face of considerably more numerous opponents and if reconnaissance was inadequate.

Mysore also had effective light cavalry, and Mysore armies defeated British forces in 1780 and 1782. The British advance on Seringapatam, the Mysore capital, in 1791 failed for different reasons. Having reached the city, defeating a Mysore force outside it, the British found themselves short of supplies, in part because of an epidemic among the bullocks that supplied transport, and, with the monsoon about to break, before a strongly fortified position. They fell back in disorder, abandoning many of their cannon.

Individual successes and failures had different causes, but the overall lesson was that Indian military systems were not foredoomed to failure. The light cavalry of Britain's opponents could best be thwarted only if the British recruited local allies. This put a premium on the political skill of British leaders, on the financial resources of Britain's Indian possessions, and also on the factors encouraging Indian rulers to help Britain. Thus the 1792 and 1799 advances on Seringapatam were more successful than that of 1791 largely because local allies had been secured. The failure of Hyderabad, Mysore and the Marathas to make common cause against the British was crucial.[1]

Politics were also involved in the cohesion of opposing states. Like China, the European powers had great strength as a result of the continuity of administrative organization and government identity. Opponents who were largely dependent on the leadership of a single individual were weaker. This was a problem for Mysore, while the Marathas were greatly weakened by periods of civil war that in general reflected disputed successions.[2] There was a considerable shift in power from the centre to the peripheral Maratha states, and this eventually made the British task easier because it hindered cooperation between their opponents.

In 1803, the British waged war with the Marathas in a very different fashion than in 1778–79. A far larger force was deployed: 60,000 men on a number of fronts. The commander in the Deccan was General Arthur Wellesley, later Duke of Wellington, a master of methodical yet rapid warfare, who understood the importance of logistics without allowing them to preclude mobility. Wellesley was able to achieve what had eluded his predecessors in the American War of Independence; the decisive victory. At the battle of Assaye on 23 September 1803, Wellesley, with 4,500 men, 17 guns and 5,000 unreliable Indian cavalry, successfully confronted 30,000 cavalry, 10,000 infantry trained by French officers, and over 100 well served and laid cannon, a disparity greater than that faced by Napoleon in his major battles.

The British infantry had to advance through the heavy fire of the Maratha artillery and the battle was a confused and hard-fought one in which successive British infantry and cavalry attacks eventually forced their opponents to retreat. At Assaye, Wellesley demonstrated the speedy attack he believed essential for campaigning in India.[3] This compensated for his numerical inferiority and for poor intelligence about the location of the Maratha forces. Wellesley's success in the battle owed much to bayonet charges, scarcely conforming to the standard image of Western armies gunning down masses of non-European troops relying on cold steel.[4] Casualties accounted for over a quarter of the British force, but, crucially, the fearsome Maratha cannon were captured.

There were fewer British losses in their victory at Argaon (Argaum) on 29 November, but, again, the Maratha artillery, although it opened fire at too great a range, was effective and checked the first British attack. Wellesley eventually succeeded with a second attack supported by light artillery. This victory, and Wellesley's continued ability to take the initiative and to sustain the range and mobility of his force, were instrumental in leading Dowlut Rao

Sindia, Maharaja of Gwalior, to accept peace terms on 30 December 1803. The weak command structure and lack of money of the Marathas had disrupted operations, and the absence of regular pay had destroyed discipline and control.[5]

Further north, the British were commanded by General Gerard Lake, who defeated the Marathas outside Delhi on 11 September 1803, at Laswari on 1 November 1803, and at Farruckhabad on 17 November 1804. Lake was also a firm believer in mobility because only thus could the British hope to counter the Maratha cavalry and impose themselves on such a large area. Lake benefited from the Experimental Brigade of Horse Artillery, created by the Bengal Army in 1800, a step which reflected the influence of the formation of the Royal Horse Company in the British Army in 1793.

Despite their increasing flexibility, the British had a number of serious setbacks. Colonel William Monson lost his guns when forced to retreat in July–August 1804, in the face of the vastly larger cavalry force of Jeswunt Rao Holkar, Maharaja of Indore, a key Maratha leader.[6] The following year, Lake lost heavily in four unsuccessful attempts to storm Bháratpur. As at Assaye, the British were outgunned. Lake had only four 18-pounders and insufficient ammunition and was unable both to neutralize the defensive fire and blow the gates in, as he had done at Aligarh the previous year. The need to combine sufficient firepower to offset opposing cannon and make an impact on fortifications, and at the same time to achieve mobility, was a serious command and organization problem. Nevertheless, defeated at Farruckhabad, and eventually driven to take refuge in the Punjab, Holkar finally sought peace and a treaty was signed in January 1806.[7]

Westernization was both a challenge and an opportunity for the British in India. It was a challenge, because the already formidable military difficulties presented in particular by Indian light cavalry were accentuated by the well trained artillery and infantry units that Indian states in large part owed to European advisors. European-style infantry forces were created by, for example, the Nizam of Hyderabad, Tipu Sultan of Mysore and the Marathas. French experts taught Indians to cast cannon in the French style and also played a role in local fortification techniques. Thus, Benoît de Boigne, commander of a corps for the Maratha leader Sindhia, constructed French-style fortifications at Aligarh east of Delhi, after 1788. French engineers also helped fortify Seringapatam, and other Mysore fortresses.[8] This was part of the history of Western warfare in this period, for its global impact was not simply achieved by the direct action of Western forces.

Westernization was also an opportunity, because the fusion of European training and Indian manpower was to be a basis of British military power in the nineteenth century, helping in the creation of a South Asian imperial state of hitherto unprecedented range. The mostly native East India Company army was 18,200 strong in 1763 and numbered 154,000 in 1805. This army was supported by the resources of the fertile areas that were under British control: Bengal and the Carnatic. Their banking networks were also crucial, because they helped the British to tap resources outside the combat areas.

The resulting army was capable by the 1800s not only of defeating the most powerful of Indian forces, but also of acting as a maritime imperial force in the Indian Ocean in a way that no previous Indian state had managed. The nearest comparison was with the Chinese amphibious expeditions of the early fifteenth century, but these had not been sustained. During the Napoleonic Wars, expeditions were also sent from India to Egypt, Ceylon (Sri Lanka), Mauritius, the Persian Gulf and the East Indies in order to fight both Western and non-Western opponents.

The former involved attacks on Western bases, as well as an attempt to resist French pressure on Egypt. About 3,000 sepoys served in the successful attack on Mauritius in 1810. The following year, 5,770 Indian as well as 5,344 British troops took Batavia, the leading Dutch position in the East Indies. The British landed on 4 August and the Dutch governor rapidly abandoned vulnerable Batavia in order to concentrate on holding the well fortified lines of Cornelis, but they fell on 28 August after they had been out-flanked and attacked from the rear. After another defeat at Samarang on 8 September, the Dutch surrendered. This was a fast-tempo war comparable to that of Napoleon in Europe. British forces from India were also deployed against non-Western opponents. In the Kandyan War of 1803, the British were thwarted in Ceylon by guerrilla attacks, logistical problems, inhospitable terrain and disease. The garrison in Kandy was obliged to surrender in June and was then massacred on its retreat to the coast; imperial retreats were always hazardous. In 1815, however, 900 British and 1,800 Indian troops conquered the kingdom of Kandy in the interior of Ceylon as a result of concerted operations by independently moving columns. Three years earlier, British forces had deposed the Sultan of Palembang on Sumatra and stormed the Sultan of Yogyakarta's *kraton* (royal residence), despite its far larger garrison and numerous cannon. Pangeran Arya Panular, a Sumatran whose diary recorded the assault, was impressed by the British combination of discipline, bravery and determination.[9]

The use of Indian military resources was very important as it enabled the British to overcome the demographic imbalance that affected European forces in South and East Asia and, albeit to a lesser extent, Africa. As such, the British role was not too dissimilar to earlier empire builders in India from central Asia.[10] However, the British were less willing than earlier conquerors to absorb Indian political and military values and more determined to deploy Indian resources in accordance with a wide ranging strategy. The British also benefited from ambitious, determined and skilful leadership, able generalship and a high degree of military preparedness in a period of near-continual conflict. The increase in British commitments in South Asia led to an expansion in the military there and to greater willingness to consider a resort to force to push boundaries further.

This led to a renewed bout of activity in 1814–18. War was declared against the Gurkhas of Nepal in 1814. Initial failures in 1814–15 owed much to poor British generalship, unfamiliarity with mountain warfare and the Gurkha combination of defensive positions, especially hill forts and stockades, with attacks on British detachments. British success was far from inevitable, but victories at Almora (1815), Malaun (1815), and Makwanpur (1816) eventually brought the conflict to a successful conclusion in March 1816. The victories owed much to the effective use of bayonet attacks, but also reflected luck, the skill of some commanders, and the failure of the Marathas and Sikhs to support the Gurkhas.[11]

The Marathas were more rapidly crushed in 1817–18, thanks to victories at Kirkoe, Sitabaldi, Mahidpur, Koregaon and Satara. At Mahidpur (21 December 1817), the British infantry advanced under heavy fire from the Maratha artillery. The Maratha infantry mostly retreated, but the gunners continued to fire until bayoneted beside their cannon. The infantry advance was supported by a cavalry attack before which the Marathas retreated, the British horse being supported by 3,000 Mysore cavalry. The subsequent treaties led to major acquisitions of territory, and the remaining Maratha leaders had to accept treaties that brought them under British protection.

These victories brought to an end the challenge posed by one of the most dynamic elements in Indian society. The Marathas had successively resisted and eventually supplanted the Mughals, but could not do the same to the British. Between 1799 and 1818, Mysore, Nepal and the Marathas had all been humbled. There still remained other formidable powers in South Asia, especially Burma (Myanmar) and the Sikhs. However, more of India was now under a greater degree of British power than hitherto, and this provided the British with a secure reservoir of soldiers, not least because they had come to dominate the market for military manpower.[12]

At the same time, the pace of Western expansion in the New World had increased, as the newly independent United States of America pushed westward far more strongly and continuously than the colonial powers had done. Furthermore, unlike in India, expansion was far more closely linked with a growing Western population and with a major extension of the cultivated area. Initially, the Native Americans had held their own during the American War of Independence. Many had supported the British, and they had not been defeated or outfought; in fact, the frontier of European settlement had been pressed hard, particularly in New York and Pennsylvania in 1778. The Native Americans maintained the initiative at the close of the war, defeating the Patriots in Kentucky and on the shores of Lake Erie in 1782. Patriot expeditions, such as John Sullivan's campaign against the Iroquois in 1779, were often unsuccessful, in Sullivan's case in large part because of the logistical problems facing expeditions into the interior, especially a lack of transport. Nevertheless, thanks to careful reconnaissance, Sullivan's army was able to avoid ambush.

The Native forces were militarily sophisticated, but the cumulative pressure of sustained conflict damaged Native society and disrupted their economies. In 1779, Sullivan destroyed many villages and 160,000 bushels of corn, causing much suffering.[13] Furthermore, the lessening of British support after American independence left Native Americans more vulnerable when the pace and pressure of settlement accelerated. The importance of foreign support was shown in 1786 when the Creeks of Alabama and Mississippi used arms supplied by Spanish governors to check the Americans' westward advance from Georgia. However, in 1795, Spain accepted the thirty-first parallel as the northern border of West Florida, opening the way for American penetration into the lands of the south-eastern tribes.

Despite some successes, including the victory of the Miamis under Little Turtle on the Maumee river in western Ohio (18–22 October 1790) and the defeat of Arthur St. Clair's army on the Wabash river in Ohio (4 November 1791), the Native Americans found it difficult to cope with the casualties and consequences of defeat. The Native position in the "Old Northwest", the lands south of the Great Lakes, was broken by Anthony Wayne's victory at the battle of Fallen Timbers on 20 August 1794, a victory that allowed expansion into the region. An American bayonet charge played a crucial role in this victory. The Natives were malnourished and, in part, taken by surprise, and they were also affected by a withdrawal of British support.[14]

The American advance was consolidated by their victories in the 1810s over tribes with close ties to the British in Canada: the Shawnees at Tippecanoe on 7 November 1811 and at the battle of the Thames (near London, Ontario) on 5 October 1813.[15] Mounted riflemen played a major role in the American victory. Further south, the Creeks were attacked in 1813 and defeated at Tallasahatchee (3 November) and Talladega (9 November). The following year, Andrew Jackson attacked the centres of Creek power and stormed their fortified camp at Horseshoe Bend (27 March).

North of Mexico, the Spaniards faced pressure from tribes on the Great Plains moving south, especially the Comanches and the Utes. Well mounted and armed with Western firearms, tribes such as the Apaches were able to thwart the Spanish expedition sent against them in 1775. The following year, there were only 1,900 Spanish troops to defend a 1,800 mile frontier of Spanish North America. A successful Spanish attack on the Comanches in 1779 was followed by treaties with them in 1785–86; peace was now the Spanish goal and they used goods and trade to lure the Native Americans into their way of thinking. Once they were allied with the Comanches, the Spaniards pressed the Apaches hard; in the 1790s they persuaded many of them to settle on "peace establishments", the precursors of the later reservations. Further west, in 1781 the successful Yuma rebellion thwarted Spanish plans for expansion through the Colorado valley and into central Arizona.

Pressure was less intense on the Pacific littoral where limited European numbers were linked to remoteness, an emphasis on fur trapping and the need to win the support of Native American allies. The newly established Spanish base on Vancouver Island was not attacked in 1790–91 because of rivalries between the local bands and their desire to trade with the Spaniards. There were, however, minor clashes. Twice, Spanish launches were repelled; the second time, arrows were countered by muskets and swivel guns, and the light artillery of the launches made a dramatic impact. Spanish advances in coastal California from 1769, Russian pressure in Alaska and the British presence in what was to be British Columbia were all either dependent on, or assisted by, command of the sea. As so often across the world in this period, this could not be challenged effectively by non-Europeans; European powers were able to apply direct military pressure from the sea, and, more significantly, support their forces and integrate new acquisitions into global trading networks, making the process of advance both possible and profitable. This was crucial to the Russian quest for furs in the Aleutian Isles, southern Alaska and down the coast towards California, and in Australasia where the first European colony – the British base at Botany Bay – was established in 1788.

The last was to lead to the rapid establishment of a new military and political order. The Aborigines were not in a position to mount sustained resistance in areas where the environment encouraged large numbers of European settlers: they lacked numbers, fire-power and large-scale organization, and were being exposed to new diseases.

This was also true of the interior of South America, but there the environment did not encourage large numbers of settlers. In the tropical forests, Native American resistance was at its most effective when it was practised by apparently "primitive" peoples using dispersed warfare; not probably as a consequence of deep reasoning, but because they were skilled in hunting. Such techniques were often successful in frustrating more sophisticated, cohesive and concentrated European formations, although more infrequently beating them. If the peoples were nomadic or had scattered settlements, they obviously presented the Europeans with fewer or poorer fixed assets to threaten. The British in India found this a fundamental problem: the more sophisticated, "civilized" peoples were easier to conquer than the "primitives". However, the "primitives" too were eventually generally contained or controlled if it was worthwhile for the Europeans.[16]

Successful resistance to European advance was difficult, but native rebellion against control that had already been achieved was more so. In part, this was because rebellion produced economic dislocation and occurred where ethnic solidarity and political practices had already been breached by European conquest and settlement. Probably the largest rebellion by those not of European descent prior to the 1790s was the general insurrection in Peru in 1780–83. Provoked by the rigorous collection of taxes, and headed by Tupac Amaru, a descendant of the last Inca rulers, the uprising was crushed, with over 100,000 people dying in the conflict. Divisions within the native population played as important a role in this defeat as fire-power. The Comunero revolt in New Granada in 1781 was also defeated.[17]

Divisions and a lack of weapons were also important in limiting slave resistance to Western control in North and South America and the West Indies. The whites limited the availability of firearms and horses to slaves. Thus, those plotting what was to be known as Gabriel's Conspiracy in Virginia in 1800, had first to consider how they could acquire guns, horses and swords.

The most successful slave rebellion occurred on the French colony of St. Domingue in August 1791. Troops were sent from France in 1792 and slavery was abolished in the colony in 1793 (and in all the French colonies the following year), but, greatly assisted by the impact of yellow fever on French troops, the determination of the black population not to remain under French rule ultimately prevailed. In 1793, Spain went to war with France and provided aid to the rebels. British troops intervened in 1794 only to withdraw in 1797, leaving the colony divided between black forces under Toussaint L'Ouverture and mixed race forces under André Rigaud. Toussaint defeated Rigaud in 1800 and overran neighbouring Spanish Santo Domingo in 1801. A force of 20,000 men under Napoleon's brother-in-law, Charles Leclerc, was sent to restore French control. Toussaint was treacherously seized during negotiations in 1802.

Napoleon hoped that St. Domingue would be part of a French empire in the west that would include Louisiana, Florida, Cayenne, Martinique and Guadeloupe. However, resistance continued, and in 1803 the resumption of war with Britain led to a blockade of St. Domingue's ports. Hit by yellow fever and their food supplies cut, the French lost the initiative and were pushed back. Driven back to Le Cap, the French force agreed a truce with the black army under Toussaint's successor, Jean-Jacques Dessalines, and in November 1803 was transported by British warships to Jamaica. The surviving white settlers fled to Cuba. The independence of Haiti, the second independent state in the New World, was proclaimed on 1 January 1804.[18]

French failure owed much to the intractability of the task: the re-conquest of St. Domingue was far more difficult than the Spanish conquest of Cuba in 1511–13. The impact of the hostility of other European states, especially the leading naval power, Britain, was also important. More generally, this serves as a reminder that use of Western expansion as a gauge of the respective military capability of Western and non-Western states has to be considered in a number of contexts, including that of the other commitments of individual Western states.

This, for example, affected French attempts to establish their power in the Middle East and South Asia. Interested in doing so, in 1798 Napoleon invaded Egypt, intending to make it a French base from which India could be threatened. Like Julius Caesar, Napoleon also wished to win glory and to retain his own military position. Fearing his ambition, the government wished to keep him out of France. Having first easily overrun Malta, a vulnerable target then ruled by the Knights of St. John, Napoleon landed in Egypt on 1 July. After capturing Alexandria, he defeated the Mamelukes, the *de facto* rulers of Egypt, at Shubra Khit (13 July) and Embabeh, the Battle of the Pyramids (21 July); victories for defensive firepower over shock tactics. French rifles were described as "like a boiling pot on a fierce fire".[19]

Cairo fell, but the French fleet was destroyed by the British on 1 August. This stranded the French, but Napoleon continued to consolidate his position, albeit in the face of a hostile population, which mounted an unsuccessful rising in Cairo on 21 October. One force under Desaix was sent up the Nile to control Upper Egypt, while, with inadequate preparations, Napoleon and most of the army invaded Palestine, then ruled by the Turks. El Arish and Jaffa were successfully captured, the latter by storm (7 March 1799), but Acre successfully resisted, helped by British naval gunners. Napoleon's siege-train had been captured by British warships, he had underestimated his opponents, and successive French assaults all failed.[20]

Napoleon fell back on Egypt, where, on 25 July, he defeated a newly landed Turkish army at Aboukir, storming the earthworks with a cavalry charge. This was of scant benefit. In the face of British naval power, the French were still isolated. Napoleon abandoned his army and fled back to France by sea. The army left in Egypt was finally defeated by a British expeditionary force in 1801. Napoleon had sought more than Egypt. He asked Piveron de Morlat, who had served as French agent in Mysore, to join his staff in Egypt, and also sought to win the alliance of the Pasha of Acre by promising help against Turkey. Napoleon's secretary, Louis Antoine Fauvelet de Bourrienne, thought that the general wished to repeat the triumphs of Alexander the Great by marching overland against India.[21]

However, British successes in 1798–99 over the French navy and Tipu Sultan – at the Battles of the Nile and Seringapatam respectively – followed by their victories over the French army in Egypt in 1801, made it clear that Napoleon would not be able to project his power successfully along the Egypt–India axis. As a result, his victories in Egypt were of no lasting value in increasing French power projection, although they did encourage a sense of French superiority and the idea that the Mediterranean should be made into a French lake, which were both to be of lasting importance.[22]

Failure in Egypt checked, but did not end, thoughts of the East. In 1803, General Decaen sailed from Mauritius to try to reoccupy Pondicherry, the leading French base in India. His squadron carried some 1,250 men, many of whom were young officers intended to continue France's earlier policy of raising and training forces for native rulers, and thus extending French influence in India. They could not land at Pondicherry, however, because it was occupied by the British, and that year Lake destroyed the "Brigades françaises de l'Hindoustan" of de Boigne and Perron in north India.[23]

At war with Britain, the leading maritime power, for most of the Napoleonic period, France was unable to enjoy the benefits of the European hegemony it had gained. The colonial empires of its European allies were outside its (and their) control, and the resources that Napoleon deployed could not be used to project French power. Western European empires were dependent on maritime links back to the metropolitan lands and thus vulnerable to naval attack. This in effect limited the expansion of the states that were weak at sea. Maritime vulnerability did not prevent peacetime expansion and, also, was less of a factor where colonies were large and able to support expansionism, as in Spanish America.

Whether dependent on maritime links or not, forces confronted opponents across cultural as well as political divisions. In the New World, as in India and the Balkans, the defeat of non-Western forces, especially on the battlefield, had more to do with superior hierarchical command and control in European armies than it had to do with superior weapons, although weapon manufacture, precision and standardization were improving all the time. Chaos usually threatened as soon as battle was joined, but Westerners tended to keep cohesion and control for longer than their adversaries. This enabled more effective fire and more sophisticated tactics in moving or withholding units on the battlefield, including the crucial use of reserves. These advantages were linked to more general issues of administrative and political capability.

Any discussion of relations in terms of conflict alone would be incomplete. Economic, cultural, religious and political ties crossed Western/non-Western divides, turning them into zones of interaction in which symbiosis, synergy and exchange are analytical terms that are as helpful as conflict and war. These terms also enhance the understanding of why the West more often than not prevailed in conflict with non-Western states and peoples. Much of the violence across Western/non-Western divides also involved an important measure of collaboration between Westerners and local power brokers.

This was especially true of the slave trade, which would not have been possible without the active cooperation of local non-European potentates. Indeed, the slave trade encapsulated much of the reality of the European military impact. It was destructive, served the needs of a European-dominated global economy and would have been impossible without local support. Slavery was also important to the demographics of Western expansion. For example, in 1788–89 the French West Indies contained 594,000 slaves: 406,000 were on St. Domingue, in contrast to 28,000 whites and 30,000 free blacks.[24] It was not until the technological transformations of the mid-nineteenth century – in communications, firepower and medicine – that the Western states would be able to seize control of much more of the world, and even then native cooperation was still important, especially in filling the ranks of imperial armies.

CHAPTER TWO

Two Episodes of Modernity? The American War of Independence and the French Revolutionary Wars

These people show a spirit and conduct against us they never showed against the French, and everybody has judged of them from their former appearance and behaviour when joined with the King's forces in the last war [Seven Years' War, 1756–63] . . . They are now spirited up by a rage and enthusiasm as great as ever people were possessed of and you must proceed in earnest or give the business up. A small body acting in one spot will not avail, you must have large armies making diversions on different sides, to divide their force. The loss we have sustained is greater than we can bear. Small armies can't afford such losses, especially when the advantage gained tends to little more than the gaining of a post.

> General Gage, British Commander-in-Chief in North America, to the Secretary at War, after the battle of Bunker Hill, 1775.[1]

If the origins of modern war are being sought, then attention tends to focus on these two conflicts. Thus, for example, the Arnold Modern Wars series began with Stephen Conway's study, *The War of American Independence 1775–1783* (1995). The conflict is presented as a Revolutionary war whose "defining characteristics are those of modern warfare . . . The real innovation was the first appearance, on a significant scale, of a people's war".[2] This argument is then amplified for the French Revolutionary Wars, which broke out in 1792. They are seen as the product of a more sweeping revolution, and as marking and making a greater change in the waging of war.

For both wars, there are also images of battle that encode ideas of different ages in conflict at the same moment. In each war, the neat linear formations of *ancien régime* (pre-Revolutionary European) warfare are contrasted with more fluid forces, in the first the Patriot (American Revolutionary) marksmen relying on individual fire, and in the second the massed attacking columns of

Revolutionary soldiers. The new shock tactics are seen as the product of social forces and as, at once, the expression of respective capability and the contrast that ensured the result. Such an interpretation is not without some force, but it is also overly simplistic. This chapter seeks to provide a brief narrative of the major events of both wars, but also to qualify the notion of Revolutionary change.

The American war (1775–83) was indeed the first example of a transoceanic conflict fought between a European colonial power and subjects of European descent. It was also a major example of a Revolutionary war; a struggle for independence in which the notion of the citizenry under arms played a crucial role. The new state was accompanied by a new army that was a more egalitarian and dynamic army than any in Europe; although not for the sixth of the population who were slaves. Although many of the commanders of the leading Revolutionary force, the Continental Army, were from the wealthier section of society, the social range of the American leadership was far greater than that in European armies, and discipline was different. Although the social composition of the Continental Army was similar to that of the British regulars, this was an army of citizens, not subjects. The degree to which the army represented a new political identity and social practice helped to sustain its cohesion and even the continuation of the Revolutionary cause when the war went badly, as in the winter of 1777–78, when the army camped at Valley Forge after the loss of the capital, Philadelphia.[3]

Yet it would be misleading to ignore earlier parallels, not least the creation of the Swiss Confederation and the United Provinces (Netherlands), in the fourteenth and sixteenth centuries, respectively. Any overthrow of authority potentially entailed the creation of new military organizations and these could be regarded as revolutionary in their social, political or military character. Thus, for example, the New Model Army of the English Civil War, created in 1645, had a different social politics and ethos to its Royalist opponents. The successful Genoese rising against Austrian control in December 1746 was a popular rising that prefigured much that was to be associated with the Revolutionary warfare of the last quarter of the century.

It would also be misleading to exaggerate the novelty of the War of American Independence in terms of battlefield operations. It was essentially fought in terms that would have been familiar to those who had been engaged in the Seven Years' War (1756–63). The American response to battle was to adopt the line formations of musketeers of European warfare. This course was advocated by George Washington (1732–99), the commander of the Continental Army, who had served in the Virginia forces in the Seven Years' War, taking part in advances against the French in 1754, 1755 and 1758. He had learned the value of mobility and irregular warfare. Washington was not a military genius, but his character and background were very useful. A member of the Continental Congress and a native American, Washington looked like a natural leader. He did not wish to rely on militia but instead wanted a regular army that could provide America with legitimacy. Washington also stressed drill and discipline. He was a believer in position warfare (the location of units in order to protect particular positions), although he was also willing to use the militia as partisans.

The alternative strategy, advocated by Major-General Charles Lee (1731–82), centred on irregular warfare, especially the avoidance of position warfare and battle. The British would have found it difficult to identify targets had such a strategy been followed, but it was not, except in 1781 after defeats in the south. Lee was a former British regular officer who had served in North America and Portugal before transferring to the Polish army, which had to confront the greater strength of Russia.

The decision to form a Continental Army was not simply a matter of military options: it was a political act. The army, a force that would not dissolve at the end of the year, even if individual terms of service came to an end, symbolized the united nature of the struggle by the Thirteen Colonies and was a vital move in the effort to win foreign recognition and support. It was not necessary to have such an army in order for individual colonies/states to assist each other militarily. Prior to the American Revolution, military units had been deployed outside the boundaries of individual colonies, against Indian attacks and French and Spanish forces. During the Revolution, militia units under the control of state governments were sent to assist other states, as indeed they were sent to the Continental Army. However, by having such an army, military decisions were in large part taken out of the ambit of state government. In theory, this made the planning of strategy easier, freeing generals in some measure from the direction of state governments and allowing them to consider clashing demands for action and assistance.

In practice, the creation of the army, although essential to the dissemination of a new notion of nationhood, did not free military operations from the views of state governments, nor from the political disputes of the Continental Congress. In addition, the army did not enjoy the support of a developed system for providing reinforcements and supplies, let alone the relatively sophisticated one that enabled the British armed forces to operate so far from their bases. The provision of men and supplies created major problems, preventing or hindering American operations, and producing serious strains in the relationship between the new national government and the states. Accounts of how the militia served to suppress or inhibit Loyalist activity need to be complemented by an awareness of the extent to which local communities were not therefore disciplined to provide what was deemed to be necessary by Congress.

Both the Americans and the British fought in a more open order with more significant gaps than was the norm in Europe because the general absence of cavalry made the infantry less vulnerable to attack, while the enclosed nature of much of the terrain encouraged deployments that reflected the topography. Heavily encumbered regular units manoeuvring and fighting in their accustomed formations were vulnerable in the face of entrenched positions and unsuited to the heavily wooded and hilly terrain of the Canadian frontier; they were also not ideal for the vast expanses of the south. Artillery and fortifications played a smaller role than in conflict in western Europe, while, as more generally with transoceanic operations, the force–distance relationship was different: here relatively small armies operated across great distances in a war in which there were no real fronts.

Although the British had extensive earlier experience of campaigning against the French in North America, American tactics were still able to pose major problems for them, especially when the Americans took advantage of the terrain. William Evelyn was part of the relief force sent to help the British retreat from Concord and Lexington in 1775:

> they were attacked from the woods and houses on each side of the road and an incessant fire kept up on both sides for several hours, they [Americans] still retiring through the wood whenever our men advanced upon them . . . we were attacked on all sides from woods, orchards, stone walls, and from every house on the road side.

Blockaded by land in Boston, Evelyn felt that a new kind of war was taking place and that a new response was required:

> five or six thousand men are not sufficient to reduce a country of 1500 miles extent, fortified by nature, and where every man from 15 to 50 is either a volunteer or able to carry arms . . . some other mode must be adopted than gaining every little hill at the expense of a thousand Englishmen.

He advocated total war, arguing that the sole way to win was by "almost extirpating the present rebellious race".[4]

At the battle of Long Island on 27 August 1776, Captain William Congreve of the British artillery recorded:

> I found the enemy numerous and supported by the 6-pounders [cannon]. However, by plying them smartly with grapeshot their guns were soon drawn off but the riflemen being covered by trees and large stones had very much the advantage of us, who were upon the open ground . . . [had] not the light infantry of the Guards . . . come up in time I believe we should all have been cut off.[5]

Bunker Hill showed the hazard of frontal assaults on American hazards. British casualties in that battle helped to account for Gage's subsequent caution in the face of steadily more extensive American entrenchments. They were also responsible for Howe's caution, for Howe had commanded the actual assaults. The terrain of much of America was appropriate for such defences. Narrow valley routes were flanked by dense woodland, deep rivers often had few crossing points, and in the north the omnipresent stone walls created ready-made defences.

Yet this did not make the Americans invulnerable. The struggle between offence and defence is a constant theme in military history, endlessly replayed and at the same time difficult to evaluate as a number of factors are involved in capability and success. In the period covered by this book, improvements in fire-power appeared to give an advantage to the defence, but, as any detailed study will reveal, the situation was in fact more complex. Secondly, there were means to counteract defensive positions, ranging from the "counter" fire of artillery to manoeuvre warfare, especially movements round the flanks or flank attacks. Thirdly, frontal attacks could still be successful, as the British were to show at Guilford Court House (1781) and the French Revolutionaries repeatedly demonstrated. Finally, it is necessary not to pre-date the shift towards a defensive fire-power that dictated open deployments such as those of the Prussians in the Franco-Prussian War of 1870–71.

In positional warfare, the Americans could be defeated, their troops outflanked, as at the battles of Long Island and Brandywine (11 September 1777), or their strongholds captured, as at Fort Washington (1776) and Charleston (1780); but, elsewhere, the more mobile American units could operate with deadly effect.

The major role of the American militia created a problem, both in operational terms, for example by restricting the range of the British supply gatherers, and in the political context of the conflict, especially in harrying Loyalists, the large number of Americans who supported continued allegiance to the British crown. This helped give the Americans strategic depth. The militia could provide at least temporary reinforcements for the Continental Army. It helped to ensure that the British were outnumbered and thus limited their effectiveness as an occupation force. At the outset of the Revolution, militia overcame royal governors and defeated supporting Loyalists. Thus, in December 1775, the Earl of Dunmore, the last royal Governor of Virginia was defeated by Virginia militia at Great Bridge, Josiah Martin, his North Carolina counterpart, following two months later at Moore's Creek Bridge.

It is only too easy to assume that the war was a foregone conclusion, that the British could not conquer the Thirteen Colonies, and that their defeat was inevitable because they employed an anachronistic method of warfare. Instead, the British understood the need for mobility, while any reading of the correspondence of American generals underlines the difficulties of their task. In October 1774, Gage reported:

> they affect to despise our small numbers and to overwhelm us with forty or fifty thousand men . . . if you would get the better of America in all your disputes, you must conquer her, and to do that effectually

> to prevent further bickerings, you should have an army near twenty
> thousand strong, composed of regulars, a large body of good irregu-
> lars such as the German huntsmen, picked Canadians etc. and three
> or four regiments of light horse. These exclusive of a good and suffi-
> cient field artillery.[6]

The British faced serious problems, especially with logistics and with
defining an appropriate strategy.[7] However, Washington's correspondence
shows that there was no major capability gap in favour of the Revolutionaries. Furthermore, the British managed to maintain a major war effort at a
great distance, and did so for eight years without excessive problems or
disruption. This was the largest military force that Britain had hitherto sent
abroad. For much of the war, the British occupied the major American ports
(save Boston) and controlled coastal waters, so that they could move troops
and supplies along a north–south axis.

By the time of French entry into the war in 1778, the Americans had forced
the British out of New England (March 1776), challenged the occupation of
New Jersey at Trenton (25–6 December 1776) and the British capture of
Philadelphia by mounting a riposte at Germantown (4 October 1777), and
defeated Burgoyne's advance south from Canada (Saratoga capitulation, 17
October 1777). Yet they had also been driven from Canada (1776) and Philadelphia (1777).

The Americans probably benefited in the long run from being driven from
Canada. Such extended lines of communication and supply, and the commitment of manpower required, would have bled their army. Without Canada,
the Americans maintained their advantage of interior lines, and this was
important in responding to the British offensives in 1776 and 1777. The fall
of New York in 1776 was a major blow, but the initiative was regained by
Washington's success at Trenton.

Although he was a "Fabian" commander, who understood the value of
(and need for) a defensive strategy, and the value of conceding space in order
to preserve his forces, Washington could also take the offensive. This had a
military value, helping to throw the British off balance, but was also important in maintaining political support for the Revolution. This serves as a
reminder of the need to consider political factors when assessing strategy; a
similar point could be made about Robert E. Lee's offensives in 1862–63
during the American Civil War.

Aside from at Trenton and Princeton (3 January 1777), Washington also
displayed an aggressive side in the Philadelphia campaign of 1777–78, attacking at Germantown and Monmouth Courthouse (28 June 1778). Far from
feeling that time was on his side, Washington wished to exhaust the British
before America grew too weary and weak to continue. For example, during
the war of attrition in New Jersey in January–May 1777, the frequent and
devastating attacks by American forces on British outposts and foraging

parties demonstrated their capability. Washington's increasing employment of light infantry enhanced American strength, as did British delay in mobilizing the Loyalists.

At the same time, the American cause was greatly handicapped by the problems of creating an effective war machine. This was not due to poverty, as the colonists were relatively affluent, but to the problem of mobilizing and directing resources. The anti-authoritarian character of the Revolution and the absence of national institutions made it difficult to create a viable national military system. Much of Washington's correspondence is an account of organization and improvisation under pressure. For example, in early 1777, when the British had pulled back across New Jersey after the battles of Trenton and Princeton, and Washington had taken up a protective position at Morristown, his army was badly affected by desertion, expiring enlistments and supply problems. There were difficult negotiations over the Militia, as seen for example in Washington's letter to the Pennsylvania Council of Safety on 29 January: "If some Mode is not adopted for obliging the Officers of the Militia to return the Arms and Accoutrements that are lent to them, we shall be in the greatest want of them when the regular Regiments are raised". On 3 February, he wrote to Jeremiah Wadsworth:

> The present unsettled State of the Commissary's department in this quarter, makes me fearful, that unless some Measures are fallen upon to reconcile the jarring Interests of these who act, or pretend to act, under the Appointments of Colo. Trumbull, that the Army will in a little while want Supplies of every kind.

That spring, Washington was similarly affected by a high desertion rate and handicapped by unhelpful state authorities. He was helped, however, by the absence of a British spring offensive. Again, there are reiterated signs of weakness. Brigadier-General George Clinton wrote from Fort Montgomery on 1 May, "The Garrisons of this and the other Fortresses in this Neighbourhood being already rather Weak considering their Importance and their defenceless Situation on the Land Side where we are now buisilly [busily] employed in erecting proper works". Major-General Horatio Gates added his contribution of gloom from Albany on 30 May: the garrison at Ticonderoga had a "shameful deficiency" and "Artillerists are likewise much Wanted".[8] Success in the war appeared far from clear. These problems did not disappear. In 1780, Nathanael Greene resigned as Quartermaster General because of his anger with civilian politicians and what he saw as their responsibility for his failure to meet the logistical demands of the Continental Army.

Richard Henry Lee wrote to Washington on 27 February 1777:

> I realy think that when the history of this winters Campaign comes to be understood, the world will wonder at its success on our part.

> With a force rather inferior to the enemy in point of numbers, and chiefly militia too, opposed to the best disciplined troops of Europe; to keep these latter pent up, harassed, and distressed – But more surprizing still, to lessen their numbers some thousands by the sword and captivity![9]

Checking the British was not, however, the same as shaping the war through a proactive strategy.

The relative capability of the two sides changed greatly in 1778, as French intervention added to the range of urgent British military commitments elsewhere in the world. The French also threatened British naval control of North American waters, and thereby challenged the application of British resources and the articulation of the British imperial system. The French also sent an expeditionary force, while in 1779 Spain entered the war and began the conquest of West Florida, one of the more successful campaigns of the war, which culminated with the capture of Pensacola in May 1781.

The more serious nature of the military challenge increased the pressure on British leaders. They had no additional resources, while the customary problems of poor communications in the age of sail, and the consequences both for command and control and for transport and supply, were accentuated by the scale of the war and the interconnections between different spheres, most obviously naval operations in the Caribbean and off North America, which in 1781 lost Britain command of Chesapeake Bay.

French intervention did not automatically lead to British defeats. Franco-American attacks on British positions at Newport (1778) and Savannah (1779) were unsuccessful. Nevertheless, British moves had now to be made against the background of a possible French response. The absence of major engagements in the middle colonies in 1779 and 1780 should not be taken to indicate a disinclination to fight. However, the manpower situation in both armies was a testimony to the strains they were suffering from. The British had lost one army at Saratoga, and now had other pressing commitments, while the Americans were finding it increasingly difficult to sustain a major army. As a result, both sought new support: the British looked to the Loyalists, their opponents to French intervention in America, rather than the West Indies. The war therefore became a curious interplay of cautious moves and bold aspirations, as increasingly exhausted participants played for stakes that had been made higher as a consequence of the new factor of the intervention of French naval power and in an atmosphere that the changing arithmetic of naval strength helped to make volatile for both sides.

French entry led the British to abandon Philadelphia (18 June 1778), and to concentrate on the southern colonies. There, they succeeded in capturing the major cities – Savannah (December 1778) and Charleston (May 1780) – but found it difficult to consolidate their position in South Carolina. Victories – over Horatio Gates at Camden (16 August 1780) and, less easily, over

Nathanael Greene at Guilford Court House (15 March 1781) – did not bring permanent control; on the contrary, a partisan war broke out over much of the south.

The extension of the war to the south created problems for both sides, especially of manpower, logistics, and command and control. It also showed that the British still had options. For their enemies, 1780 was a year of disappointment. The French expeditionary force that arrived in Newport achieved nothing, while Washington was unable to shake British control of New York. His troops were increasingly demoralized and some units were to mutiny in the new year. The British still controlled the sea, and, if their impact in the interior was limited, they revealed at Charleston and around the Chesapeake an ability to use their amphibious forces to considerable effect, taking the initiative, harrying their opponents and disrupting the American economy. Nevertheless, this achievement was precarious. The close of 1780 saw the central themes of the 1781 campaign already clear: the need for Franco-American cooperation if a major blow was to be struck against the British; Cornwallis's problems in the south; the rising importance of the Chesapeake; and the crucial role of naval power. However, the contrasting results of the campaigns of 1780 and 1781 indicate that these circumstances and problems made nothing inevitable.

Despite the anxieties expressed in 1778, French entry had not obliged the British to abandon New York, nor had it led to another attack on Canada, nor to the permanent postponing of operations in the south. Similarly, the British position had not collapsed outside America. The Franco-Spanish attempt to invade southern England in 1779 had failed; although more due to poor leadership, disease and inadequate supplies than to the role of the British navy. By the beginning of 1781, Britain had lost few possessions outside North America. The government had won the general election of 1780 and was able to finance massive expenditure on the war, substantially by borrowing.

In May 1781, Lord Cornwallis pressed north overland to Virginia, in the hope that he could thereby improve the situation. Once there, however, he failed to crush American resistance and soon surrendered the initiative, establishing himself that August at Yorktown, a poor defensive position but with an anchorage that would permit withdrawal. At this point, the war in America was far from over, although it was apparent that neither the British southern strategy nor the advance into Virginia had brought the anticipated gains. Nevertheless, as earlier around New York, the British had shown that they could gain and hold important points and defeat American forces. Furthermore, the economic burden of the struggle was becoming more punishing for the Americans.

Given the weak state of the armies of Greene and Washington, and French concern with the West Indies, it is probable that Clinton and Cornwallis could have preserved their positions and waited on the defensive while Britain pursued her maritime war outside America. This would not have brought victory, but might have resulted in negotiations with the Bourbons and the consequent collapse of the anti-British coalition. In early 1781, the British had sent an expedition by sea to the Chesapeake and had retained the initiative because they had preserved naval superiority.

There was to be no repetition that autumn. Washington's ability to see an opportunity led to a concentration of American and French land and sea forces against Yorktown, without any matching British action, which placed Cornwallis in an untenable position. The failure of Admiral Graves to defeat the French off the Virginia Capes and force his way into the Chesapeake on 5 September 1781 was indecisive in terms of losses, but, as it prevented the relief of Cornwallis, it was an important success for the French. Yorktown was lost not because the naval dimension was ignored, as a demonstration of its importance was hardly necessary, but because the British got it wrong, for which Admiral Rodney must bear much of the blame thanks to his failure to send sufficient ships from the West Indies. Blockaded and under a heavy bombardment that could not be countered, Cornwallis surrendered on 19 October 1781. This success – a decisive battle won with few casualties – was greatly to impress Helmuth von Moltke, the architect of Prussian success in 1864–71.

Although the British still held Charleston, Savannah and New York, as well as having substantial forces in America, this was effectively the end of the war in North America. News of the defeat led to the replacement of Lord North's ministry by a government more ready to accept American independence. Thereafter, although American advances on British bases in 1782 were held off, and Washington had to abandon his plan for an attack on New York, the British concentrated on their conflict with the Bourbons and, in the eventual Treaty of Versailles of 1783, agreed to accept American independence and to surrender Charleston, Savannah and New York, as well as the "Old Northwest".

To return to the issue of modernity, in terms of the politicization of much of the American public there was an obvious contrast with most European warfare of the previous century. The Americans owed their independence to the willingness of some of the people to continue fighting when the struggle became more widespread, bitter and sustained than had at first seemed likely, before the British sent a major army to crush the Revolution. The Americans subsequently had to face British determination to continue the struggle on land even after French intervention. Casualties were heavy, about 0.9 per cent of the population in 1780, compared to near 1.6 per cent for the Civil War, 0.12 per cent for World War One and 0.28 per cent for World War Two.

Much about the war, however, for example the weaponry, was conventional. The motivation of the troops was the major aspect of modernity. In addition, as with the tactics of the French Revolutionary armies, it is necessary to note earlier examples. The American snipers, whether deliberately or not, could be seen as an extended development of the skirmishers and sharpshooters sent out in front of the line on the battlefield in most later eighteenth-century armies in Europe. The French Revolutionary attack harked back to the sixteenth-century Swiss pike square, although now combining a shock weapon, the bayonet, with a fire weapon, the musket. But the new forms could not be easily adopted by their opponents, because both in part depended on enhanced commitment (initiative in the American case and élan in the French) by the individual infantryman, which derived from the fact that they were fighting for a cause they believed in – different kinds of freedom. In the American war, there was little of the emphasis on large armed forces and the mass production of munitions that was to be such an obvious aspect of the "industrial warfare" of the late nineteenth and early twentieth centuries.

Warfare and the military in pre-Revolutionary Europe

As the columns of French citizen-soldiers charged down their opponents in the 1790s, it was easy to see change in effect and to claim that the political Revolution in France helped bring about a military "revolution" and was dependent on the latter for its survival. Alongside an awareness of such change, both in the scale of forces and in the political and social context of warfare, it is also necessary to note that the current of change in European armies was already strong, for this helps to explain the successes of France's opponents.

The sources and interactions of this current of change were various, but three were particularly important: first, widespread demographic and economic expansion in Europe from the 1740s; secondly, an emphasis on the value of reform and the rational approach to problems that characterized Enlightenment thought; and, thirdly, the impact of the protracted warfare of 1740–62. The first produced the resources for military expansion, the second encouraged an emphasis on novelty, and the third, a period of testing, led to a determination to replace what had been found deficient and to ensure that armies (and societies) were in a better state for future conflicts. The last were seen as likely: in the 1780s, Europe's rulers were preparing for major conflict, for example those that seemed imminent between Austria and Prussia in 1786 and 1790, France and Prussia in 1787, and Prussia and Russia in 1791. In addition, Austria, Denmark, Russia, Sweden and Turkey were all involved in conflict during all or part of the period 1787–92. Russia was the most successful, beating the Turks and thwarting Swedish attack.

It is necessary not to offer too static an account of *ancien régime* warfare, just as a static account of Revolutionary/Napoleonic warfare would be misleading. Far from the situation being a question simply of precursors to Revolutionary warfare, focusing on French innovators, it is important to allow for a more fluid situation during the *ancien régime*. Supporters and effective practitioners of the offensive included Charles XII of Sweden (ruled 1697–1718) and Frederick II, the Great, of Prussia (ruled 1740–86). Despite the close association, the French did not invent columns or the massed use of artillery.

Generals were able to respond to situations with a variety of tactical ploys. Far from *ancien régime* tactics being stable, let alone stagnant, there had been considerable flexibility and experimentation. Commanders digested and sought to benefit from the development of new weapons: the socket bayonet and the flintlock musket in the late seventeenth century and the elevating screw for cannon in the eighteenth, as well as the introduction of conic ramrods which allowed the reduction of the difference between the muzzle calibre and the ammunition calibre and thereby promoted more precise targeting. The rapid introduction of successful inventions or modifications in most European armies suggests that the importance of closing technological gaps was well recognized.

The introduction of the socket bayonet helped to change the face of the European battlefield. Prior to that, infantry had been divided between musketeers and pikemen. The former were more numerous and provided fire-power, but the pikemen were necessary in order to protect the musketeers from cavalry and from other pikemen. The combination of the two was complex and led to a degree of tactical inflexibility, as well as a density of formation that limited the possibilities of linear deployment over an extensive front.

The development of socket bayonets, which were attached to a metal ring around the barrel, led to an increase in fire-power and tactical flexibility, as all the infantry were now armed with muskets. The change permitted more effective drill, and drill and discipline were essential to enhanced fire-power. More linear infantry formations were employed on the battlefield. Battalions were drawn up only three ranks deep and firings were by groups designed to maximize the continuity of fire and fire control. Soldiers fired by volley, rather than by individual aim, although, in battle, such control often broke down. The large bore of muskets and their lack of rifling, or spiral grooves, in the barrel, ensured they could take ammunition of several calibres. The loose fit of the ball helped ramming and thus contributed to the rate of fire, but ensured that accuracy was lost with distance. Problems were also caused by poor sights, eccentric bullets, heavy musket droops, overheating, stiff triggers, powerful recoil and poor performance in wet weather if the powder became damp. Muskets had a low rate of fire, a short range and had to be re-sighted for each individual shot. Non-standardized manufacture and wide clearances (windage) meant that the ball could roll out if the barrel was pointed towards the ground, while, at best, the weapon was difficult to aim or to hold steady. Balls were rough cast and the spherical bullets maximized air resistance. The developments of iron, instead of wooden, ramrods was believed to increase the rate of musket fire, but these often bent and jammed in the musket, or broke or went rusty; and frequent use of the ramrod distorted the barrel into an oval shape.

Tactics focused on the deployment of infantry in close-packed, thin, linear formations in order to maximize fire-power. Linear formations and an increase in the numbers of officers and non-commissioned officers (NCOs) also lessened the problems of command and control posed by the limitations of information and communication on the battlefield. Despite the failings of the muskets, casualties could be substantial, because the combatants were densely packed and fought at close range. Low muzzle velocity led to dreadful wounds, because the more slowly a projectile travels the more damage it does as it bounces off bones and internal organs.

Bayonets increased fire-power, but did not greatly encourage attacks because bayonet drills were for a long time modelled on pike drills, with the weapon held high and an emphasis on receiving attacks. Hand-to-hand fighting on the battlefield was relatively uncommon, and most casualties were caused by shot. The greater battlefield mobility of the infantry put a premium on a more mobile field artillery (lighter guns drawn by horses), which was developed in most armies.

Infantry was flanked on the battlefield by cavalry units, although the proportion of cavalry in European armies declined during the century as a result of the heavier emphasis on fire-power and the greater cost of cavalry. Cavalry was principally used on the battlefield to fight cavalry; cavalry advances against unbroken infantry were uncommon, because they were costly in casualties, although infantry was vulnerable to attack in flank and rear or when retreating. Cavalry played a crucial role in some battles, but, in general, was less important than it had been in the past.

Unbroken infantry was more vulnerable to artillery than it was to cavalry, especially because of the close-packed and static formations that were adopted in order to maintain discipline and fire-power. The use of artillery on the battlefield increased considerably during the century, and, by the end of the Seven Years' War, Frederick II, who had not, initially, favoured the large-scale use of artillery, was employing massed batteries of guns. The greater standardization of artillery pieces led to more regular fire, and thus encouraged the replacement of the largely desultory and random preliminary bombardments of the seventeenth century by more efficient exchanges of concentrated and sustained fire. Artillery was employed on the battlefield both to silence opposing guns and, more effectively, in order to weaken infantry and cavalry. Grape and canister shot were particularly effective; they consisted of a bag or tin with small balls inside that scattered as a result of the charge, causing considerable numbers of casualties at short range.

The leading generals of mid-century, Frederick II, the Great, of Prussia (1712–86) and Hermann, Count of Saxe (1696–1750), the outstanding French general of the 1740s, were both concerned to keep ahead of their opponents, and saw tactical flexibility as a key. Frederick had been particularly enterprising in the 1740s and 1750s, but after 1763 he showed a greater degree of rigidity, in part because the pressure of wartime competitiveness was replaced by peacetime manoeuvres. In 1768, Frederick considered an advance in open order, but, in general, there was little change in Prussian methods after the Seven Years' War.[10]

In the War of the Bavarian Succession (1778-79), the European war that, in part, coincided with the War of American Independence, the Prussians were unable to defeat Austria and were affected by desertion and a growing caution in Frederick's generalship. He advanced into the Habsburg dominions, but, thereafter, did not fight an offensive war. The tactical offensive-strategic defensive that he had employed so successfully in the Seven Years' War was not repeated. In 1778-79, the Austrians relied on strategic defensive-tactical defensive, which led to a safe but less than sparkling conflict that both denied Frederick the opportunity to catch advancing forces at a vulnerable moment and ensured that Prussia was not knocked out of the war. More generally, Frederician tactics were most suited to the particular environment of east-central Europe, especially the unenclosed tracts of Bohemia and Silesia. Their limitations were to be revealed in the French Revolutionary Wars from 1792, in the face of French troops fighting in open order in the enclosed and wooded country of the Austrian Netherlands and the Rhineland.

Nevertheless, thanks to the Seven Years' War, the prestige of the Prussian military was high. Foreign observers flocked to attend Prussian military reviews and the annual manoeuvres in Silesia. Louis-Alexandre Berthier, later Napoleon's chief of staff and minister of war, was much impressed by those he attended in 1783, three years before Frederick's death. The Prussians demonstrated their continued effectiveness in 1787. A rapidly advancing Prussian army under the Duke of Brunswick overran the United Provinces in order to re-establish the authority of William V of Orange. Invading and advancing to Nijmegen on 13 September, the Prussians entered Utrecht on 16 September after the principal Patriot force had abandoned it in panic. They pressed on to enter Dordrecht on 18 September and Delft on 19 September. The last Patriot stronghold, Amsterdam, was protected by opening dykes, but a Prussian force crossed the Haarlem Lake and the city surrendered on 10 October. The Prussians were helped by the poor quality of the resistance and by the failure of the French to come to the assistance of their Dutch allies, but, nevertheless, this was a striking display of military capability. It is easy to see why it was widely anticipated that Brunswick would have another rapid success against Revolutionary France in 1792.

Indeed, in the summer of 1792, the Russians overran Poland in ten weeks. An invasion force of 100,000 made quick work of a badly armed and equipped and largely inexperienced defending army of half that size.

Reform in the French army

Tactical development after the mid-century conflicts was best shown by Russia, as a result of the need to defeat the Turks; and in France, having been beaten in the Seven Years' War, there was a willingness to experiment in theory and practice and to challenge the operation, organization, equipment and ethos of the army. This also reflected the pre-Revolutionary governmental culture in France in this period with its testing of assumptions and consideration of new methods.

There was considerable interest both in different fighting methods and in military organization. The former in part developed earlier ideas by writers such as Saxe. His *Mes Rêveries* had criticized reliance on fire-power alone, advocating, instead, a combination of individually aimed fire (instead of volley firing by command) and shock: charging with a bayonet. Saxe was not alone in encouraging fresh thoughts about tactics and strategy. Jean-Charles Folard and François-Jean de Mesnil-Durand stressed the shock and weight of forces attacking in columns, rather than the customary deployment of fire-power and linear tactics. Manoeuvres in 1778 designed to test the rival systems failed to settle the controversy, but the new tactical manual issued in 1791 incorporated both.

In addition, the concept of the division, a standing unit maintained in peace and war, and including elements of all arms and, therefore, able to operate independently, was developed in France. Such a unit could serve effectively, both as a detached force and as part of a coordinated army operating in accordance with a strategic plan. The divisional plan evolved from 1759, and in 1787–88 army administration was arranged along divisional lines.

The French army was also given better weaponry. Jean-Baptiste Gribeauval (1715–89) standardized the French artillery from 1769, and was appointed Inspector General of Artillery in 1776. He used standardized specifications: 4-, 8- and 12-pounder cannon and 6-inch howitzers in eight-gun batteries. Mobility was increased by stronger, larger wheels, shorter barrels and lighter weight cannon, more secure mobile gun carriages and better casting methods. Accuracy was improved by better sights, the issue of gunnery tables and the introduction of inclination markers. The rate of fire rose thanks to the introduction of pre-packaged rounds. Horses were harnessed in pairs, instead of in tandem. This was useful, but was typical of the incremental rather than revolutionary nature of military development. There was no alternative to the use of horses to pull cannon (or supplies). In this respect, there had been no change for centuries. Horse-based transport systems were dependent on the energy of the animals. They could not pull loads round the clock and were affected by terrain and weather. Horses also required food and water. Transport problems affected mobility. Even if they chose to try to live off the country, armies required not only cannon, but also munitions, for both infantry and artillery shot was heavy and rapidly expended in battle.

The theory of war advanced to take note of these and other changes, although it would be foolish to neglect the extent to which it is difficult to establish what was an advance. There was considerable controversy over tactics, organization and other aspects of the military, such as fortification design. All these controversies displayed a widespread conviction of the value of change, and an accompanying difficulty in assessing which changes would be valuable. Hippolyte de Guibert, in his *Essai général de tactique* (1772), stressed movement and enveloping manoeuvres, advocated living off the land in order to increase the speed of operations, criticized reliance on fortifications, and urged the value of a Patriotic citizen army. In his *De l'usage de l'artillerie nouvelle dans la guerre de campagne* (Paris, 1778), the Chevalier Jean du Teil argued that the artillery should begin battles and should be massed for effect.[11]

Thanks to Gribeauval's reforms, Revolutionary France had the best artillery in the West. In several other respects, its army was a product of pre-Revolutionary changes. Napoleon, who had been taught to use Gribeauval's guns, also admired Guibert's work, which was the basis for the army ordinance of 1791. He subsequently argued that Revolutionary France was able to raise good armies so speedily because of the pre-Revolutionary foundations. Charles Pichegru was another artillery man who became a Revolutionary general. In the Revolution, the regular army was disrupted through desertion and by the emigration of officers, but it played a major role in the successes of 1792, not least because the regulars were better trained than new levies.[12]

The French Revolutionary Wars, 1792–99

Yet the political context of warfare was now very different, particularly in providing far larger armies for the French. War broke out in April 1792 when the National Assembly, fired by Revolutionary enthusiasm, declared war on Austria. An invasion of France was mounted by Prussians under the Duke of Brunswick, a veteran of Frederick II's wars, but was checked on 20 September at Valmy by a larger and more heavily gunned French force. Brunswick retreated, while the French advanced, overrunning Savoy, the middle Rhine and the Austrian Netherlands. It had taken Saxe from 1744 to 1747 to over-run the Austrian Netherlands, whereas in 1792, although the initial advances met with disaster, an invasion in November met with overwhelming success within a month.

The scope of the war broadened in 1793: the National Convention decided on 1 February to declare war on Britain and the Dutch; and added Spain on 7 March. The Austrians recaptured the Austrian Netherlands in 1793 after their victory at Neerwinden (18 March), but by the end of 1794 the French had again conquered it. The larger numbers, once organized, told, especially as Allied cohesion was limited. Victories at Tourcoing (18 May) and Fleurus (26 June) led to the conquest of the Austrian Netherlands. The French could afford their greater losses at Fleurus. Battles were particularly impor- tant because sieges played a smaller role than in wars in the region over the previous three centuries. This owed something to the poor state of the avail- able fortifications, not least as a consequence of the decision by the Emperor Joseph II to dismantle much of the fortress system in the Austrian Netherlands in 1781. He did so in order to force their Dutch garrisons to leave, but this political objective helped to ensure military vulnerability in 1792–94. Once Austrian armies had been defeated, they lacked the shelter of fortresses, and the French did not need to tie up much of their army in sieges.

The French pressed on to overrun the United Provinces, capturing Amster- dam on 20 January 1795, while in late 1794 other French forces overran the left bank of the Rhine. Superiority in numbers was important in battles such as Valmy, Jemappes (6 November 1792) and Wattignies (15–16 October 1793), as well as in successful offensives, such as that against the Spaniards in Roussillon.

The French were also greatly helped by divisions about goals and means among their opponents, divisions that combined with differences in success and failure to affect their determination to continue the struggle. Frederick William II of Prussia rapidly lost his enthusiasm for the conflict, and Prussia was driven in the Peace of Basle of 5 April 1795 to accept French occupation of the left bank of the Rhine. On 16 May 1795, the Dutch accepted satellite status as the Batavian Republic, and that July Spain agreed terms.

Numbers came from the large French population, the largest in Europe after Russia, and as a result of the *levée en masse*, the general conscription ordered on 23 August 1793: the entire population could be obliged to serve the war effort and all single men aged between 18 and 25 were to join the army, where they would be deluged with Revolutionary propaganda. The armies raised were both larger than those deployed by France hitherto and enabled it to operate effectively on several fronts at once, to sustain casualties and to match the opposing forces of much of Europe. Feeding and supplying forces on this scale, however, created new logistical and organizational problems.

Tactics were also important. The characteristic battlefield manoeuvre of French Revolutionary forces, and the most effective way to use the mass of inexperienced soldiers, most of whom went into the infantry, was in independent attack columns. This was also best for an army that put an emphasis on the attack. Column advances were far more flexible than those of lines, although frontal attacks by columns led to heavy casualties. At Jemappes, the French were able to advance in columns and to get back into lines at close range, defeating the greatly outnumbered Austrians.[13] The number of cannon in the field was increased, enhancing fire-power. The

French combination of artillery, large numbers of skirmishers, and assault columns was potent; a successful *ad hoc* combination of tactical elements matched to the technology of the times and the character of the new republican soldier. An ability to move quickly between line and column formations also proved important.

The role of the skirmishers should not be underrated. They were sent in advance of the main assault force. Deployed in open order, the skirmishers were not vulnerable to volley fire or to cannon. However, they were able to use individual fire in order to inflict casualties on the close-packed lines of their opponents. This hit enemy morale and could also disrupt their formations. However, as with the use of rifles by the American Revolutionaries, it is important not to exaggerate the impact of a particular weapon, tactic or deployment. None was unique to the French, and each faced particular problems. For example, skirmishers were vulnerable to cavalry, although far less so in broken terrain, and were also used by the Allies. The Russians were experts in the use of columns.

There were also important organizational changes in the French army, including a more "democratic" command structure, at least at battalion level. The greater dispersal of units ensured that command and coordination skills became more important, and the French benefited from young and determined commanders. The rapidly expanded army and the departure of many royal officers provided numerous opportunities for rapid promotion, ensuring a young officer corps. Many NCOs from the royal army were promoted to command positions. Those who failed, or were suspected of treachery, were executed: 17 generals in 1793 and 67 in 1794. This put a premium on energy and success. Talent flourished: commanders included Jean-Baptiste Jourdan, a former private, Louis Lazare Hoche, a former corporal, Napoleon Bonaparte, a junior artillery officer from Corsica, a recent French acquisition, and Pichegru, a sergeant major in the artillery from a peasant background.

The armies were systematized by Lazare Carnot, head of the military section of the Committee of Public Safety, who brought a measure of organization to a situation made chaotic by Revolutionary change. This also fulfilled the political objective of enhancing central control.[14] Success in forming and training new armies was instrumental in the transition from a royal army to a nation in arms. The *amalgame* of 1793 combined the battalions of the ex-royal or "line" army with those of the National Guard in new "demi-brigades". This offered a degree of uniformity and rationalization necessary to cope with the impact of Revolutionary disruption. The expertise of the regulars was also seen as a valuable addition for the National Guard. A number of these "demi-brigades" formed a division. Carnot used the idea of the division to create an operational flexibility that enabled the Revolutionary government to respond rapidly to domestic and external challenges. Grouped together, divisions constituted an army. In addition, Carnot's Topographical Bureau acted as a General Staff. The new logistics brought about by the partial abandonment of the magazine system or reliance on fixed depots helped the aggressive style of war – both in strategy and in tactics – of the Revolutionary armies, which relied on numbers and enthusiasm. If you did not win, you did not eat. The way was open for the ruthless and skilful boldness and high-tempo war that Napoleon was to show in defeating the Austrians in north Italy in 1796–97.

Yet it is necessary to consider other aspects of the warfare of the 1790s, and to avoid any simplistic account that exaggerates the novelty and success of French methods. It is arguable that a focus on the war-fighting methods of the French underrates other related aspects of the French Revolution that were as important. For example, it is difficult to assess the impact of ideological considerations, but they appear to have been important. It has been argued that the French soldiers were better motivated and, hence, more successful and better able to use the new methods. This is hard to prove, but, initially at least, Revolutionary enthusiasm does seem, by its nature, to have been an important element in French capability. It was probably necessary for the higher morale required for effective shock action, for crossing the killing ground produced by opposing fire-power. Patriotic determination was also important to counter the effects of the limited training of many of the Revolutionary soldiers. Nevertheless, numbers may have been more important. The French only tended to win if they had a clear numerical superiority.[15]

At the same time, it is important not to underrate the motivation of France's opponents, nor the military value of the professionalism of their forces. The Austrians bore the brunt of fighting France on the Continent. The rapid success of the French in overrunning the Austrian Netherlands in November 1792 was not to be an indication of the future course of the conflict, no more than the initial successes of the American Patriots in 1775 culminating in their forcing the British to leave Boston in March 1776 signalled the future of that war. Instead, the Austrians proved tough and resourceful opponents. This was particularly so in Germany under Archduke Charles in 1796, with victories at Wetzlar (15 June), Amberg (24 August) and Würzburg (3 September), Amberg stopping a French advance on Austria; but, earlier, the Austrians had also displayed impressive fighting qualities.[16] Their disciplined fire initially checked the French at Jemappes and Hondschoote (8 September 1793), and helped to defeat them at Weissenburg (13 October 1793) and Neerwinden. The Prussians, under the Duke of Brunswick, had won victories at Pirasens (14 September 1793) and Kaiserlauten (28–30 November 1793). In 1795, the French in Germany were pushed back across the Rhine: Würmser and Clerfayt successively defeated Pichegru, and Würmser recaptured Mannheim.

If the Austrians (and their allies) could not in the end preserve the Austrian Netherlands, then it is worth noting that *ancien régime* French forces had also been successful in this area, for example in 1676–78 and 1745–48. Similarly, the French were able to advance into Germany, but they had also done so before the Revolution. Then, for example in 1703–1704 and 1741, they had, however, been helped by the alliance of Bavaria, and there was no equivalent in the mid 1790s. Prussia abandoned the allied camp in 1795, but it did not join the French. French advances into Germany were contested. There was no equivalent in the 1790s to Napoleon's successful advance in 1805 in which the Austrian army was forced to surrender at Ulm, allowing the emperor to press on to Vienna.

To judge the Revolutionaries by pointing out that Napoleon achieved more far-flung and rapid triumphs, is harsh for two reasons: first that Napoleon's military fame and system was a creation of the 1790s; and, secondly, that the situation facing the French was more difficult in the 1790s than it was to be in the 1800s. In part, Napoleon was the solution, although, as already suggested, the situation was more complex.

The difficulties were both domestic and international. Revolutionary governments faced a situation of instability and opposition within France that was not to confront Napoleon in the 1800s. This had direct military consequences. It was necessary to deploy sizeable forces to overcome domestic opposition, for example the Federalist revolt of 1793, which temporarily captured Lyon, Marseilles and Toulon, and the royalist Chouans in western France, who also rose in 1793. A British-backed *emigré* invasion was smashed at Quiberon Bay in July 1795, while, that April, Pichegru suppressed a Jacobin rising in Paris. In 1799, there were also royalists uprisings within France, including near Toulouse, and in the west. However, it proved difficult to coordinate uprisings, and the rebels lacked the military experience of the government forces. The uprisings were rapidly suppressed.

In addition, governmental instability interacted with military factionalism. The army leadership was already politicized as a consequence of the Revolution, but the inability to produce a stable government ensured that this politicization became a cause of continual difficulties. The views and ambitions of many of the generals were not limited to the conduct of war and many were contemptuous of civilian authority and involved in politics. Pichegru and Hoche played a role in the 1797 Fructidor coup and Napoleon, who had used artillery firing at point-blank range, the famous "whiff of grape shot", to help put down a rising in Paris on 5 October 1795, himself seized power with a coup on 10 November 1799: the conduct of the war had created an atmosphere of expediency in which it became easier for him to mount a coup.

Political instability also exacerbated the serious problems of supporting such a lengthy struggle. In large part, the burden was transferred to conquered areas, but military exactions there undermined the acceptance of French control. This led to violent responses that further helped develop a vicious cycle of exaction, and also undermined the universalist and liberal aspirations of France's supporters. The cause of Revolution became the practice of repression.[17] The brutal exploitation of Lombardy in 1796 led to a popular uprising that was harshly repressed, and there were also serious popular uprisings in Swabia and Franconia.

Thus, the very conduct of the army and the organization of its supply system helped to defeat France politically and to make it totally reliant on military success. Supply problems also affected French operations and hit the quality of its forces. For example, an absence of pay and new clothing hit the Army of Italy in 1799, exacerbating desertion and disease.

It was difficult for the Army of Italy to find adequate food in 1799, because it had already devastated much of the countryside in 1796–97 when under the command of Napoleon (1769–1821). A Corsican who had become a Second Lieutenant in the pre-Revolutionary artillery, Napoleon had taken part in an unsuccessful expedition against Cagliari in February 1793, but made his name later that year when his successful command of the artillery in the siege of Toulon had played a major role in driving British and royalist forces from the port. Napoleon was promoted to brigadier general in December 1793, and was made artillery commander for the army in Italy the following February. However, he suffered from the political instability in France, being imprisoned in August 1794 after the fall of Robespierre. Released in September, Napoleon refused command of the artillery of the Army of the West the following year, instead being appointed to the Topographical Bureau.

Appointed first general of division and then to the command of the Army of Italy as a reward for his "whiff of grape shot" in Paris, Napoleon developed and demonstrated in 1796 the characteristics of his generalship: self-confidence, swift decision-making, rapid mobility, the concentration of strength at what was made the decisive point, and, where possible, the exploitation of interior lines. Invading Piedmont from the south across the Ligurian Alps, Napoleon seized a central position between the Austrians and the leading independent Italian ruler, the king of Sardinia. The Austrians were defeated at Montenotte (12 April) and Millesimo and pushed back, and the Sardinians knocked out of the war after the battle of Mondovi (22 April), in which French columns beat the outnumbered defenders. Success in advance won the French food, money and captured military supplies, including cannon.

Napoleon then turned on the Austrians, turning the line of the Po by infringing the neutrality of Piacenza, where he crossed the river. The Austrians fell back; their rearguard covering the crossing of the Adda at Lodi was defeated on 10 May, winning Napoleon much glory and helping both to create the legend of Napoleonic generalship and to exalt his already high sense of his own ability. He pressed on to occupy Milan, and to seize Modena and the papal cities of Bologna and Ferrara. The Austrians fell back on the Tyrol and Venetia, but left a force in their major north Italian fortress, Mantua. Successive Austrian attempts to relieve it were defeated at Lonato (4 August), Castiglione (5 August), Arcola (15–17 November) and Rivoli (14 January 1797), and Mantua fell on 2 February. Napoleon's tactical genius and ability to manoeuvre on the battlefield brought victory over the Austrians, and associated Napoleon with military success. His siting of the artillery was particularly important.[18]

Furthermore, Napoleon's military successes brought a political verdict. Marching his men through Klagenfurt to within seventy miles of Vienna, Napoleon forced Austria to accept the Truce of Leoben on 18 April 1797, and to avoid the resumption of war it was obliged to accept the Treaty of Campo Formio on 18 October 1797. This left France dominant in Lombardy and forced Austria to give up the Austrian Netherlands. France was also left with the prospect of gaining most of the left bank of the Rhine. The First Coalition of powers against Revolutionary/Napoleonic France had been brought low. The location of the treaty's signing, at a village near Udine, in what is now north-east Italy, was a testimony to the range of Napoleon's advance. Further north, Hoche and the Army of Sambre and Meuse had beaten the Austrians at Neuweid (18 April 1797).

Neither under Revolutionary governments nor under Napoleon was France able to learn restraint. Repeatedly, victory was followed by a peace settlement that was only temporary. Military convenience, lust for loot, the practice of expropriation, ideological conviction, the political advantages of a successful campaign, and strategic opportunism all encouraged aggressive action, both before and after Campo Formio, as with the occupation of Venice in 1797, and the Papal States and Piedmont in 1798, and the invasion of Switzerland and Egypt in 1798. The invasions of Switzerland and Egypt helped precipitate the formation of the Second Coalition of Austria, Britain, Naples, Portugal, Russia and Turkey against France. In 1799, the French under Jourdan were defeated by the Austrians under Archduke Charles in Germany at Ostrach (21 March) and Stockach (25 March) and driven back across the Rhine. Charles defeated Massena at Zurich (4–7 June).

With Poland partitioned out of existence by the Third Partition in 1795, and Russia at peace with Turkey, the Russians were able to intervene effectively in western Europe, but this was only possible as a result of their defeat of the Polish rising of 1794. Proclaimed at Cracow on 24 March, the rising gathered pace with Tadeusz Kościuszko's victory over Tormasov at Raclawice on 4 April 1794. Warsaw rose and defeated its Russian garrison in street fighting on 17 April, and the Russians were driven from Vilna on 22–3 April. However, Prussian and Russian forces defeated a greatly outnumbered Kościuszko at Szczekociny (6 June) north of Cracow, and then besieged Warsaw unsuccessfully (27 July–5 September). The Prussians occupied Cracow on 16 June and a fortnight later Austrian forces joined in. Vilna was retaken by the Russians on 12 August. However, the army besieging Warsaw was badly hit by disease and hunger, and a rising in west Poland threatened Prussian communications. Frederick William II called off the siege on 5–6 September.

Meanwhile, a fresh Russian army under Suvorov advanced on Warsaw from the east, defeating Sierakowski at Krupczyce (17 September) and Terespol (19 September) near Brest Litovsk, and capturing the city. Russian success reflected superior military resources and Prussian support. The

Russian advance on Warsaw in late 1794 was decisive, thanks in particular to Fersen's victory over the outnumbered Kościuszko at Maciejowice (10 October 1794) and Suvorov's defeat of Mokronowski at Kobilka (23 October) and his storming of the Warsaw suburb of Praga (4 November). The Polish army retreated from Warsaw, which surrendered on the 5 November, and then largely dispersed on 16 November, the remaining senior officers surrendering three days later. Kościuszko himself had been wounded and captured at Maciejowice. Courland, which had risen in June, was regained by the Russians in September.[19] The defeat of the Poles, as also of the Irish rising against British rule in 1798, indicated that Revolutionaries could be rapidly defeated by *ancien régime* regulars. This underlines the variety of successful fighting methods in the period, and the importance of particular political contexts in affecting the success and failure of Revolutionary forces.

The range of power of the Russian military was demonstrated in a number of spheres in the 1790s. Under Suvorov in 1799, the Russians advanced into northern Italy, the first time that they had operated there. Suvorov's victories, particularly Cassano d'Adda (27 April), Trebbia (17–19 June) and Novi (15 August 1799), were brutal battles, in which repeated attacks finally found weaknesses in the French position.

Like Napoleon, Suvorov was a believer in the strategic and tactical offensive and had little time for sieges. Just as Wellington was to use in Portugal and Spain methods he had developed in India, so Suvorov employed techniques developed in conflict with the Turks. Willing to accept a high rate of casualties and to mount costly frontal attacks, Suvorov relied on bayonet attacks, not defensive fire-power, and showed that an emphasis on aggression, attack and risk was not restricted to the French.[20]

The failure of the Coalition partners to disrupt the French home base permitted a rallying of French strength, and divisions within the Coalition became more serious. The Austrians and Russians fell out, and an Anglo-Russian amphibious invasion of Holland that landed in August failed. The Anglo-Russian advance was checked and then defeated by a skilful French defence, and, with the initiative lost, the invaders withdrew in October. The expedition demonstrated what was already apparent from earlier episodes in the century, namely that amphibious operations against the Continent were far less successful than those against overseas European bases. This reflected the room for manoeuvre and reinforcement enjoyed by defenders on the Continent, and the contrast with overseas where, on the whole, the presence of the European power rested on a narrow coastal littoral. The situation was not to change until the British intervened on behalf of Portugal and Spain in 1808: their cooperation against French invaders helped provide room for manoeuvre.

Elsewhere, the Allied cause was also collapsing in 1799. On 25 September, a victory by Soult at Zurich over Korsakov led to the French regaining the initiative in Switzerland. This undercut Suvorov's bold advance there. He stormed the St. Gotthard, but, outnumbered and without supplies had to abandon Switzerland.[21] The government of France, the Directory, was, however, discredited by division and unpopular. Napoleon and Sieyès seized the opportunity to seize power, replace the Directory and establish the Consulate on 18–19 Brumaire (9–10 November). Napoleon became First Consul and General in Chief.

CHAPTER THREE
Napoleon and His Opponents

The Napoleonic Wars dominated the historical military consciousness of Europe until the Franco-Prussian War of 1870–71. Paintings, many commissioned by the Napoleonic government, left a powerful account of conflict.[1] These wars seemed to show the character, potential and limitations of Western warfare. The analysis of Napoleonic generalship and strategy attracted considerable attention and Baron Antoine Jomini was a particularly influential exponent. Furthermore, the wars were of great importance to the memories, careers and political location of the leading European commanders and militaries. As a result, they repay particular study.

As First Consul, and, from 1804, Emperor, Napoleon was in a position not only to act as an innovative general, but also to control the French military system and to direct the war effort. He enjoyed greater power over the army than any French ruler since Louis XIV (1643–1715). Decision-making was concentrated.

Furthermore, in many respects, Napoleon was more powerful than Louis.[2] His choice of commanders was not constrained by the social conventions and aristocratic alignments that affected Louis, and both armies and individual military units were under more direct governmental control than had been the case with the Bourbon dynasty. In addition, Napoleon was directly in command of the leading French force throughout the wars of his reign. Although he had to manage many campaigns from a distance, they were always those of subsidiary forces.

Under Napoleon, French resources were devoted to the military with a consistency that the Revolutionary governments had lacked. The conscription system, which had become less effective in the late 1790s, was strengthened, necessarily so as there were very few volunteers after 1799. Napoleon raised 1.3 million conscripts in 1800–11 and 1 million in 1812–13 alone.[3] In August 1813, he had a reserve of 18 million musket cartridges.

Napoleon also developed the corps; a unit at a level above that of the division, that could include all the arms (cavalry, artillery and three infantry divisions) and also be large enough to operate effectively. Both corps and divisions were given effective staff structures. Thus, the corps added to the flexibility of the earlier divisional system the strength necessary both for the punishing battles of the period, where opposing forces would not collapse rapidly as a result of well planned battlefield moves, and for Napoleon's campaigns of strategically applied force. The formal introduction of the corps system, on 1 March 1800, followed soon after Napoleon's seizure of power. Corps operated effectively, both as individual units, for example against the Prussians at the battle of Auerstädt (14 October 1806), and in concert. His opponents were to adopt the corps structure and thus improve their organizational resilience. The ability of corps to operate separately increased the frontage of any advance, but also made cooperation between corps important. As battle approached, it was necessary to bring corps together, achieving a dynamic mass. This made battles on an hitherto unprecedented scale possible. The division helped in the coordination of infantry, cavalry and artillery, providing a more integrated fighting force than that of France's opponents. However, the combination of corps in an *ad hoc* manner created particular problems of command. These were seen in French operations in 1813 when marshals Macdonald, Ney and Oudinot each found it difficult to control their armies.[4]

Greater numbers and operational flexibility ensured that skilled staff work was important to Napoleon. It was necessary to deploy rapidly and effectively the massive resources he controlled, in particular to be able to move many large corps by different routes, yet enable them still to support each other. In 1805, Napoleon speedily moved 194,000 men and about 300 cannon from northern France, where they were preparing to invade Britain, eastwards, in order to attack the Austrians in south-western Germany. The logistical basis of the campaign in 1805 was inadequate and the French were forced to resort to ravaging the countryside, but they were still able to move rapidly enough to surround the Austrians in Ulm.

More generally, better roads and better map-making facilitated the swifter movement of troops. Napoleon's Chief of Staff, Louis-Alexandre Berthier, a veteran of the French expedition to North America in 1780–82, was a crucial figure in a French command structure that was better than those of its opponents. Henri Clarke, minister of war from 1807, was an effective and energetic administrator, responsible for the drafting of troops, the organization of new units and the management of the armies of occupation.

However, there was no General Staff to match that which the Prussians were to develop under Moltke in the second half of the century. Napoleon planned both strategy and operations, but although this offered coherence it was also a formidable burden that placed great pressure on his abilities and resilience. Napoleon's centralized direction of campaigns became a problem from 1809, when he limited the autonomy of his commanders in the distant Peninsular War, and it even proved difficult to control effectively the large armies of his later years that were under his direct command. Several of his commanders, including Davout and Masséna, were talented, but Napoleonic intervention lessened their capability for effective independent command. This was serious as the corps system required talented subordinates capable of independent command. As a separate problem, the French commanders were of variable quality. Several good fighting generals, such as Ney, proved poor planners. In addition, the absence of an effective hierarchy among the commanders pushed decision-making, indeed arbitration, back on Napoleon, and also caused problems when, as in Spain, he was absent.

The French organizational and command structures were vital to Napoleon's characteristic rapidity of strategic and tactical movement, and his troops also travelled more lightly than those of Frederick the Great. Napoleon employed this mobility to strategic effect. He concentrated on a single front, seeking in each war to identify the crucial opposing force and to destroy it rapidly. This, not the occupation of territory, was his goal. For temperamental reasons, and because he wanted glory, and rapid and decisive results, Napoleon sought battle. He attacked both in campaigning and in battle. Although he fought for much of his reign, his individual wars with Continental opponents were over fairly rapidly. Warfare (incorporating diplomacy, preparation and the campaign) might be a long-term process for Napoleon, but war became an event. Thus, for example, wars with Austria in 1805 and 1809 ended the same year, while the war with Prussia that began in 1806 ended in 1807. Such rapid results were the product of a concentration of military resources on a single front, a contrast with the situation in the 1790s.

The pressure for a rapid close also reflected Napoleon's weakness in logistical planning, in particular his emphasis on improvisation. In practice, this meant heavy pressure on France's allies and occupied territory to produce resources, and a stress on troops living on the country. This encouraged a movement into fresh pastures, but was no solution where supplies were limited, as in Russia and Spain, or already exhausted by frequent campaigning, and was also of limited value when forces rested on the defensive.

On campaign, Napoleon took a central position in order to divide more numerous opposing forces and then defeat them separately. A strategy of envelopment was used against weaker forces: they were pinned down by an attack mounted by a section of the French army, while most of the army enveloped them, attacking them in flank or, in preference, cutting their lines of supply and retreat, the *manoeuvre sur les derrières*. This put the opponent in a disadvantageous position if they wished to fight on rather than surrender; a similar technique was to be employed by the Prussians under Moltke against the French in 1870.

Napoleon was a strong believer in the value of artillery, organized into strong batteries, particularly of 12-pounders. He increased the number of field guns and the ratio of guns to infantry. Nevertheless, Napoleon had fewer cannon than he wanted: the expansion in his forces helped to keep the ratio below his target of five per thousand troops. Napoleon compensated for this by using his cannon as an offensive force, making them as mobile on the battlefield as possible, by the use of effective horse-drawn limbers. The French pieces were carefully deployed, in order to give effect to tactical planning. Each corps was allocated a number of batteries, but Napoleon kept the Army Artillery Reserve under his own control. This gave him a vital reserve for use on the battlefield, maintaining his tactical flexibility. Austrian cannon was less well deployed. At Wagram (5–6 July 1809), Napoleon covered the reorganization of his attack with a battery of 102 guns.[5] Before attacking the Saxons, then backing Napoleon, at Grossbeeren on 23 August 1813, Bernadotte bombarded his opponents with 62 cannon he had massed together.

Napoleon also massed his cavalry for use at the vital moment, as with Murat's charge through the Russian centre at Eylau (8 February 1807). He initially successfully employed *l'ordre mixte* of the 1790s for the infantry: a mixture of lines and columns with many sharp-shooters to precede the attack. The use of these formations was enhanced by effective tactical plans and detailed staff planning. Napoleon thus developed the innovations and practices of the Revolutionary years and systematized them. He moved from a position in which these tactics had been adopted as an *ad hoc* reaction to the crisis situation of 1792–93, to employing them as a considered response to the military situation; they were more flexible than Austrian tactics. However, French tactics degenerated later on, and it can be argued that Napoleon devoted insufficient attention to tactical details. He was limited by the continual need to adapt tactics to his large numbers of inexperienced troops. As the French army, due to continuing heavy casualties, began increasingly to fill up with raw, unwilling conscripts, its tactical finesse was coarsened and became less effective. Napoleon, himself, his energy draining with age possibly also lost his youthful sharpness in conducting battles.[6]

On the whole, Napoleon has been applauded as a great operational genius, especially as a manoeuvrer and strategist, with a great sense of timing. He was an able planner and knew when and how to strike, although he usually left tactics to the discretion of his field officers. His campaigns and battles are still studied at West Point. Recently, however, there has been more criticism of his generalship. Owen Connelly presented Napoleon as a skilful improviser who did not care if he initially blundered, since he had confidence that he could devise a strategic or tactical plan in the field, based on the enemy's movements and/or errors, and win. He had an innate flair, which enabled him to "read" the battlefield in terms of time and space.[7] This was different to the character of improvisation shown by Moltke in 1866 and 1870: the Prussians responded to Austrian and French moves, but did so within a much more clearly structured plan, necessarily so as the command and planning system was not so heavily dependent on one individual.

Napoleon manipulated the historical record to disguise his failings and seize credit from others. He had official accounts of the Battle of Marengo (14 June 1800) rewritten in order to conceal his mistakes and to present the battle as going according to plan. In fact, Napoleon was rescued from a different situation by a detached corps under Desaix. Paddy Griffith has been blunt at the expense of Napoleon: "no greater in the strategic and operational arts than Dumouriez . . . nor, surely, did Bonaparte display any greater mastery of the central direction of war than . . . Carnot".[8] Napoleon is seen as different because he had more troops. Furthermore, it has been argued that, having changed European warfare himself, Napoleon failed to understand and respond to further developments:

> Napoleon's mistakes prior to 1809 did not have catastrophic conse-
> quences because his opponents made more mistakes and their armies
> were less effective in war. But Napoleon's usual mistakes were
> magnified as his opposition improved. Convinced that his personal-
> ity and genius could overcome all obstacles, Napoleon was blinded to
> the changing realities of warfare.[9]

The last point is a valuable reminder that, as with Gustav Adolf of Sweden, Marlborough and Frederick the Great, as well as less famous commanders, it is necessary to avoid a static account of their generalship and, instead, to consider them in terms of a dynamic situation, specifically varying relative capability and effectiveness. This was as much a case of "political" as of more narrowly "military" factors, but, even in terms of the latter the variety of opponents and the pace of change were such that it was necessary to be continuously flexible and adaptable. Thus, it is possible to add to the influential analysis of Napoleon as a failure because of the nature of his rule and the character of his foreign policy, specifically the resolute alliance that consolidated against him in 1813, the suggestion that it is also necessary to offer a military account of his military failure. This has to be found in terms both of the French and of how they compared with their rivals and changes in the latter's armies and methods, an approach that invites attention to such questions as capability gaps and developments in military systems.

Napoleon's generalship should not be simplified into a trajectory of success to failure, however attractive that might be in terms of the parallel idea of a ruler brought down by hubris. Napoleon's handling of the 1815 campaign was maladroit – his failure to drive his opponents apart in order to defeat them in detail, and his lack of flexibility on the battlefield at Waterloo – but in both 1813 and 1814 he displayed impressive generalship against superior odds. Throughout, Napoleon was dominated by the desire to engage and win. By launching campaigns and forcing battles whose likely shape was unclear, Napoleon placed great reliance on the subsequent effectiveness of his armies.

This rewarded the fighting quality of individual units, the initiative and skill of subordinates, and the ability to retain reserves until the crucial moment.

Napoleon confronted grave problems, not least the number and fighting quality of his opponents and the difficulty of establishing their positions, let alone intentions, the primitive communications of the period, and the need to raise the operational effectiveness of his conscripts. He deserves credit for developing an effective military machine, even as he undermined it by the strains of near continuous warfare, and eventually overwhelmed it in 1813–14 by failing to avoid or end a multi-front struggle. Able to adapt rapidly to changing circumstances and fresh intelligence, Napoleon had a remarkable ability to impose his will upon war. He won close to 50 major battles in his career, including the largest, most convoluted engagements hitherto seen in the gunpowder age. Most martial reputations rest only on a victory or two. Indubitably, Napoleon, like so many other great commanders, committed errors of judgement, but they were relatively few. His successes owed something to weight of numbers, but Napoleon should be given credit for the skill with which he achieved (usually local) superiority, generally by manoeuvre over vast distances. Leadership and morale were also important. The quest for glory was valued in the culture of the period, and Napoleon's search for fame had a significant military consequence in that it contributed to the morale of his troops and thus his ability to impose his will upon war. Napoleon's command of the respect and affection of troops and officers was a major resource.[10] To suggest that he was a great general is not to denigrate his predecessors and contemporaries in the 1790s, nor to ignore his faults and limitations as a commander, nor his serious deficiencies as a ruler.

Napoleonic campaigns, 1800–1807

Napoleon's opening campaign as First Consul was an invasion of northern Italy, boldly begun with a crossing of the Great St. Bernard Pass so that he arrived in the Austrian rear, capturing Milan and wrecking their communications. At Marengo (14 June 1800), however, he found the Austrians a formidable opponent when they mounted an unexpected attack and fought well. Napoleon's enforced retreat for much of the battle was only reversed because of the arrival of reinforcements – the forces he had earlier detached – and the successful counter-attack they mounted. A quarter of the French force became casualties. Thus, Napoleon's strategic skill in managing the campaign was not capped by a well managed battle.

In Germany, the French under Jean Moreau successfully advanced into Bavaria. The Austrians tried to counter-attack, but the French, flexible in defence, successfully ambushed and defeated them at Hohenlinden (3 December 1800). This led the Austrians to conclude peace at Lunéville on 9

December 1801. They recognized French annexation of the entire left bank of the Rhine. The previous year, Tsar Paul I had abandoned the war. Victory in war and peace consolidated Napoleon's hold on power.

Britain was left isolated, more so in April 1801 when a French-supported Spanish invasion of Portugal forced Portugal to break with Britain. France could not defeat the British at sea, but, with the Treaty of Amiens of 25 March 1802, they had to accept French hegemony in Western Europe. Mutual distrust and Napoleon's unwillingness to accept limits to further expansion led to the resumption of war in May 1803. Angered by aggressive French steps, Russia allied with Britain in the spring of 1805, while Napoleon's demand that Austria demobilize led it to declare war on France and, on 9 September, to invade Napoleon's ally Bavaria.

In the War of the Third Coalition, Napoleon benefited from the years of peace on the Continent from 1801. These had enabled him to train the infantry, increase the artillery and cavalry and produce better balanced corps. The earlier years of war had provided experienced troops and an officer corps sifted by merit.

The peacetime improvements were important because the battles of the 1790s and 1800 had indicated both the strength of France's opponents and also the diversity and divisiveness of the French armies, because, for political reasons, there was no overall commander-in-chief. Thus, Napoleon's strategy in 1800 was affected by his limited control over Moreau, and the sway of the latter over his Army of the Rhine. In 1804, Moreau was imprisoned for his role in Royalist plotting and then exiled to the USA. Many of his troops had already been sent to St. Domingue.

Napoleon used the peace to establish the *Grande Armée* (1802) and to give his troops and officers systematic training. In addition, both equipment and organization were overhauled. The ability to keep so many men in arms in peacetime was important. The Austrians failed to match these improvements.

Napoleon benefited from having his army ready: it had been prepared for an invasion of southern England, but the French fleet had failed to gain the necessary naval control of the Channel. Napoleon was helped in the War of the Third Coalition by the lack of cohesion in political objectives or military planning shown by his opponents. The Austrians were most interested in regaining Lombardy and sent their largest force to Italy. Another force was sent to invade Bavaria and it was then intended that it should be supported by the Russians. Napoleon was able to take advantage of this absence of concentration. He imposed his own timetable, and this superseded that of his opponents. The Austrians were preparing for an attack from the west through the Black Forest, but they lost understanding, let alone control, of the sequence of events as they were outmanoeuvred and enveloped by the rapid advance of the French from the middle Rhine to the Danube in their rear. From the outset, Napoleon hoped and planned to get behind the Austrians. The French crossed the Danube on 6 October. The overly cautious Austrian response left an army under Mack bottled up in Ulm. It surrendered on 20 October, and, with Bavarian support, Napoleon then overran southern Germany and Austria: Napoleon entered Vienna on 13 November. Success in Germany was helped by the situation in northern Italy, where a French force of only 50,000 under Masséna contained the 90,000 strong Austrian army under Archduke Charles.[11]

Napoleon's advance brought him closer to the advancing Russians, deliberately so as he wanted to inflict a heavy defeat on them. There was to be no winter break in the campaigning. On 2 December 1805, Tsar Alexander I and a 85,000 strong Austro-Russian army attacked the 75,000 strong French at Austerlitz, as Napoleon had hoped. A strong assault on Napoleon's right was held and, in a surprise attack, the French turned the weak flank of this Russian attack and divided the opposing army in order to win. The French were better able than their Russian counterparts to use numerical superiority at the point of contact they had sought. French forces also showed themselves more manoeuvrable in battle conditions. Training and organization paid off in the successful integration of different arms: aside from Napoleon's superior generalship, the French command system proved better able to integrate the different arms effectively.[12] Austria left the war by the Treaty of Pressburg of 26 December 1805. Archduke Charles's victory in Italy over Masséna at Caldiero (28–31 October) was not a sweeping success and had anyway been made redundant by Austerlitz.

The following year, French bullying and Prussian opportunism led to war between the two. Poorly commanded and outmanoeuvred, the Prussian forces were defeated at Jena and Auerstädt (14 October), although French fighting quality also played a major role at Auerstädt. At Jena, massed French artillery and substantial numbers of skirmishers inflicted heavy losses on the Prussian lines. The French pressed on to force the surrender of other Prussian forces. Frederick the Great's famous army had collapsed in less than a month. This was much more abrupt and dramatic than Prussia's failure in the French Revolutionary War.[13]

The Russians proved a tougher opponent and Eylau (6 February 1807) was a severe blow because there was a very serious loss of experienced troops. The Russians inflicted heavy casualties with their more numerous artillery and fought off successive attacks before withdrawing during the night. Napoleon's double envelopment had failed. Had the factors of distance and weather, both of which hit the French campaign in Poland, been comparable to those in Russia in 1812, then it is possible that the failure of the Napoleonic system would have been dated earlier.

Nevertheless, French victory over the outnumbered and badly positioned Russians at Friedland (14 June 1807) brought peace with Prussia and Russia. This was the first battle in which a large part of Napoleon's army had not been French. Napoleon's tactics had centred on a frontal attack: the Russian position resting on a river had not provided opportunities for an envelopment.

Napoleon used effective artillery-infantry cooperation: a 30-gun battery was advanced into close range and the French infantry exploited the impact of its canister shot.[14] Portugal was successfully invaded the same year in order to close it to British trade.

The conflicts of this period indicated the superiority of the French corps and divisional structure over the less coherent and ill coordinated opposing forces, who lacked any consistent equivalent organization. French staff work, at army and corps level, was superior to that of both Austria and Russia, and this helped to vitiate the effect of the greater numbers that France's opponents put into the field. The quality of French staff work enabled Napoleon to translate his wide-ranging strategic vision into practice, to force what might have been a segmented war into essentially a struggle in one major theatre of operations where he could use the *Grande Armée* effectively.

Napoleonic campaigns, 1808–12

Napoleon had already encountered many serious problems before his unsuccessful invasion of Russia in 1812. His attempt to seize Spain in 1808 led to a popular uprising. A surrounded French corps surrendered at Bailén (21 July 1808) and British forces landed in Portugal the following month. There, an attacking French army was stopped by the fire-power of a British force under Sir Arthur Wellesley, later Duke of Wellington, at Vimeiro (21 August 1808). Napoleon, however, intervened in Spain, defeating poorly trained, commanded and outnumbered Spanish forces, and entering Madrid on 4 December. This, however, did not end the fighting in Spain.[15]

The following year, war also resumed with Austria, and Napoleon found her a tougher military opponent than in 1805, but the Austrians were handicapped by poorly conceived war aims, inadequate and divided central leadership and a foolish strategy. Nevertheless, under the leadership of Archduke Charles, the Austrians had adopted division and corps structures and, like the French, provided them with their own artillery; the number of cannon was also increased. Infantry tactics and cavalry formations were also changed, although there was still a lack of flexibility (and of meritocracy in appointments) compared to the French. Austrian staff work was also inadequate.

The Austrians began operations in 1809, advancing into Bavaria. However, Charles squandered the initiative by moving too slowly and he failed to take advantage of the dispersed nature of the French forces. Napoleon responded vigorously, pummelling Charles at Abensberg (21 April) and Eggmüll (22 April). Charles fell back, as, in response, did Archdukes John and Ferdinand who had invaded Italy and Poland respectively. Nationalist risings against Napoleon in the Tyrol and northern Germany did not affect the campaign.[16]

Charles retreated beyond Vienna to rest on the defensive on the north bank of the Danube. Once the French had got some of their troops across, Charles attacked their bridgehead around the villages of Aspern and Essling (21 May). The French held off the attack, and on 22 May Napoleon assaulted the Austrian centre. However, he failed to break through and, under pressure, fell back from the bridgehead. As at Eylau, Napoleon had been thwarted by the strength of the defence, although at Aspern-Essling, denied room for manoeuvre, his tactical plans had been simpler. Unlike at Eylau, he had to abandon the battlefield.

At Wagram, on 5–6 July 1809, Napoleon proved the better general and the French corps commanders were superior to their Austrian counterparts. Napoleon's forces successfully crossed the Danube on 4 July, and on 5 July the French advanced, although they failed to capture the major Austrian positions. The Austrian attack on 6 July was held with difficulty, but, as the French began to advance successfully, the Austrians retreated. Napoleon's counter-attack drove the Austrians from the field, but it was no Austerlitz: the Austrians were not routed, and the French lost 33,000 dead and wounded. Thanks in part to the heavy artillery power of both sides, breakthroughs were limited. The Austrian corps structure was effective, and the French victory was essentially due to their superiority in troops and material and to the mishandling of the Austrian attack in what was a battle of attrition. In the end, Napoleon had to rely on frontal assaults, especially in the centre. Unlike in 1805, the Austrians had no Russian support, while Frederick William III of Prussia refused promised support. Austria accepted terms for political reasons; her army had not been destroyed. By the Peace of Schönbrunn of 14 October 1809, the Austrians accepted heavy territorial losses and a limitation on the size of their army.

The 1809 campaign has been seen as a turning point, although reasons vary. Focusing on organizational factors at the operational level, Robert Epstein saw the campaign as marking a revival of symmetry in Western warfare as Austria learned to counter the French corps system by using one of her own. He argued that this made a decisive stroke unlikely and, instead, put the emphasis on a more long-running process of engagement. In contrast, J. R. Arnold focused on tactics and a shift in the dynamic of the combined arms army, with, in particular, the rise of artillery and the demise of battlefield shock cavalry, at least as a decisive force.[17] These were both important developments, although whether they deserve the designation "modern war" is far less clear, and, as this study suggests, that concept is more appropriately located later. The claims advanced by Epstein are possibly more appropriate for the 1813 campaigns in Germany, and it was those that were to attract the later attention of Moltke and the Prussian General Staff. The degree to which the Austrians had adapted to French war-making techniques by 1809 is problematic. However, as this study will suggest, the elusive question of modernity can best be addressed in relation to developments considerably later in the century.

In 1812, Napoleon's hegemonic ambitions and unwillingness to consider restraint as the better option led him to war with Russia. Napoleon's closest advisers opposed the invasion which was as unnecessary diplomatically as it was foolish militarily. But for the invasion, the French might have been able to defeat their opponents in Spain and Portugal.

As with his earlier attacks on Austria, Prussia and Spain, and his planned invasion of Britain in 1805, Napoleon resolved to strike at the centre of Russian power, thus gaining the initiative and transferring much of the logistical burden of the war on to his enemy. He invaded on 24–5 June with half a million men, many of whom were allied, principally German, troops, including 36,000 Bavarians and 26,700 Saxons. Planning to envelop the Russians, Napoleon invaded on a very broad front, but this created problems of command and communication. On the left, Macdonald's corps, which included a Prussian force, was to besiege Riga, unsuccessfully. The Russians fell back, denying Napoleon a decisive battle.

With less space in which to manoeuvre in defence of their capitals, the American Confederates and the French were to follow a very different policy in 1861 and 1870: both fought on their frontiers. In contrast, in 1812, scorched earth and guerrilla activity by the retreating Russians severely reduced French supplies, losing them men through hunger, disease and fatigue in consequence. Dysentery and typhus became serious problems. Finally, at Borodino on 7 September, the Russians sought to stop the advance on Moscow. In a battle of attrition that involved 233,000 men and 1,227 cannon, the Russians gave ground after successive attacks, but without breaking. The Russians had created extensive earthworks, which Napoleon insisted on attacking frontally, rather than trying to turn their flank as Davout advised. The Russians relied on the fire-power of their defences and on counter-attacks. Eventually, Napoleon took the Great Redoubt in the centre of the Russian position, but his failure to use his reserve, the Imperial Guard, helped ensure that the Russians could withdraw successfully. Russian casualties were heavier, but Napoleon lost a quarter of his army.[18] He repeatedly pressed Clarke to forward troops from all available sources within the empire.

Napoleon followed up Borodino by entering an undefended Moscow on 14 September, but the city was set ablaze, probably by the Russians. The enormity of the task, logistical problems and the endurance of the Russians defeated Napoleon militarily, while the difficulty of securing any settlement thwarted him politically. He had no terms to propose, faced an opponent who would not negotiate, and could not translate his seizure of Moscow into negotiations.

In the face of a deteriorating supply situation and encroaching Russian forces, Napoleon began his retreat on 19 October. The retreat turned into a nightmare as heavy snowfalls, supply breakdowns and Russian attacks, especially as the French crossed the Berezina River on 26–9 November, combined to cause heavy casualties. French discipline collapsed and helped dissolve the army, but the commanders were also found wanting. Napoleon returned with only 60,000 men. Marshal Ney was the last to cross the Niemen on 14 December.[19]

This disaster was far more serious than the earlier checks at Eylau and Aspern-Essling; or the British victories in the Peninsular War in Portugal and Spain at Talavera (27–8 July 1809) and Salamanca (22 July 1812), for the French were winning the Peninsular War until 1812, at least in so far as control over much of Spain was concerned. Napoleon was fatally weakened by his failure in 1812, not least because there would never thereafter be anywhere near such an opportunity to defeat the Russians, and because the Russians were now determined to defeat him. The failure of the attempted coup in Paris on 23 October 1812 by ex-Général Claude-François Malet was scant consolation.

The Peninsular War

The Peninsular War also throws light on deficiencies in French military methods. French success in battle had turned on the exploitation of the synergy between cavalry, close-order infantry, artillery and skirmishers. A combination of attacks by different arms reduced both the enemy's physical means to resist and his will. However, in Spain, the French experienced great difficulty in trying to achieve this combination. Terrain factors frequently precluded the efficacious use of their often superior cavalry and artillery. Attacks were frequently executed sequentially, rather than simultaneously, and by only one arm, usually the infantry. French failures to weaken the British lines, by the use of artillery or skirmishers, before the column attack, left the columns exposed to heavy defensive fire. The lack of unity and mutual support among the corps commanders also hit the French hard. The French suffered from a number of poor commanders, especially, in 1810, the tired Masséna, who was well past his prime and, in 1813, Joseph Bonaparte.

Napoleon's continued interference from a distance was also a major problem. He did not understand the war, its topography and ramifications; he went to Spain only once – in overwhelming force in 1808 – and then forgot about the nature of campaigning there. Napoleon was consumed with his own projects and was jealous of his subordinates. His misguided attempt to direct plans through written instructions was compounded by the absence of a clear command structure within Spain itself. In 1810, Napoleon tried to micro-manage Masséna's campaign, ordering him to take the border fortresses first. Wellington, in contrast, had far more control over military operations and benefited from this unity of command. He was appointed commander-in-chief of all allied forces in November 1812.

French forces in Iberia outnumbered those under Wellington's effective command, but they also had to face Spanish resistance. The Spaniards were generally unsuccessful in formal conflict, and British generals could be critical of their organization, but their regular and guerrilla operations denied the French control over the countryside and, in particular, greatly harmed their communications and logistics. The French were unable to concentrate their superior forces against Wellington, but would have been able to do so had they knocked out the Spaniards, which would have been a distinct possibility but for the invasion of Russia. Spanish guerrillas also provided Wellington with useful intelligence.

The British, under Wellington, used both defensive fire-power and bayonet advances. A bayonet charge preceded by a volley had become a standard British tactic from the 1750s, used with effect in the War of American Independence, and, with his fine grasp of timing and eye for terrain, Wellington brought the system to a high pitch of effectiveness. He employed the thin red line of two ranks that the British had utilized in North America, but his men fought elbow to elbow, not in the more open order used by the British in North America and employed by Wellington's Light Infantry and Rifles.

The British succeeded in balancing the well drilled line that represented the legacy of Frederick the Great with the extensive use of light infantry in battle; the conservatism of an emphasis on linear fire-power formations with a greater role for manoeuvrability. Wellington ably executed fire and movement tactics. Like Napoleon, much of Wellington's skill lay in adapting quickly to fresh intelligence and changing circumstances. At Vimeiro (21 August 1808), the well positioned British lines succeeded in blunting the French columns, while at Salamanca, Wellington used his lines in attack with great effect. His reverse-slope ploy of locating his troops behind the crest of hills in order to protect them from artillery was important, as at Bussaco on 27 September 1810. Wellington's flexibility underlines that the variety and dynamism of tactics in this period was not restricted to France, and thus further subverts any simplistic model of military development and capability.

Napoleonic campaigns, 1813–14

The idea of Napoleonic invincibility was shattered by defeat in Russia, although the defeat was in large part attributed to General Winter. Napoleon made no real attempt to accept the military verdict and offer Russia terms that would assuage the tsar's hostility. He could conceive neither of a new ethos in French foreign policy nor of a new system in eastern Europe. This greatly contributed to Russia's determination to implement the decision in December 1812 to press on against France, and thereby put Prussia in the front line.

In the new year (1813), Napoleon's diplomatic position collapsed as the French retreated before the Russian advance. In March, Prussia, which had signed a treaty with Russia on 28 February, affected by a wave of francophobia in the army and parts of the populace, declared war on France. Nevertheless, Napoleon fought back hard in Germany, aided by concerns among the German rulers about Russian and Prussian intentions. Napoleon rebuilt his army to a force of over 400,000 plus his artillery, but the new recruits were more like the fresh troops of 1792 than the veterans of his earlier campaigns, and, unlike in 1792, France's opponents were no longer outnumbered. They also better understood French military methods. In addition, Napoleon suffered from the consequences of the losses in 1812; in particular he was unable to create a new cavalry to match the troops and over 175,000 trained horses[20] lost in Russia. His victories over the Prussians and Russians at Lützen (2 May) and Bautzen (20–21 May), thanks to which he cleared his opponents from Saxony, were achieved over outnumbered forces, and neither was decisive; they might well have brought success had Napoleon pressed on, but he could not, in part for lack of cavalry. Instead, Bautzen led both sides to agree to an armistice.

The number of Napoleon's opponents was growing; a product of political and military failure. He suffered from his unwillingness to compromise and thus to bring any stability to the inherently unstable French hegemony across much of Europe. This instability was exacerbated by the invasion of Spain and the situation there collapsed as a consequence of failure in 1812–13; but that failure was military. Many European rulers and much of the social elite had been willing to compromise with Napoleon. The large numbers of Germans, Italians and Poles that invaded Russia in 1812, and the Saxons and Danes who supported him in 1813 were, however, led to defeat, and many began to lose faith in him.

Defeat exposed Napoleon's character flaws. To be unwilling to compromise when triumphant was serious enough: to fail to do so when defeated was far more so. In January 1813, Napoleon harshly rejected Prussian terms. That summer, he mishandled Austria, and in early 1814 he ruined the chance to use the negotiations at Châtillon to bring peace. The political will of Napoleon's opponents stiffened: anger with Napoleon took precedence over their own serious divisions.[21]

This would have mattered less had there been an issue both to divide or distract, as Poland had in 1793–95. The equivalent for Britain might have been failure in the war of 1812, American conquest of Canada, and the threat of American intervention in the West Indies or Ireland, but none of these were plausible; the Americans lacked long-range amphibious capability and the unity and resources for a major war. There was no equivalent to Poland in Europe, and Turkey had ended its war with Russia in 1812.

In the summer of 1813, when Napoleon rejected peace terms, Austria and Sweden joined his opponents and the French became heavily outnumbered. In the late summer and autumn of 1813, Napoleon confronted his enemies again. Austrian, Prussian, Russian and Swedish forces exceeded 600,000, while Napoleon's total field army was only 370,000. The allies adopted the

Trachenburg Plan, probably drawn up by Josef Radetzky, the Austrian quartermaster: battle with Napoleon was to be avoided while independent forces under his subordinates were to be attacked. The plan reflected the Allies' respect for Napoleon's generalship. The Prussians defeated detached French forces at Grossbeeren (23 August), on the Katzbach river (26 August), and at Dennewitz (6 September); and the Austrians won at Kulm (30 August). Napoleon's failure to train his marshals to operate as independent commanders, and their lack of supporting staffs cost the French dear. The marshals could not concentrate their armies at the decisive point in order to achieve victory, and they were unable to operate in order to fulfil strategic objectives. The scale of war was too great for Napoleon to control everything, and he also suffered due to the raw nature of many of his troops.

Only at Dresden, where Frederick William III insisted on fighting on 26–7 August, was Napoleon victorious, thanks to strong attacks by his flanks. Nevertheless, this was not the triumph of envelopment that the French required in order to win a major triumph. By failing to concentrate his forces during the campaign, Napoleon had allowed their attenuation, and this had preserved neither the territory under French control nor the strategic advantage; he had neglected his maxim that the main enemy force, not territory, should have priority. Threatened with Austrian invasion, Bavaria, long a stalwart of French interests, allied with Austria in October.

It was Napoleon, not his opponents, who was outmanoeuvred, his line of retreat threatened by the converging Allied forces. At the Battle of the Nations at Leipzig (16–19 October) Napoleon was heavily outnumbered: 195,000 to 365,000 by the time both sides were fully engaged. Napoleon had hoped to defeat his opponents in detail, but the Austrians were helped on 16 October by the arrival of the Prussians. On 18 October, the Russians and Swedes also joined the attack and Napoleon was pressed back on Leipzig with heavy losses and pressure on his ammunition supplies. On 19 October, Napoleon ordered a retreat, but the premature destruction of the Elster bridge trapped four corps, leading to French losses of 68,000 in the battle.

After Leipzig, Napoleon's position in Germany collapsed, as former allies, such as Württemberg, deserted and the French fell back. Too many troops, however, were left in fortresses in Germany and Spain, a sign of Napoleon's refusal to face facts, and one that was to be matched by Hitler in 1943–45. In France, Napoleon's capability was debilitated by falling tax revenues, widespread draft avoidance, a serious shortage of arms and equipment, chaos in the Ministry of War and a marked decline in the morale and efficiency of officials. The economy was in a parlous state, hit by British blockade and by the loss of Continental markets.

In the early months of 1814, Austro-Prussian-Russian forces invaded eastern France: there was no winter break to campaigning, and this lessened Napoleon's ability to mount an adequate response. Nevertheless, he took the initiative and, with some success, attacked the converging forces of the invaders, manoeuvring with skill in order to defeat the most exposed units, at Champaubert (10 February), Montmirail (11 Februrary), Vauchamps (14 February), Montereau (18 February), Craonne (7 March), and Rheims (13 March). Numbers, however, eventually told. In place of the 80,000 opposing troops he had anticipated, there were about 200,000, while his own army was 80,000 strong, and not the 120,000 men he had anticipated.[22] Both Napoleon and his subordinates were defeated at Laon (9–10 March) and Arcis-sur-Aube (20–21 March).

Finally, the Austrians and Prussians marched on Paris, ignoring Napoleon's position on their flank and his threat to the supply lines. After its defenders were driven back in the suburbs, Paris surrendered and Marshal Marmont, who had been pressed hard at Montmartre on 30 March, agreed an armistice the following night. This allowed the Allies to occupy Paris. A provisional French government deposed Napoleon. He wanted to march on Paris, but Marmont had already joined the Allies. With his other marshals, led by Ney, unwilling to fight on, Napoleon abdicated on 6 April 1814. Four days later, the British army under Wellington that had earlier driven back the French in Spain, crushing them at Vitoria (21 June 1813), defeated Marshal Soult at Toulouse.[23]

The Waterloo Campaign, 1815

Napoleon was exiled to Elba, but he returned to France in March 1815 and seized power from the weak and unpopular Louis XVIII, Louis fleeing before his arrival. Napoleon was able to reimpose his authority relatively easily: he entered Paris on 20 March without firing a shot. The Vendée rose again, but the rising was crushed at the battle of Rocheservière.

Napoleon's return united the European powers against him. On 25 March 1815, they renewed their alliance to overthrow the restored emperor and pledged a total force of 700,000 men. Napoleon, meanwhile, sought to strengthen his army, by raising both volunteers and renewing conscription, but was not allowed time, by the threatening invasion, to realize his plans in terms of size or proper preparation. Furthermore, the campaign was to reveal serious deficiencies in French staff work.

Rather than wait for his opponents to invade in overwhelming force, and, in particular, for the Austrians and Russians to advance, Napoleon attacked their nearest concentration, invading the Low Countries on 15 June. He planned to separate the opposing forces, an Anglo-Dutch-German army under Wellington and a Prussian army under Blücher, and defeat them in detail, necessarily so as his force was outnumbered two to one. This would create a window of diplomatic and military opportunity before invasion by Austrian and Russian forces, which was not expected until July.

Short of information about French dispositions and intentions, Wellington mistakenly gave Napoleon his opportunity by moving his army west towards Mons, in order to cover his links with the Channel Ports, instead of moving towards the Prussians as he had agreed. On 16 June, French forces were able to engage Wellington and Blücher separately but not to bring their whole strength against either one of them. Napoleon planned to attack Blücher in front, flank and rear at Ligny, but Ney, who was to fulfil the latter two functions, moved slowly and was blocked by Wellington at Quatre Bras: repeated attacks failed to dislodge the British. The Prussians were pushed back at Ligny, their line broken, but, having held out until nightfall, they were able to retreat in good order; furthermore they were to retreat north, not away from the British. The French failed to keep an adequate grip on Prussian moves and strength; indeed Napoleon over emphasized the impact of his attack at Ligny. On 17 June, with the Prussians in retreat, Ney failed to destroy Wellington. Instead, Wellington was able to disengage and to fall back to the ridge of Mont St. Jean.

There, on 18 June, in the battle of Waterloo, Wellington's 67,000 strong force was attacked by 74,000 French troops. Wellington was encouraged by a promise from Blücher that four Prussian corps would be sent to his help. Neither Wellington nor Napoleon was fighting with armies that were as good as those they had commanded at the peak of their careers; instead, the forces were in several respects scratch armies: many of the troops had little combat experience and many of the units had no experience of fighting together. This was a particular problem for Wellington: he was justifiably dubious about many of the Dutch and German units in his army. This unevenness helped encourage him to rely on a defensive deployment anchored on British units. Nevertheless, Napoleon was in a weak position, in part of his own making: he had underestimated his opponents' generalship and French intelligence and staff work were inadequate.

In the battle, defensive fire-power beat off successive French frontal attacks. There was no effective coordination of French infantry, cavalry and artillery. Wellington was correct to describe the battle as a "pounding match". In part, this reflected the tactical control wielded by Ney; Napoleon was ill. Napoleon also had no experience of commanding against Wellington, and ignored the warnings of those such as Soult who had done so in the Peninsular War. He was also frustrated by the overnight rain, which had left the clay soil soggy and delayed (perhaps fatally) the start of the battle as the artillery was hauled into position. Flank attacks, which Napoleon neglected, or yet more frontal assaults might have succeeded. However, the arrival of the Prussians on the French right spelled the end. The detached force under Grouchy intended to prevent this had signally failed. Realizing this, Napoleon still continued to order frontal attacks but they were defeated by the steadiness of the defending infantry. Wellington still had reserves, but most of Napoleon's had had to be used against the Prussians.[24]

Napoleon fled back to Paris, arriving on 21 June. As his regime collapsed, and the Allied forces advanced, he was urged by some advisers, including Davout, to fight on, but, instead, abdicated on 22 June. The French army had been ruined by Waterloo. Only 27,000 troops assembled at Laon on 24 June. Anglo-Prussian forces occupied Paris on 7 July. British forces cooperated with local royalists to occupy Marseilles and Toulon. Davout successfully held the line of the Loire against the Austrians before submitting. Elsewhere, the French had put up a creditable resistance to invading forces. In command of the Army of the Alps, Suchet had held off the Piedmontese, while the Army of the Rhine under Rapp initially put up a strong performance in Alsace, driving back the Austrians on 28 June and 8 July, and major fortresses, such as Verdun and Strasbourg remained in French hands. However, Waterloo had truly been a decisive battle. For example, Rapp's victory on the river Souffel north of Strasbourg on 28 June could not be exploited, not only as Rapp was heavily outnumbered, but also because Napoleon had already been defeated. On 22 July, a truce was concluded for Alsace.

The deployment of a large Russian army against France, following the units already sent in 1814, underlined one aspect of the geopolitical legacy of the Napoleonic Wars: Britain and Russia, the two "peripheral" powers had become relatively far stronger within Europe. Napoleon sought to take refuge in the USA, but found French ports blockaded by the British. He surrendered to Captain Frederick Maitland of HMS *Bellerophon* and was taken to St. Helena, a distant British possession, where he was held prisoner until his death in 1821.

A novel form of war?

How novel was the character of the French Revolutionary and Napoleonic Wars, looking both forwards and backwards? If the context for judgement is late-nineteenth century warfare then it is possible to stress continuity rather than change, to argue that essentially all that changed was a use of yet greater resources of people, matériel and funds to pursue familiar military courses. Looking back, much that Napoleonic warfare is noted for had been anticipated in earlier conflicts in the later eighteenth century: large armies, a strategy of movement, a preference for battles over sieges, a greater emphasis on artillery, light infantry. In this context, Napoleon was more of a consolidator than an innovator.

However, if the political and social context is to be seen as crucial, then the period was more of a departure than in the narrower realms of weaponry and naval conflict. Large conscript armies, organized into corps, were a new development in western Europe, made possible by greater state control of society. Possibly the greatest tactical difference was that of scale and the resulting organizational, operational and logistical problems. The military effectiveness, in the widest sense, of European states, increased, as ever greater resources, made possible partly by economic growth, were devoted to warfare. Both the mobilization of a large proportion of national manpower and warfare became more insistent. This greater effectiveness of the state military posed a serious problem for popular uprisings, such as those in and south of Rome in 1798. Such uprisings were not new, but they were more important in the period, in part because the French destroyed or took over existing power structures leaving rebellion as the only way to express discontent, and because the French also accelerated processes of reform that the population had already found inimical.

Conclusions

Although coming close to Gettysburg in 1863, Waterloo was closer to the battle of Pavia of 1525 than it was to the battle of Kursk of 1943. Furthermore, the notion that ways of warfare were not fixed and that states needed always to be seeking ways to get a military "edge" over likely opponents was already well established from the fifteenth century, so that the interest in novelty that was an important characteristic of thought in Enlightenment, Revolutionary and Napoleonic periods affected a society already receptive to the possibility of change in military affairs.

However, although change, more specifically the benefits of more sophisticated creation and control of standing armed forces, was already well established from the late fifteenth century, the warfare of the period did not yet witness the coordination of large-scale operations that was to characterize land and sea warfare in the Napoleonic period. The potential effectiveness of the military system was demonstrated by Napoleon's ability to force Austria, Prussia and Russia to terms in 1805–1807, and by the simultaneous large-scale French operations against Austria and Spain in 1808–1809. The role of coordinated land and sea power was demonstrated in 1798–1815 by the British. They suppressed rebellion in Ireland, made extensive gains in India, fought a war with the USA and resisted France and her allies, eventually playing a major role in Napoleon's overthrow.

In Britain, France and more generally in Europe, the war reflected the growing ability of governments to tap economic resources and demographic potential. In 1808, Austria introduced a militia, the *Landwehr*, that could serve as a large reserve force: all men between 18 and 45 in Austria and Bohemia were enrolled, although in 1809 they were revealed to be of limited military value. By 1813, the Prussians had 100,000 regulars and 120,000 men in their *Landwehr*.

War increasingly became a matter of exploiting the nexus between capitalism and government. This was a nexus that was mediated by political processes and social practices that reflected the dynamic cooperation of rulers and political elites. The Napoleonic enterprise was defeated not by an unreconstructed *ancien régime*, but by states that had absorbed many of France's developments. Across much of Europe, the modernization of political structures and administrative practices was influenced by French occupation or models, or by the need to devise new political and administrative strategies to counter the French. The changes introduced in the Prussian army and society after defeat by Napoleon in 1806 are an important example, although there was also considerable continuity with the Enlightenment reforms of the pre-Revolutionary period.

Gerhard von Scharnhorst, Minister of War and Chief of the General Staff in 1808–10 and Chief of Staff to Blücher in 1812–13, was the key figure in creating a General Staff system that provided both coherent central direction and an effective system of links between the centre and individual units designed to ensure unity in command. Each Prussian corps and division contained a group of staff officers headed by a chief who was responsible both for advising its commander and for links with the centre. This was a corporate system unlike the essentially personal command system used by Napoleon.[25] Scharnhorst was succeeded by August von Gneisenau (1760–1831), who also played a role in the development of the General Staff: he introduced in 1813 a practice of "joint responsibility" in which the chiefs of staff of individual forces were to turn to the chief of the General Staff if their force commanders did not heed their opinion. Gneisenau was determined to keep up the military pressure on Napoleon, and not delay operations for diplomatic considerations.[26] Scharnhorst was a patron of Clausewitz, a graduate of the War Academy that Scharnhorst had helped create at Berlin in 1801. In 1813, Clausewitz served as liaison officer between Russian and Prussian forces, and in practice as Scharnhorst's intelligence officer.[27] In 1831, Clausewitz was to be chief of staff in the Observation Army sent under Gneisenau to resist Polish separatism; both men died of cholera.

It is important not to exaggerate the effectiveness of military administration in this period. Despite manufacturing large quantities of munitions, including 110,000 muskets in 1812 and raising the number of cannon to 1,699 by that year, Russia was short of arms and ammunition and musket calibres were still not standardized. Yet, in part, this was due to the pressures created by the mass recruitment of the period. The year 1812 was an exceptional one for Russia, but it saw 420,000 regulars recruited, along with a 200,000 strong militia.

The resources devoted to conflict created long-term demographic problems for France, but were part of the major transformation of warfare in this period. There had also been important increases in resource use in the period 1689–1714 and 1740–63, but in 1792–1815 an unprecedented level was reached. This helped to accentuate long-term logistical and command and control problems, and these encouraged an emphasis on attack, to get a quick decision, contributing to the high-tempo warfare of the period. The latter posed major problems for the coordination of forces. Periods of intensified warfare, as in northern Italy in 1796, Germany in 1813, France in 1814, or even the three battles of Quatre Bras, Ligny and Waterloo on just three days in June 1815, posed severe problems for both strategy and logistics, as issues of prioritization and coordination came to the fore.

War involves far more than resources and governmental structures, but both impacted on the features that tend to absorb more attention. They also played an important role in Napoleon's failure. It was far from inevitable, but he was gravely weakened both by the ability of Britain to use the resources of world-wide trade to finance opposition to France and by the precarious nature of the new imperial system and the limited support it enjoyed across those parts of the continent that he dominated militarily. Napoleon's failure to bring lasting peace was in part a testimony to his unwillingness to compromise, but was also the product of a widespread reluctance underpinned by strong separate political identities to accept his forced unification of much of Europe. Others, before and since, the Habsburg Emperor Charles V and Hitler, faced similar situations and failed, but, in each case, the explanation must lie in the particular character of each period in military and political history.

Napoleon benefited from the operational and organizational advantages that the French enjoyed over their opponents from the outbreak of war in 1792, and from the commitment of the Revolutionary political system to war. These relative advantages were, however, eroded in the 1800s, such that in 1807–1809 the French encountered formidable opposition from Russian, Spanish, British and Austrian forces. The French lacked a lead comparable to that enjoyed (although not without anxiety) by the British at sea after Trafalgar, and the circumstances of land warfare were not such as to permit a replication of a lead of this type. As so frequently in European military history, a capability gap within Europe had been closed and, in combination with political factors, the consequence was the end of a drive for hegemonic power. Opposition to French hegemony required a skilful response, both military and political. His apologists notwithstanding, Napoleon could not provide this.

CHAPTER FOUR

Naval Power and Warfare

It is always difficult to decide how best to present naval power and warfare within the context of general military history. Usually they are treated as different subjects to land warfare and covered by other scholars responding to the methodology, conceptualization and historiography of a distinct subject, with its own institutional structures. This reflects the scope, importance and detailed work on naval history. It also has its limitations, not least a failure to search for comparisons, contrasts or connections with land warfare or to probe a wider context within which the relative value of naval force can be assessed. This study does not pretend to a high level of naval expertise, but seeks to include a discussion of the naval dimension, albeit one that focuses on the particular interests of this book.

Global context

First, it is important to consider the global context. The Western powers enjoyed an effective monopoly of long-distance naval strength, not least transoceanic, globe encircling capability. There were other naval powers, but none matched those of the West. For example, despite its enormous resources and the strength of its governmental structure, China no longer engaged in long-range naval activity as it had in the early fifteenth century. Similarly, neither Japan nor Korea matched their naval activity of the 1590s.

Turkish naval power in the Persian Gulf and Red Sea was not what it had been in the sixteenth century, but it remained significant in the Black Sea and the eastern Mediterranean. In the mid-1780s, the Turks employed French experts on ship construction. In both seas, there was the rising challenge of Russian naval power. The Turks were heavily defeated at Cesmé in the Aegean in 1770 and in the Black Sea at the battles of the Dnieper (1788) and Tendra (1790). In 1790, the British feared that the Russians would be able to send a fleet to the Red Sea via Madagascar in order to open up a new sphere of naval operations against the Turks.

The naval strength of the north African powers – Morocco, Algiers, Tunis and Tripoli – consisted essentially of privateering forces, appropriate for commerce raiding, but not for fleet engagements. Occasionally, privateering bases were attacked, but they generally proved difficult targets. In 1784, when a large Spanish fleet attempted to destroy the privateering base of Algiers, a line of Algerian warships prevented the Spaniards from coming inshore. An earlier attack in 1775 had been repelled on land when exposed Spanish troops were subjected to heavy fire and their artillery was delayed by the coastal sand. In contrast, on 27 August 1816, a British squadron fired 40,000 round-shot and shells when Algiers was bombarded by an Anglo-Dutch squadron into accepting the abolition of the enslavement of Christians.

In India, Maratha naval power had been cut short by British action in 1755, while in 1783 the British took the ports belonging to Tipu Sultan and stopped the development of a Mysore navy. Further east, there were important regional naval powers in the East Indies but their fleets of heavily armed galleys were more appropriate for inshore operations than the deeper-draught sailing ships of Western powers.

As long as the Western powers had nothing beside such warships with their wooden hulls and reliance on wind power, they found it difficult to operate in tropical estuary, delta and river waters and most tropical inshore waters. Thus, although there was no naval balance, nor any frontier of capability and control between Western and non-Western powers on the oceans of the world, the situation was different along the coasts. The absence of any challenge to Western naval power on the oceans was dramatically demonstrated in the 1770s, 1780s and 1790s as European warships under naval commanders such as James Cook, Jean-François de la Pérouse, António Malaspina and George Vancouver, explored the Pacific. They charted and (re-)named the world, considered where to establish naval bases, and established the first European colony in Australasia: Botany Bay in 1788. There was still much of the world's land surface where European military strength and models were unknown, but the warships that showed their flags and ran out their guns around the globe were the forceful edge of the first real integration of the world, an integration made by Europeans and to their own ends and profit.

Western navies

Western navies continued the pattern of development begun in the mid-seventeenth century, with a concentration on specialized warships instead of armed merchantmen. Numbers, organization and infrastructure were interlinked and mutually sustaining changes whose net effect was an increase in naval force. The growth in Western naval power was not simply a matter of developments afloat. New naval bases were created and existing ones enhanced, affecting the geography of naval power. Thus, for example, in response to the French development of Cherbourg in the mid-nineteenth century and the construction of steam-powered warships, the British created a naval base at Portland to cover the coast between the existing bases of Plymouth and Portsmouth.

In the late nineteenth century the notion of command of the seas was much discussed (on A. T. Mahan's inspiration) in navalist literature. Its value as a concept at that point is open to debate, but it was certainly questionable prior to the development of steam power. Wind-powered warships were dependent, both tactically and strategically, on the weather. Ships could only sail up to a certain angle to the wind. Too much or insufficient wind were serious problems. For example, reliance on the wind alone made inshore naval operations much more chancy undertakings than they were to be in the steam era. Yet, there were also specialized wooden sailing ships, in particular bomb ketches, designed with coastal operations in shallow waters during the sailing era foremost in mind. It is also possible to adduce examples of successful campaigns in precisely such waters; for example the Chesapeake campaign of 1814. Thus, it is important not to exaggerate the operational limitations caused by wind and, particularly, wood.

It was far harder to counteract the impact of current and tide than it was to be after the advent of steam power. For example, French ships could only leave their major Atlantic port – Brest – with an easterly wind. This was not all that prevalent and that helped British blockaders.

In addition to the problem of motive power, there were serious limitations in the surveillance and command and control capabilities of naval power. These made it very difficult to "see" or control in any strategic sense and certainly limited the value of any blockade. It was generally possible for a lookout to see only about 15 miles from the top of the main mast in fine weather.

This had implications not only for operations between fleets, but also in terms of trade protection. This commercial dimension was important in relations between imperial systems with maritime links: British, French, Spanish and Dutch. An ability to wreck the foreign trade of rivals could cripple their imperial systems, greatly hamper their economies and seriously damage their ability to wage war. During the Napoleonic Wars, the British blockade inflicted serious damage on the French economy. Even if it was not possible to inflict this degree of damage, higher insurance premiums, danger money for sailors, and the need to resort to convoys and other defensive measures could push up the cost of trade. Logistical factors were an important limiting factor on blockading operations. Only with Portsmouth and Plymouth close at hand could the British maintain an effective blockade of the French Channel and Atlantic ports.

Vessels were seized by warships and by privateers: private vessels given licences to take enemy ships. Privateers were smaller and less heavily gunned than ships of the line, but they were more manoeuvrable and of shallower draught, and were thus more appropriate for commerce raiding. The major role of privateers and of light warships – frigates, sloops, ketches, and so on – and not only in commerce warfare, is a reminder of the danger of concentrating on ships of the line, and battles, in any account of naval history. The analogous situation is that of the major role of light cavalry in raiding, cutting communication routes and challenging any notion of control on land. To press the analogy further, the limited effectiveness of countermeasures – fortified bases and lines against light cavalry, and blockades and amphibious operations against privateer bases – should be noted. French bases, especially Dunkirk and St. Malo, proved difficult to contain, and the British suffered greatly from the *guerre de course* (privateering war); although, in the French Revolutionary and Napoleonic Wars, the regional economies in French ports and their hinterlands suffered more economic harm as a result of the prolonged British blockade.

Throughout this period, the leading naval power, Britain, had the largest and most successful navy in the world. This success was not due to any superiority of British ships, for the British navy was very similar to its opponents in the weaponry it employed. The greater effectiveness of the Royal Navy was largely due its capacity to build and maintain more ships, its extensive and effective administrative system and dockyards infrastructure, the strength of public finances and good naval leadership. The British also had a more meritocratic promotion system and a more unified naval tradition than that of France, the second naval power.

Britain also devoted a greater proportion of national resources to naval than to land warfare. This was a political choice that reflected the major role of trade, a growing overseas empire and the fact that, as an island, the sea was its front line in a war and it had an extensive coastline to defend but no land frontiers, as well as the national self-image. Trade was less important to the government and political culture of France, and to those of the world's two leading land powers, China and Russia. They were very different politically, geopolitically and militarily from Britain. Both geopolitical circumstances and political culture were important. The British could afford to prioritize the navy above the army in a way that most continental powers could not, thanks to their relative security.

American War of Independence, 1775–83

The first major war in our period, the American War of Independence, developed a naval dimension when it became a stage in the Anglo-Bourbon struggle for maritime hegemony. Due to the weakness of the navy of the American
Revolutionaries, the naval war after France's entry into the conflict in 1778
was a conventional one, fought between European powers, and there was no
distinctive character or "modernity" to the conflict comparable to the war on
land. Prior to that, the British enjoyed many advantages from their naval
strength, not least that of taking the initiative. In August 1777, George Washington commented on Howe's force, then sailing from Staten Island towards
the Chesapeake:

> They have stood out to sea again, but how far, or where, they are
> going remains to be known – From their entire command of the water
> they derive immense advantages, and distress us much by harassing
> and marching our troops from post to post – I wish we could fix on
> their destination – in such case, I should hope we would be prepared
> to receive them.[1]

Although Britain still had the largest single navy in the world, by 1780,
thanks to much shipbuilding in the late 1760s and 1770s, especially by Spain,
France and Spain combined had a quantitative superiority in naval tonnage
over Britain of about 25 per cent. Partly as a result, the British were unable to
repeat their success of the Seven Years' War (1756–63).

Instead, the British navy in 1778–83 had full control of neither European
nor American waters, and, unlike in 1759, was unable to defeat the French
before Spain entered the war. On 17 July 1778, Augustus Keppel failed in his
attempt to destroy the Brest fleet off Ushant. British naval strength was
concentrated on defending home waters, so the French Mediterranean port
of Toulon was not blockaded and the Toulon fleet was able to sail to American waters and threaten New York in 1778. The following year, France and
Spain sent a fleet into the Channel; this attempt to invade Britain was
thwarted by disease and poor organization rather than by British naval action.
The British position in the West Indies was also challenged. Yet, at the same
time, the British naval blockade of the American colonies greatly weakened
their economy. Furthermore, the British retained a considerable "lift" capacity: amphibious operations were mounted both in North America and in the
West Indies.

There was no major decisive British naval victory until the Battle of the
Saints on 12 April 1782. It was a testimony to the rising importance of
colonies and transoceanic operations, and the British failure to maintain an
effective blockade, that this was fought in the Caribbean, off the Iles des
Saintes, south of Guadeloupe. The outnumbered French, under their

commander, François de Grasse, were soundly defeated by George Rodney, who, by abandoning traditional parallel line tactics and adopting a head-on attack, broke through the French line, capturing five ships of the line, including the flagship. This was a great British achievement, all the more decisive in light of the failure of the British fleet (in Rodney's absence) to defeat de Grasse and rescue Cornwallis in 1781. At the Saints, although there were 36 British ships of the line against 30 French ships, the French ships were larger and the total displacement of the two fleets was roughly equal; in most fleet actions, the number of ships of the line present tends to overestimate British strength and underestimate French strength, as French ships were on average larger than the British ships. The same applies to numbers of cannon, as the French pound was heavier than the British pound, and the larger French ships had 36-pounders as against British 22-pounders. However, the British gradually obtained a qualitative advantage in cannon. The head-on attack can be compared with the attack column that French Revolutionary armies were to use with great success on land from 1792.

The war was followed by a general European naval race in the 1780s. Britain, France and Spain all launched a formidable amount of tonnage. These huge naval forces dwarfed those of non-European powers far more decisively than they had when Christopher Columbus and Vasco da Gama sailed forth in the 1490s. Some other powers also greatly expanded their navies in the 1780s. This was particularly true of Russia and the Dutch, which became the fourth and fifth largest naval powers. Denmark, Sweden, Naples, Portugal and the Turks all increased the size of their navies.[2]

Programmes of naval construction and enhancement registered not only the growing resources of European governments but also the capability of their military-industrial complexes and the ability of their administrative systems to plan and implement changes.[3] For example, progress in British metallurgy improved their gunnery towards the end of the century, and the impact of British naval gunfire on enemy hulls and crews markedly increased during the war period 1793–1815, when enemy ships were reduced to wrecks in a comparatively short time. Britain had an advantage in technology, as well as benefiting from superior seamanship and well drilled gun crews.

Fleets of warships were powerful and sophisticated military systems, sustained by mighty industrial and logistical resources based in dockyards that were among the largest industrial plants, employers of labour and groups of buildings in the world. These dockyards were supported by massive storehouses, such as the vast Lands Zeemagazijn in Amsterdam, which was destroyed by fire in 1791. Naval bases also required considerable investment. As soon as the Russians had seized a Black Sea coastline and the Crimea, they began to develop bases there.

These military-industrial complexes also demonstrated a capacity to stimulate change. There were numerous innovations, which were put to good use. Improvements in seaworthiness, stemming in part from the abandonment of earlier top-heavy and clumsy designs, increased the capability of warships both to take part in all-weather blockades and to operate across the oceans. After the War of American Independence, the French adopted recent British naval innovations, such as copper-sheathing ships' bottoms in order to discourage barnacles and boring worms and so increase manoeuvrability and lengthen service life. Standardization was increasingly apparent prior to the changes brought by steam power and armour plating; in 1786 the French adopted standard ship designs for their fleet. Furthermore, the incremental process of improvement continued in the last decades of sail. For example, diagonal framing, introduced in the latter stages of the Napoleonic Wars, increased the resilience of ships, and thus their sea and battle-worthiness. In addition, better signalling in the period 1790s–1810 helped to enhance the potential for tactical control. These improvements helped make earlier ships appear redundant, certainly for the line of battle. Although the first operational use of a submarine occurred off Staten Island, New York in 1776, it was not followed up. As yet, the very basis of successful underwater existence, such as compressed air, did not exist.

Europeans also took their naval military-industrial capability abroad, developing major shipyards at colonial bases such as Havana and Halifax. The growing British naval and mercantile presence in the Indian Ocean owed much to shipyards in India, where merchantmen averaging 600–800 tonnes and capable of carrying very large cargoes were constructed, as well as naval vessels, including several ships of the line; the last, HMS *Meeanee*, was launched in 1848. Western navies organized the charting of much of the world's coastlines, to the benefit of trade as well as the assertion of power. In the 1780s, for example, the French navy charted the coast of Asia from Suez to Korea.

However, logistical limitations, along with disease and climate, substantially circumscribed European "power projection" outside European waters. Notwithstanding Halifax, Bermuda and Jamaica, the Royal Navy lacked the requisite support bases to mount an effective blockade of the east coast of North America, either in 1775–83 or in 1812–14. Naval operations outside Europe, especially in the Indian Ocean and the Caribbean, remained greatly conditioned by climate and disease. Despite improvements in some spheres, the general conditions of service at sea remained bleak. Aside from cramped living conditions and poor sanitation, food supplies could be inadequate and inappropriate, with a lack of fresh food, fruit and vegetables, and thus of vitamin C. The cumulative impact was both to make naval service unattractive and to ensure serious losses among those already in service, although neither point should be exaggerated.

The next major conflict after the War of American Independence was not fought on the oceans, but in the inshore waters of the Baltic and the Gulf of Finland. In 1788–90, Gustavus III of Sweden attempted, unsuccessfully, to win back territory in Finland lost to the Russians in 1743. This war demonstrated the need to understand that even within the West and at sea, there was an important variety in ship types. The Swedish ship designer Frederick Henrik af Chapman developed oared archipelago frigates whose diagonal internal stiffenings enabled them to carry heavy guns in light, shallow-draught hulls, and oared gunboats: small boats with great fire-power and a small target area. The guns were moved on rails and used as ballast when the boats sailed in open waters. Gunboats proved particularly effective against the Russians, who also built a large number of oared frigates. In the USA in the 1800s, Thomas Jefferson encouraged the development of inshore gunboats, although for political and ideological, rather than strategic reasons.[4]

French Revolutionary and Napoleonic Wars

The first conflict after the War of American Independence between powers whose naval strength focused on deep-water operations and deep-draught ships-of-the-line began in 1793 when Britain joined in the French Revolutionary War. The French fleet was badly affected by the political and administrative disruption stemming from the Revolution, although there had also been important problems earlier caused by financial difficulties. Despite the building of numerous warships in the 1780s, the Treasurer of the Navy was unable to fund any sustained naval operational activity. The Revolution brought first violence and then civil war. In November 1790, a mob killed the Count of Macnamara, commander of the French squadron in the Indian Ocean.[5] In 1793, the British Mediterranean fleet was invited into Toulon by French Royalists, before being driven out again by Revolutionary forces benefiting from the well sited cannon of Napoleon, then a young artillery officer.

The British went on to grasp the controlling maritime position by winning victory at the battle of the Glorious First of June in 1794. Richard, Earl Howe, with 25 ships of the line, successfully attacked a French fleet of 26 of the line sent to escort a grain convoy from America. Howe, who had gained the weather gauge through skilled seamanship, could not fully execute his plan for all of his ships to cut the French line, each passing under the stern of a French ship and engaging it from leeward. Nevertheless, enough ships succeeded and superior British gunnery was at close range for long enough to cost the French seven warships (one sunk, six captured) and 5,000 casualties; although the vital convoy reached Brest.

This maritime advantage was lost on land in 1795–96 when the French forced the Dutch and Spanish into alliance and forced the vulnerable British to evacuate the Mediterranean. Able again to threaten invasion, the French and their allies were nevertheless repeatedly outfought at sea between 1797 and 1805. Victories over the Spaniards at the battle of Cape St. Vincent (14

February 1797), the Dutch at Camperdown (11 October 1797), the French at the Nile (1 August 1798), the Danes at Copenhagen (2 April 1801), and the French and Spaniards at Trafalgar (21 October 1805),[6] left the British with a clear superiority in ships of the line and sailors, and with the important psychological edge of success; effectively, the Royal Navy now had command of the seas, at least in European waters, until the end of the war.

In these battles, the fighting quality of individual ships was combined with a bold command culture that emphasized manoeuvre and seizing the initiative in order to close with the opposing fleet and defeat it in detail after it had been divided by intersecting the opposing line. These tactics were recommended in the influential *Essay on Naval Tactics* by John Clerk of Elden, a work that greatly impressed Horatio Nelson, the most successful of the British admirals.

Off Cape St. Vincent, Rear-Admiral Sir John Jervis and 15 of the line successfully attacked a superior and far more heavily gunned Spanish fleet of 27 of the line under Don José de Cordova, using tactics similar to those of Napoleon on land, to operate on interior lines and concentrate his strength on attacking one part of the Spanish fleet. Nelson, on his own initiative and followed by others, kept the two parts separated. British captains took advantage of the mêlée Nelson created to win a number of individual ship encounters: their greatly superior rate of fire had a deadly effect. The Spaniards lost four ships of the line captured, and had ten more badly damaged. At Camperdown, two advancing British lines of warships broke the Dutch line into three segments preparing the way for individual actions in which the Dutch lost seven of the line.

At the Nile, Nelson unexpectedly attacked an inshore anchored line of French ships on both sides: on the shallow, inshore side they were not prepared for battle. The nature of the French position gave Nelson a battle of annihilation, first defeating the ships in the French van and then pressing on to attack those moored behind; the latter had been unable to provide assistance. French gunnery proved inadequate, and the French were not only poorly deployed, but also failed to respond adequately to the British attack. The British navy worked as a well integrated force. Nelson had ably prepared his captains to act vigorously and in cooperation in all possible eventualities, and had fully explained his tactics to them. This was a style of command that was similar to that of Moltke with the Prussian army in 1864–71.

At Copenhagen, the Danish fleet was battered into submission after Nelson had boldly attacked from an unexpected direction. At Trafalgar, Nelson attacked the larger Franco-Spanish line in two divisions in order to split his opponents into smaller groups. By using his windward position to attack the Franco-Spanish rear and centre, Nelson achieved numerical superiority because his opponent's foremost ships could not intervene effectively. The line was penetrated as planned, making it difficult for Admiral Villeneuve to retreat or regroup, and the battle became a series of small struggles in which British gunnery and seamanship prevailed, albeit at the cost of heavy casualties, including Nelson.

Napoleon sought, with some success, to rebuild his fleet after Trafalgar, but the loss of trained sailors was harder to recoup. Furthermore, the blockaded French navy was unable to build up maritime experience. The French and allied squadrons that did sail out were generally defeated, for example off Rochefort in September 1805 and off St. Domingue in February 1806.

Thanks to this naval strength, the British were able to maintain an effective convoy system that helped them increase their proportion of world mercantile shipping and to deny access to world markets to the French and their allies. More generally, the strength and nature of British naval power and maritime resources enabled Britain to resist Napoleon's attempt to isolate her commercially from the Continent in 1806 and subsequently. Naval strength also supported Wellington in the Peninsula and permitted amphibious operations, leading to the capture of French and allied overseas bases, which further lessened their ability to challenge the British. Cape Town fell in 1806, Martinique in 1809, Réunion and Mauritius in 1810 and Batavia in 1811. In 1808, Napoleon planned to take over the Spanish overseas empire, not only in the New World but also the Philippines. These hopes were thwarted by Spanish resistance, but would, anyway, have been inhibited by British naval power.[7]

British naval strength was also crucial in the War of 1812–15 with the USA. Naval blockade hit the American economy, amphibious forces were able to approach Baltimore and burn Washington (1814), and it was possible to send reinforcements to Canada in order to resist successfully poorly led and uncoordinated American attacks. An unsuccessful British attack was mounted on New Orleans in January 1815, but the British were able to send a force there, and when hostilities ceased an expedition was being planned against first Savannah and then Charleston, both of which were blockaded.

Nevertheless, the British suffered initially from overconfidence, inaccurate gunnery and ships that were simply less powerful and less well prepared than those of their opponents. Although the Americans had no ships of the line and their total fleet at the outset contained only 17 ships, they did have the most powerful frigates in the world. The Americans captured three British frigates in 1812, but the other British naval losses were of smaller ships, and British naval effectiveness improved during the war, as did their gunnery. Over half the American navy was destroyed in the war; losses would probably have been greater had not the Royal Navy been massively distracted by the war in Europe.[8]

The War of 1812 showed that light naval forces were able to inflict considerable damage but not to sever the vital arteries of imperial power. To operate in North America, the British were dependent both on routes across the Atlantic and on an ability to act in coastal waters. Neither was really challenged by the Americans in this war, or in the War of Independence. In the earlier conflict, French support had been crucial, but in 1812 Napoleon was in no position to intervene. That was the year of his fatal invasion of Russia. The choice was a reminder of the role of options in military history. Equally, the British could not overthrow Napoleon without the help of powerful land allies. There were none such in North America.

If naval power has to be seen in such wider contexts of military potential and political purpose, that does not undermine the effectiveness and achievement of the British navy. This rested on a sophisticated and well financed administrative structure, a large fleet drawing on the manpower of a substantial mercantile marine and fishing fleet (although there were never enough sailors), and an ability to win engagements that reflected widely diffused qualities of seamanship and gunnery, a skilled and determined corps of captains and able leadership. This was true not only of command at sea, as with Nelson's innovative tactics, but also of effective institutional leadership that developed organizational efficiency.

To support the fleet, which by the end of 1808 totalled 113 of the line and 596 other ships, the infrastructure developed and became more far flung. New naval facilities were developed both in Britain and abroad. Thus two new deep docks were created at Portsmouth in 1796–1800, while Barbados, Bermuda, Bombay, Cape Town, Madras, Malta and Trincomalee were developed as bases, enhancing Britain's power projection capability.[9] Signalling at sea, crucial to operational effectiveness, communications and coordinated action improved from the 1780s, and a quick and flexible numerical system of signals was created. The Admiralty Hydrographic Office was founded in 1795 to improve charts world-wide.

Thanks to its naval resources and organization, Britain was able to turn tactical triumphs to strategic advantage. As on land, mobility, firepower and determination were crucial in battle, although at sea these were most readily applied in the offensive. The effectiveness of the British blockade in 1803–15 was crucial to Britain's strategic success. The naval battles in part can be understood with reference to the blockade, and its economic consequences should not be ignored. Successive victories, especially Trafalgar, conditioned British and foreign expectations about the nature of naval power and of Britain's maritime role, and, indeed, allowed her throughout much of the nineteenth century to get grudging unofficial recognition of Pax Britannica (the doctrine of the Royal Navy keeping the peace of the seas for all to benefit).

These assumptions, however, were at least in part misleading. The number of British ships of the line considered fit for service was actually lower than the supposed number. Furthermore, the size of the navy fell rapidly from 1815, in part because many wartime launchings had been of ships rapidly built from unseasoned wood and they swiftly deteriorated. In contrast, postwar launchings using seasoned wood produced ships that lasted. Thanks to new systems of internal bracing it was possible to build large ships that were stronger than those built hitherto. The British felt no need to maintain their wartime rate of construction or maintenance, because, unlike after the Seven Years' War, the Bourbons after 1815 did not launch a major programme of naval construction. The French decided to concentrate on frigates and, in the event of another war, to attack British trade.

Post-1815 naval warfare

Technological development does not dominate the agenda of the naval history of the eighteenth century through to 1815, but the situation changes thereafter.[10] This reflects the enormous changes that were rapidly wrought, and the high tempo of change. As a consequence, much of the following section will be devoted to technology. However, other less obviously apparent circumstances were also important. The most important was the absence of naval warfare between the major naval powers. In 1845, Sir George Cockburn, an experienced British admiral, noted that "from the period when the first large seagoing steam vessel was successfully completed, it became evident to every body that a facility never before existing, must be afforded thereby for sudden invasion of this country [from France]". Nevertheless, despite much concern within Britain, and periodic invasion panics, especially while Napoleon III controlled France (1848-70),[11] there was no war between the two powers. Nor was there one between the USA and either Britain, for example over the Canadian frontier or during the American Civil War, or France, for example over Mexico. From 1815 until the revival of French naval strength from the mid 1820s, the British Admiralty saw the American fleet as its most likely rival. However, the two powers implicitly cooperated on crucial issues, not least in opposing Spanish control in Latin America. Furthermore, neither attempted to win colonies there. Britain and the USA collaborated to suppress the slave trade.

The Spaniards tried to build up a fleet to help in Latin America, not least by buying Russian warships in 1818-19, but the Spanish fleet was far smaller than that of Britain, and it declined greatly in the 1820s and 1830s. The Wars of Liberation in Latin America did not lead to conflict between the major naval powers, and in the Crimean War (1854-56) the British navy was essentially opposed to Russian coastal defences. The Russians had been bold at the expense of the Turks off Sinope in 1853, but they felt themselves totally outclassed by the Anglo-French fleet that entered the Black Sea in 1854. The Russians had more warships in the Baltic, but there also they did not challenge the allies: the Russians initially had no screw ships of the line. The French sent a fleet into the Adriatic during their war with Austria in 1859, but the Austrians did not risk conflict.

Indeed, the major naval clashes between Western powers, those in the American Civil War and the Austro-Italian war of 1866, did not involve the leading navies and the Battle of Lissa in 1866 was incidental to the struggle on land. The Franco-Prussian War also did not lead to significant clashes at sea. In 1870, the French declared German ports to be under blockade, but the war was settled on land; there were no landings on the German coast.

Although the Wars of Liberation in Latin America did not lead to conflict between the major naval powers, they did entail naval warfare. The new Chilean republic created a navy that in 1818 captured a Spanish frigate and transport fleet bringing reinforcements. Thereafter the Chilean fleet blockaded and attacked Spanish-held Peru, playing a crucial role in the successful invasion of 1820–21.

Western navies were involved in operations against non-Western powers and totally overpowered them. A bombardment of Algiers by an Anglo-Dutch fleet in 1816 led to an agreement to end the taking of Christian slaves. The previous year, an American squadron had forced Algiers to pay compensation for attacks on American trade. The threat of naval bombardment led the Dey of Algiers to capitulate to British demands in 1824. Thanks largely to superior British gunnery, an Anglo-French-Russian fleet under Sir Edward Codrington destroyed the Ottoman and Egyptian fleets at the battle of Navarino Bay in 1827, the last great battle of the Age of Fighting Sail, and one in which the Western fatalities were far lower than those of their opponents: 177 to about 17,000. The British naval bombardment and capture of Acre, in which a shell caused the main magazine to explode, was a decisive blow in the expulsion of Egyptian forces from Syria in 1840.

As a consequence of the absence of major naval conflict between Western powers, elements in naval power and warfare other than those of technology have been underrated. Furthermore, the lessening of the dominant role of technology that occurs due to symmetrical conflict – when both sides are similarly armed – is not as readily apparent as it was during the Anglo-French wars that ended in 1815.

Steam power

Allowing for this, the technological changes were still important. Steam was most significant. The steam engine developed in the eighteenth century was harnessed to the cause of marine propulsion. The first steam warship, *Demologos* (Voice of the People), later renamed *Fulton*, was laid down in the USA by Robert Fulton in 1814. Intended for the defence of New York Harbour, she carried 26 guns. The *Comet*, the first steamship in the British navy, began work in 1822. Her task – towing men-of-war – was modest. The first purpose-built British steam warship, the *Dee*, followed in 1830. Early steamships suffered from slow speed, a high rate of coal consumption, and the problems posed by side and paddle wheels, which included the space they

71

took up and their vulnerability. Thus steamships carried few guns. In the 1820s, French innovation in steamships was hampered by the difficulty of manufacturing reliable engines.

It was not until the 1840s that the screw propeller was to offer a better alternative to the paddle wheel. The adoption of the screw propeller made the tactical advantages of steam clear-cut. The British quickly followed suit when the French laid down *Nápoleon* in 1847. By the Crimean War, the British battle fleet was steam powered. However, the British remained confident in the capability of their sailing ships of the line and they stayed in use both in the Crimean War and thereafter. The strategic advantage of steam was less clear cut than the tactical advantage, although it had become equally apparent in European waters by about 1875, a decade before the triple expansion marine engine and nearly two decades before the water tube boiler. By 1885, only distant service ships still required sail.[12]

The potential of steam power for naval operations was rapidly appreciated and developed. In the introduction to his *On Naval Warfare under Steam* (1858), General Sir Howard Douglas claimed, with reason, that "the employment of steam as motive power in the warlike navies of all maritime nations, is a vast and sudden change in the means of engaging in action on the seas, which must produce an entire revolution in naval warfare".

Douglas correctly focused on the tactical dimension. Now able to manoeuvre in calms and make headway against contrary winds, the operational independence of individual warships in a fleet action was greatly extended (although improvements in signalling were to ensure that Jellicoe's fleet at Jutland in 1916 was more tightly controlled than Nelson's at Trafalgar). Furthermore, steam increased the manoeuvrability of warships as far as coastal positions were concerned, while long-range artillery and armour plate made the warships more effective against coastal forts. This range of factors is an example of the inter-linked nature of change, which makes the isolation of individual factors for assessment somewhat problematic.

Evidence of the inshore capability of steamers was provided by the useful role they played when the British fleet bombarded Acre in November 1840, forcing out the garrison. Steamers also towed into position the British warships that breached the forts defending the Pearl River below Canton in January 1841. Besieging Venice in 1849, the Austrians paired bombarding frigates with steamers able to act as tugs. This proved more successful than the attempt to apply firepower from balloons launched from the Austrian fleet. Six years later, during the Crimean War, an Anglo-French bombardment of Sveaborg, the fortress covering the approach to Helsinki (then ruled by Russia) destroyed six ships of the line in the harbour.

In contrast, within the Western world, the well fortified Confederate position at Vicksburg was not reduced when bombarded from the Mississippi by Farragut's Union fleet in 1862. In 1863, Charleston also resisted Union bombardment. However, Vicksburg and Charleston had unique geographic advantages, and it is possible to point to numerous successful coastal and river assaults by Union warships in the Civil War, including at Port Hatteras, Port Royal, New Orleans, Mobile Bay, Fort Henry, Island No. 10 and Memphis. Gunboats played a major role in the American Civil War, for example Union boats on the Cumberland and Tennessee Rivers in the critical campaign in western Tennessee in February 1862.

Steam capability changed the geopolitics of naval power as well as its strategy and operational and tactical geography. It led to new senses of vulnerability and opportunity. For example, British governments felt vulnerable to an invasion by French steamships and, in response, carried out major coastal defence works on the south coast of England and in the Channel Isles. In 1849, the French had been able to move 7,500 troops and supplies rapidly by steamships from Toulon to Civitavecchia, leading to the fall of the Roman Republic. The increased manoeuvrability of ships made it easier both to sound inshore and hazardous waters and to attack opposing fleets in harbour, and so destroy them, and therefore led to much fortification of harbours and dockyards.

The ability of ships to operate in rivers and during bad weather was also enhanced. Steam was extremely important for interior navigation. This was demonstrated in the First Burmese War of 1824–25, when the 60-horsepower engine of the British East India Company's steamer *Diana* allowed her to operate on the swiftly flowing Irrawady. The *Diana* towed sailing ships and destroyed Burmese war boats and was crucial to the British advance 400 miles up river; this led the Burmese to negotiate and accept British terms.

Iron ships were more useful than their wooden predecessors: far less vulnerable to tropical parasites, less prone to catch fire, lighter and stronger, although they also required more frequent maintenance. A Greek raid on Alexandria in 1827 failed when the steamer was hit by engine problems.

Steamships were able to cope with bad weather. The *Nemesis*, a British iron steamer that sailed through the winter gales off the Cape of Good Hope to China in 1840, was the first such warship to reach Macao, although two lesser warships had crossed the Pacific from Chile the same year. In 1842, the *Guadalupe*, an iron-hulled steam frigate, was built in Britain for Mexico.

The process by which steam technology revolutionized naval warfare after 1815 was not one of instantaneous change. Instead, there was a series of innovations, each with its own chronology and pattern of diffusion. These included the paddle wheel and more powerful naval ordnance in the 1820s, the screw propeller in the 1840s, followed by the combination of the screw propeller and armour from about 1860, and the ensuing development of ever more lethal arms countered by ever thicker wrought-iron armour.

As the diffusion of new methods took time, especially but not only among navies not of the first rank, the chronology of naval change was complex. The first steamship of the line, the *Napoléon*, a screw ship, was ordered for the French navy in 1847, but was not launched until 1850 and was not ready for sea for another two years. This caused great anxiety in Britain and led to political pressure for a shift to steam in the battle fleet. As with other innovations, there were conversions as well as new ships; indeed cost factors encouraged conversions. Thus, by the start of 1854, France had the *Napoléon* and eight conversions, while the British had constructed three new screw ships of the line and converted another seven. When the Crimean War broke out, the British had two steam battleships, *Agamemnon* and *Sans Pareil* in the Mediterranean, and the French had three there, *Montebello*, *Charlemagne* and *Napoléon*. The British fleet sent to the Baltic in 1854 included no fewer than nine steam line of battle ships, two (*St. Jean D'Acre* and *James Watt*) designed as steam battleships and the other seven converted from sailing ships of the line. The British also sent four 60-gun steam blockships and six sailing line-of-battle ships to the Baltic, another four 60-gun blockships following later that year. In contrast, the French 1854 Baltic fleet contained only one line-of-battle ship, *Austerlitz,* and eight sail of the line.

Elsewhere, the pace was slower. By the end of the war, in 1856, only Russia and Sweden also had screw ships of the line; although Austria, Denmark and Turkey followed later. As a reminder of the difficulty of determining what was progressive, the British conviction that paddle steamers were obsolescent for this task was not shared elsewhere; the Russians expanded their paddle tonnage in the early 1850s. Furthermore, a reminder of the danger of focusing on ships of the line is provided by the continued importance of paddle steamers for auxiliary purposes.

The Crimean War encouraged the use of screw gunboats. Carrying two to four heavy guns, they could be used for coastal bombardments, but were quickly found to be also suitable for tropical expeditions against non-Western forces. Relatively inexpensive, these gunboats were seen as an alternative to larger warships and (given their heavy artillery) also capable of engaging in defence of coastal waters. As a result, many were laid down in the late 1850s and early 1860s, for example 23 in Prussia in 1859–61.

Improved gunnery and armoured ships

Heavier guns were introduced from the 1820s. In 1826, the British decided to introduce 32-pounders for all their ships of the line. They demonstrated their effectiveness at Navarino Bay the following year. These guns fired solid shot, but naval ordnance was to change radically thanks to the work of the French gunner Colonel Henri-Joseph Paixhans, who used exploding shells, not solid shot. In the early 1820s, he constructed a gun and a gun-carriage steady enough to cope with the report produced by the explosive charges required to fire large projectiles and to give them a high enough initial speed to pierce the side of a big ship and explode inside. Paixhans's innovations were demonstrated successfully in 1824, and their impact was increased by his publications, including *Idées pour le Blindage du Batteries Flottantes* (1821), *Nouvelle Force Maritime et Artillerie* (1822) and *Expériences faites sur une Arme Nouvelle* (1825). Paixhans pressed for the combination of his new ordnance with the new steamship technology. He intended that shell-firing paddle steamers should make sailing ships of the line obsolescent. An awareness of the potential of new developments combined with the culture of print to ensure the rapid dissemination of new ideas. Giovanni Cavalli, a Sardinian, was the first to construct an effective rifled naval gun. In 1837, the French established the Paixhans shell gun as a part of every warship's armament; the British adopted a shell gun as part of their standard armament the following year; although their limited range encouraged continued reliance on the 32-pounders firing solid shot. Furthermore, the French at first found it difficult to manufacture reliable shell-firing guns. As a consequence, the hopes of Paixhans's supporters that new technology would enable France to threaten Britain's naval hegemony proved abortive in the 1820s and 1830s.

Nevertheless, these developments posed a terrible threat to wooden ships. A wooden Turkish squadron was surprised and destroyed at Sinope on 30 November 1853 by a Russian fleet of eight warships under Vice-Admiral Pavel Nakhimov, carrying in total 38 Paixhans shell-firing guns. Of the 4,400 Turkish present, 3,000 were killed, and nine of their ten ships were lost. The battle helped make the name of the shell gun, although it is important not to exaggerate its effectiveness: the Russians took six hours to win, the Turks had only frigates and corvettes, and given the disparity between the two fleets, the same outcome would have been expected with solid shot.

Shells helped lead to armoured warships, although it can be asked why, if the shell gun revolutionized naval warfare, the antidote (armour) took so long to appear. Anglo-French naval bombardments of Odessa and Sevastopol in 1854 had underlined the vulnerability of wooden warships to effective defensive fire from shore batteries. Off Odessa in April, a French warship was set on fire by red-hot shot, and the same fate affected five warships off Sevastopol on 17 October 1854, despite their greatly superior number of cannon. As a result, on 17 October 1855, Kinburn was attacked by a force that included three newly built French 1,575-ton armour-plated wooden floating batteries, which had been towed from France by steamships. Their 3,000 rounds helped destroy the fortifications; in contrast, Russian fire had scant effect on the 4-inch wrought iron plates. This bombardment helped the drive toward armoured warships.

In November 1854, Napoleon III had suggested armoured ships of the line, a move that would make redundant any further conversion of existing sailing ships of the line to steam; no more were ordered after 1855. The first iron-clad warship was *La Gloire* (laid down in March 1858) and launched in November 1859. This was merely a wooden ship fitted with 4½-inch-thick metal plates, since the French were handicapped by a lack of iron-working facilities. Nevertheless, Napoleon III ordered five more ironclads. He was determined to challenge the British and benefited from the support of an effective Ministry of Marine, which sought to overcome industrial limitations and to give iron and steam to his hopes.[13]

The British were worried that their naval lead was being destroyed. The *Gloire* was matched by a British armoured frigate, the *Warrior*, laid down in May 1859 and completed in October 1861. With its 4½-inch-thick armour plating and displacement of 9,140 tons, this was more significant than the *Gloire* as she had an iron hull (i.e. was all iron rather than iron-clad), and was generally more powerful. The *Warrior* was a revolutionary ship design, actually a true iron ship with watertight compartments below, the first large seagoing iron-hulled warship. She was capable of over 14 knots. The British also moved on from their first shell guns to 7-inch Armstrong breech-loading rifled guns. Nevertheless, both ships retained sail rigs, as did most early steamers.[14] Ironclads made redundant the wooden screw steamers built in large numbers in the 1850s and the very beginning of the 1860s. They also interacted with developments in naval ordnance.

Anglo-French rivalry also pressed forward the development of other new technologies. From 1879 the British pioneered steam torpedo boats. The French responded. In this way, typical of many fields, one breakthrough prompted another, as powers sought to maintain and expand their techno-logical lead. However, the interface of technology, tactics and operational considerations was very complex. Torpedoes had substantial ramifications in both the strategic/operational sphere and in that of ship design. In the first, it was unclear whether blockade was now too hazardous an undertaking, while, in the second, the late 1870s and early 1880s saw growing doubts about the viability of heavily armoured and armed capital ships, which seemed to contemporaries to be dangerously vulnerable to underwater weapons.

Steam transport not only increased amphibious capability, but also enhanced the possibilities of commerce raiding. This was grasped by Stephen Mallory, the Confederate Secretary of the Navy, and he, accordingly, ordered speedy raiders built in Britain. Ships laid down in British and French yards, which the Confederacy could not pay for, ended up in the navies of those countries, as well as in those of Denmark, Prussia and even Japan.[15]

The new steam-driven iron-clad warships were used against each other in the Austrian victory over a larger Italian fleet in the Adriatic at the battle of Lissa on 9 May 1866, the largest naval battle between Trafalgar (1805) and Tsushima (1905). The battle of Lissa reflected the new-found territorial range of Italian interests. Instead of just Venetia, the Italian government was also interested in Istria and Dalmatia on the other side of the Adriatic. It first planned to seize the island of Lissa, but on 20 July its fleet was attacked by a smaller, older and less heavily armed Austrian fleet under Baron Wilhelm von Tegetthoff. He tried to compensate by ramming, but instead the battle became a confused mêlée of ship-to-ship actions. In these, the Italian unpreparedness played a role in leading to their heavier losses. In contrast, during the Franco-Prussian War, the French did not translate ideas of Baltic landings into action; nor did two German squadron sorties from Wilhelmshaven lead to action. The victory of the Chilean ironclads over the Peruvian ironclad *Huáscar* off Punta Angamos on 8 October 1879 was crucial in the War of the Pacific of 1879–83.

American Civil War

In the American Civil War, ironclads played an important role, helping to end debate elsewhere about their value. The inconclusive duel between the *Monitor* and the *Merrimack* (renamed the *Virginia* by the Confederates) in Hampton Roads on 9 March 1862, was the first clash between ironclads in history. Cannon shot made little impact on the armoured sides of the two ships. The year 1864 saw the first effective attack by a submersible, mounted in Charleston Harbour, when the *Hunley* sunk the Union screw sloop *Housatonic*, although she herself sank soon afterwards, probably as a consequence of the stress of the explosion. Later that year, the first successful torpedo boat attack occurred in Albemarle Sound, North Carolina, when, with a spar torpedo fitted to a steam launch, the Union sank the ironclad *Albemarle*.

However, much of the naval action did not involve ironclads or other aspects of new naval technology. Wooden steamers played a major role, especially on inland waterways. In 1862, Farragut led such a force to take New Orleans, overcoming the single Confederate ironclad and two substantial forts in defence. Yet, on the waterways, the Union also added iron armour to many of its ships. Some were "tinclads", with only thin iron armour, but others had 2½-inch-thick armour. The Confederate loss of New Orleans and Memphis in 1862 reduced its ability to build or convert warships for service on the Mississippi and other inland waterways, although the mobilization of the Confederate economy and the adaptability of the available manufacturing resources led to building ships at other river shipyards such as Selma and Shreveport. This permitted the construction of ironclads at places away from the coast and major rivers, and thus not as vulnerable to capture by Union forces. However, it was quite an ordeal for the Confederates to get their ironclad *Tennessee* down the Alabama River from Selma to Mobile Bay.

Most of the naval conflict involved clashes between warships and shore defences or between individual ships The dispersed nature of the Confederate fleet and Southern interest in blockade running and privateering ensured that larger actions were uncommon. The last was in Mobile Bay on 5 August 1864 when four Confederate ships were defeated by 18 Union ships, despite the help of mines, which claimed one ironclad. The single Confederate ironclad was bombarded into surrender. Again, the fortifications at the Bay's entrance were the principal Confederate defensive assets.

It would be mistaken to present New Orleans and Mobile as naval battles only and to neglect the coastal assault aspects of both actions. Indeed, the chief obstacle to Farragut's passage of the head of the Mississippi was not the paltry Confederate naval force, but Fort Jackson and Fort St. Philip. The same was true of Mobile, where Fort Gaines and Fort Morgan could have kept the Union squadron out of the Bay. Once they were successfully passed, a Union victory was assured.

The Union navy turned from being a small force of deep-sea sailing ships to a far larger and more varied navy that was powered by steam and included many coastal gunboats able to mount a blockade and to support amphibious attacks. Ultimately, it became the second largest navy in the world, with (figures vary) 650–75 warships, including 49 ironclads. The blockade mounted by the Union fleet demonstrated the continued strategic value of sea power: 295 steamers and 1,189 sailing ships were destroyed or seized. This blockade, while permeable by small, fast steamships until late in the war, did grievous economic harm to the Confederacy.[16] At the same time, Confederate privateering was a threat to Union commerce. Alongside blockade, the Union fleet provided an amphibious capability that was useful in specific instances, leading to the capture of New Orleans, for example, in 1862, and also tied up large numbers of Confederate troops in coastal defence. Furthermore, the strength of the Union navy helped to keep Lee from fighting near where warships could make a direct impact, although this was not true on the Mississippi. The Union's sea-borne and riverine campaigns were more than incidental to the conflict's outcome.

The rapid demobilization of the Union fleet after the war was an important event in naval history. So also, earlier, was the avoidance of British entry into the war. Relations had been tense, as the British government expressed sympathy for the Confederacy. The British fleet in North American and Caribbean waters was strengthened. However, war was avoided. Furthermore, the threat posed by the Americans should not be exaggerated, as their ironclads were not really suited for distant service on the high seas, while their ships were also inferior in battle conditions, because their naval ordnance had too low a muzzle velocity to be effective against British armour, while American armour was inferior because of the incapacity to roll thick iron plates.[17]

Change from the 1860s

The naval warfare of the 1860s was followed by no pause in the process of change that had been continuous from the 1810s. There continued to be developments in ship design and armament, tactics and strategy. The tension between armour and armament, weight and manoeuvrability, not least the mutually interacting need for more effective guns and stronger armour, led to changes in armour. Wooden-hulled ironclads, still laid down in the early 1860s, were quickly superseded. The iron navy was followed in the late 1870s by one using compound armour plate: the iron and steel navy. In the British navy, large hull components, like the keel, stern post, and stern, continued to be iron until the 1880s, but there were also moves towards the first all-steel battleships in the 1870s. Ship designers began to face the problem that armoured knights had confronted in the fifteenth century and that afflicted tank makers in the twentieth: juggling the three desirable, but mutually antagonistic, qualities required of a weapons platform – speed, armament and armour. One could only be enhanced at the expense of the others because of the weight problem.

There were also important changes in armament. In place of warships designed to fire broadsides came guns mounted in centreline turrets, that were able to fire end on, as well as to turn. This owed much to the changing surface of ships: masts were eliminated and a single superstructure put in the centre, with turrets built fore and aft. The revolving turret began with the American *Monitor* in 1862 and the practice of locating heavy piloting guns in an armoured casement with the British *Research* in 1864. Guns became more effective. Off Punta Angamos on 8 October 1879, armour-piercing Palliser shells were used for the first time. Fired from the 9-inch Armstrong guns of Chilean warships they forced the badly-damaged Peruvian *Huáscar* to surrender: the eight inches of wrought iron on its turret proved no defence.[18]

The increasing size and cost of armoured battleships from the 1870s played into the hands of the advocates of cruiser warfare and torpedo boats. In the 1880s, Admiral Théophile Aube and the French *Jeune École* provided an ideology for battleship opponents, which gained at least some support in every navy. They pressed for unarmoured light cruisers that would use less coal and be more manoeuvrable, able to protect sea lanes and attack the commerce of opponents.

Some commentators wondered if battleships had a future in the face of torpedoes. Aube's vessel of preference was the torpedo boat. The modern self-propelled torpedo originated with an Austrian invention in 1864 of a submerged torpedo driven by compressed air and with an explosive charge at the head. Adopted by the Austrian navy in 1868, the torpedo was manufactured by Robert Whitehead, a British expatriate. Britain (in 1872) and most European navies bought the right to manufacture it. The first successful attack with a Whitehead torpedo occurred in January 1878 when the Russians sank a Turkish gunboat at Batumi with two torpedoes fired from launches; the British had launched an unsuccessful attack the previous May on a Peruvian warship that had seized British merchantmen. Torpedo boats developed in the late 1870s. Two Chilean ships, part of the squadron blockading Callao, were sunk by Peruvian torpedoes in 1880.

There were also developments in mines and with submarines. In the American Civil War, Confederate mines sank seven armoured Union ships, compared to one lost to shore batteries. In 1868, Russia designed a more effective mine, a glass tube battery electrolyte detonation device. The first steam-powered submarine, the 30-ton *Resurgam* was launched by George Garrett in 1879. Working with the Swedish arms manufacturer, Thomas Nordenfelt, Garrett began work in 1882 on the *Nordenfelt I*, a 60-ton submarine, the first to be armed with self-propelled torpedoes.

The naval history of the period was of course about more than new technology, and any focus on such technology has to note its limitations as an account of naval history and of why change occurred. The deficiencies of any linear account of development are readily apparent, not least if contemporary debates and disagreements about particular innovations are continued. Experimentation was of course designed to ensure improvement. In 1845, Cockburn explained the reason why he supported getting rid of the cumbersome paddle wheel: "The proof we have lately had of the efficiency of the screw as a propellor on board the *Rattler*", adding "with all these efforts and improvements in continual progress, in which we are decidedly taking the lead, and are therefore in advance, I feel very confident".[19] Yet there were also failures. For example, the British even reverted for a while from the early 1860s to muzzle-loading artillery because they found the new Armstrong breech-loaders too unreliable, as their screwed breech-blocks blew out. More generally, the absence of conflict between the major powers ensured that technologies and theories of naval war could not be adequately tested.

It is also important not to read backwards. Despite the earlier appearance of steam, iron armour and breech-loading guns, the true ocean-going modern (all-steam) battle fleet did not really emerge until the 1890s. The marine turbine engine was not invented by Sir Charles Parsons until 1884 and nickel-steel armoured warships were a development of the 1890s, as, more generally, was an emphasis on battleships in naval doctrine.

In addition, it is important to remember the global context. Until the 1890s, even the strongest navies employed fully rigged screw steamers to show the flag on non-European stations. Navies were faced with the dilemma of maintaining fairly distinct forces in home waters and on colonial/overseas stations. The *Imperieuse*, the last big British warship designed with the ability to sail, was laid down in 1881, although it speedily lost its brig rig. These distant deployments did not only occur in peacetime. The Crimean War witnessed a confrontation between European naval forces in the Pacific. In July 1854, an Anglo-French force that included four frigates sailed from Honolulu in search of Russian frigates reported to be at sea: the Russian Pacific squadron included three frigates. On 4 September, the force attacked Petropavlovsk, in Kamchatka, the Russian base. However, it was well fortified and the men landed were repulsed. That winter the British and French retired to Vancouver and San Francisco respectively, and on their return the following spring found Petropavlovsk abandoned. Sailing on to Sitka, Alaska, then a Russian possession, they again found no Russian forces. The campaign

NAVAL POWER AND WARFARE

indicated the difficulty of operating with effect in such a vast body of water: it was impossible to find, let alone fix, opposing warships.

In the same period, an American squadron of four ships under Commodore Matthew Perry had entered Tokyo Bay on 8 July 1853 in order to persuade Japan to inaugurate relations. The following year, he returned with a larger squadron and negotiated the Treaty of Kanagawa (31 March 1854), which allowed American diplomatic representation and the right for American ships to call at two ports.[20] In 1854–55, another American naval expedition, the North Pacific Surveying Expedition, greatly expanded hydrographic knowledge of Japanese waters.

In the American Civil War, the Union sent an ironclad, the *Camanche*, to San Francisco in order to protect California from Confederate raids. This deployment marked the domination of the Atlantic in American naval strategic thinking at the time. The ship was built in 1862–63, then divided into parts and shipped around Cape Horn – as yet there was no transcontinental railway. Once at San Francisco, it was reconstructed. In 1865–66, another ironclad steamed round Cape Horn to California. In the Civil War, clashes between Confederate privateers and Union warships occurred over a vast range: off France and Brazil in 1864. The following year, the *Shenandoah*, the first composite (iron and wood) hulled cruising warship wrecked much of the New England whaling fleet in the northern Pacific. Other naval operations in the Pacific included the French capture of Mexican ports such as Acapulco during their intervention in Mexico in 1862–7, and, in 1864, the Spanish occupation of the Chinca Islands, from whose guano (bird droppings) Peru derived much of its income. The Spanish fleet overawed that of Peru and her ally Chile, but in 1866 American pressure led the Spaniards to end hostilities, although they first bombarded Callao and Valparaíso.

Doctrine was linked to strategic need and thus geopolitics. The development of global trade and of the colonial empires of the Western maritime states helped lead to an emphasis on the value of large navies, as in J. C. R. Colomb's *The Protection of our Commerce and Distribution of our Naval Forces Considered* (1867). Concern with trade as well as status led the Germans to develop their fleet after the Franco-Prussian War. Helped by French reparations, the pace of German naval construction rose greatly in 1873. By 1883, Germany had the third largest armoured fleet in the world.[21]

Consideration of the strategic importance of trade could lead to states adopting either an offensive or defensive approach, depending on the relative vulnerability of their trade compared with others – a debate going back, at least, to Sir Francis Drake. From the 1690s, the French saw themselves facing the British with their superior naval resources but with a greater reliance on overseas trade. In consequence, they had favoured commerce raiding. Aube's *La Guerre Maritime et Les Ports Françaises* (1882) was the latest iteration of this policy; he and the *Jeune École* pressed for fast-moving cruisers, rather than more heavily armoured battleships. The British had to defend their massive overseas trade and the sea routes to their global empire and be ready to face all comers, and so had to build the biggest navy in the world. Unlike France, but like the USA and Japan, Britain, however, was not threatened over land and so all three could concentrate their defence spending on their navies. The British navy was helped by its peacetime victory in the competition with the French for naval enhancement in the 1860s, and also by the consequences of the Franco-Prussian War for French military priorities: there was a determined effort to strengthen both the army and fortifications facing Germany.

Large navies became important national symbols. It was less clear, however, how far, in the event of war, it would be possible for any of them to realize the command of the sea that was discussed by contemporaries and was the goal of governments. It was also unclear how far the earlier limitations of strong navies in preventing commerce raiding and in ensuring amphibious capability had been overcome. World War One was to reveal that this was less the case than had been believed. Furthermore, the impact of naval strength and amphibious capability on conflict on land was less direct than was sometimes suggested. Naval action was no more able to force Turkey out of the war in 1915 than it had been in 1807. Because the wars of 1861–71 had been largely waged on land, and conflict ashore had attracted the attention of commentators, these limitations had not been adequately probed. Alongside the emphasis on new naval technology and weaponry between Trafalgar and the end of the period covered in this book, it is worth noting only a limited development in doctrine and operational planning. The informed, intellectual and self-conscious German General Staff was not matched at sea (which, given the general staff's twentieth-century performance may not have been such a bad thing). There was no equivalent British naval General Staff.

Growth in international trade and in the interdependency of major economies underlined the importance of maritime routes. This had been shown in the conflicts of the 1860s and 1870s as powers sought to blockade their opponents. Both Peru and Chile sought to stop arms shipments to the other. Such economic warfare required naval strength, although circumstances varied. The more powerful naval power among the combatants had not won in the Franco-Prussian War, but had prevailed in the American Civil War.

The most important consequence of the absence of major naval conflicts, when collated with the radical technological developments in warships after 1850, was that a high degree of uncertainty grew about the likely nature of naval combat, of the strengths and weaknesses of the new ship types, and about what effect all this might have on the organization of fleets, tactics, strategy and maritime dominance. States watched each other keenly in terms of technological innovation and worried about what was the best place to put their money.

CHAPTER FIVE

The Global Context, 1815–82

Improved naval capacity was an important factor in the acceleration of European overseas expansion during this period, but obviously far more was at stake. This chapter first charts some of the major episodes in this expansion and then seeks to provide an explanation of them that focuses on military factors. At the outset, it is possible to assess the impact of Western expansion in a number of ways. A comparison of world maps in 1815 and 1882, whether of the time or historical maps, makes its results abundantly clear. At another level, I began writing this chapter just after a visit to a church in which a funerary monument provided an impressive list of the far-flung campaigning of a British junior officer in the late 1870s and early 1880s.

Britain indeed was the leading Western imperial power of the period. This largely reflected the already far-flung character of her imperial possessions in 1815 and of the challenges and opportunities that arose from them. For example, Britain's position in Bengal led to concern about Burmese expansion. In addition, after 1815 Britain played a relatively limited role in continental European politics. This enabled her to respond to opportunities further afield; and also ensured that they dominated the military imagination of the British. South Asia remained the most important area of expansion.

The Maratha and Gurkha wars of the 1810s were followed in 1824–26 by the First Burmese War. The aggressive, expansionist kingdom of Burma, keen to consolidate its frontiers and end disorder in neighbouring principalities, stirred up the East India Company's fears and its defensive determination to support protectorates in north-east India. The amphibious range of British power ensured that it was possible to avoid fighting only in the jungles of the frontier zone. In 1824, there was an advance east from Bengal and in 1826 the British moved into Manipur. The way lay open to strike directly at Burmese centres of power. Rangoon fell to assault on 10 May 1824 by a force sent from the Andaman Islands, and from Rangoon a force was sent on to

Martaban. The British were besieged in Rangoon in the second half of 1824, but resisted both that and the inroads of disease, finally smashing the Burmese investment on 15 December. Amphibious attacks were also launched on Ye, Tavoy and Mergui in Tenasserim in 1824 – this was the most effective way to seize the province – and on Negrais Island and Myohaung in 1825. In 1825–26, the British advanced up the Irrawady to Mandalay. This was a much contested advance, but the British were victorious. They benefited from the effective use of their river fleet and from the disciplined fire-power of the infantry. Britain was ceded Arakan and Tenasserim in the subsequent peace.

Within India itself, the British consolidated their position in areas in which they were already dominant (for example storming the Jat fortress of Bharatpur), as well as expanding their power into new areas. In the 1830s, Mysore was gained in 1831 and Karachi fell to amphibious attack in 1839. In the 1840s, the British expanded dramatically in north-west India. Victories over the Baluchis at Umarkot and Mirpur Khas in 1843 led to the conquest of Sind by Sir Charles Napier, and in that year also Gwalior was overrun, with battles at Maharajpur and Gwalior. Napier's victories over the Baluchis were won by smaller advancing infantry forces supported by cavalry and horse artillery attacking opposing lines supported by artillery.

The First (1845–46) and Second (1848–49) Anglo-Sikh Wars were hard-fought struggles. Like Burma, Egypt and the Zulus, the Sikhs were an expansionist power in the early nineteenth century. The Sikhs had a large army, many of whose officers were trained in European drill and tactics, armed with effective firearms and cannon. When their camp at Firozshah fell in December 1845, 73 Sikh cannon were seized. Accounts of battles emphasized the importance of artillery, although also of infantry and cavalry tactics similar to those of the Napoleonic Wars. The British relied on infantry advances. Thomas Pierce of the Bengal Army recorded, on 27 January 1846, that the Sikhs served:

> their artillery admirably . . . we were now within 300 yards of the enemys batteries which were dealing forth grape and canister without mercy. All of a sudden, they were observed to waver under our severe cannonading, and the whole line giving a wild hurrah, rushed forward, drove them from their guns, which we spiked, pursued them onwards as fast as we were able – they rallied, formed square – the 16th Lancers were ordered to charge.[1]

At the decisive battle of Chillianwalla on 13 January 1849, heavy Sikh artillery was again a feature:

> The havoc they committed was fearful . . . took place in a thick jungle, where four men, in some places, could hardly go abreast . . . At one time the grape and round shot were flying so thick that the

ground was actually covered with them; and every bush you passed out rushed a Sikh and tried to cut you down. Of course we never thought of looking into every bush we passed and thus they go in our rear.[2]

As earlier, against the Marathas, the British were helped in the wars by divisions among their opponents.

In the First Sikh War, the Sikhs had advanced across the river Sutle, but were stopped at the indecisive Battle of Mudki (18 December 1845), a hard-fought bayonet action, much of it in the night. The British under Gough then advanced, capturing the Sikh camp at Firozshah (21–22 December), where Sikh defensive fire cost about 2,400 casualties. On the British left, Sikh cannon fire had stopped the advance. The British stormed the camp on 21 December, but cohesion was lost in night-time fighting and they withdrew in order to reform and mount a further, and successful, attack the following morning. A more vigorous command by Tej Singh, the Sikh general, might well have led to British defeat. At Sobraon, on 10 February 1846, British cannon failed to silence the opposing infantry, and the battle was settled by a British infantry assault of the Sikh entrenchments. In the Second War, aside from Chillianwala, there was also a major British victory at Gujrat (21 February 1849). The Sikh army surrendered the following month. Aside from battles, there were also sieges, most importantly of Multan. Nevertheless, it was the battles that were decisive to the course of the campaign.[3]

There were also British failures in South Asia, most conspicuously the loss of an entire British-Indian division in the disastrous retreat from Kabul in 1842. British support for an unpopular client ruler was initially successful, and in 1839 they captured Kandahar, Ghazni and Kabul. However, it led to a general revolt that was mishandled. In January 1842, the force in Kabul withdrew, but met disaster in the passes. The overall failure was due to poor decision-making, a failure to understand the Afghan political system and the impact of winter. Deep snows delayed the retreat across the difficult terrain, providing an opportunity for ambush by Ghilzni tribesmen. A British force reoccupied Kabul that autumn in a punitive campaign, but it was then deemed prudent to withdraw.

Elsewhere in Asia, the British expanded in Malaya, gaining Malacca and Singapore, and moved into the Persian Gulf to stop what they saw as the piracy of the Qasimi Arabs. The Opium War of 1839–42 arose from the Chinese attempt to enforce their prohibition on the import of opium. The seizure of opium held by British merchants and their expulsion from Canton led to pressure within Britain for a response. The demand for compensation was backed up by force. Successes, including the capture of the Pearl (Zhu) River forts, Amoy, Canton, Chinkiang, Chusan, Ningpo and Shanghai by amphibious forces, led China to cede Hong Kong by the Treaty of Nanjing of 1842; British troops had advanced to its walls. Freedom of trade was enforced at the expense of China's right to regulate its economy and society. Aden had been annexed in 1839, for the first time by a European power. British naval action against Mehmed Ali in 1840 – the occupation of Beirut and Sidon and the bombardment and capture of Acre – limited Egypt's northward advance in Syria and Palestine.

In South Africa, the British expanded inland from Cape Colony. Natal was annexed in 1845, and British Kaffraria in 1847. Also in South Africa, the firepower of the Boers (descendants of Dutch settlers) smashed a Zulu attack on their wagon circle in the Battle of Blood River in Natal on 16 December 1838; they had similarly defeated the Matabele on 15 October 1836. In West Africa, a small British force under Colonel Sir Charles McCarthy, Governor of Sierra Leone, was destroyed by a much larger Asante army in 1824 after it had used up its ammunition. The governor's head became a war trophy.

No other European state could compare with Britain's transoceanic gains, but there were three spheres of significant Western expansion: first, trans-oceanic by other European powers; secondly, on contiguous land frontiers by European powers; and, thirdly, by independent Western states in the Americas. France was most important in the first case. The French began their second colonial empire when they occupied Algiers with 37,000 troops in 1830. This had been intended to win popularity for the Bourbon Charles X, not to serve as the basis of a widespread empire. It failed in this, and Charles's successor, Louis-Philippe, decided in 1834 to extend French control to the entire coastline. In the Pacific, the Marquesas and Tahiti (proclaimed a protectorate) followed in 1842, and Gabon in West Africa in 1844.

Initially, the French were successful in North Africa, seizing coastal enclaves, especially Oran in 1831 and Bône in 1833, but from 1835 they encountered strong resistance led by Abd el-Kader (1808–83) and opposition from the interior drew them in. El-Kader's troops made effective use of fire-arms. The French under Trézel were defeated at La Macta on 28 June 1835, and one poorly led French column was destroyed at Sidi-Brahim in September 1845. Nevertheless, Clausel, a Napoleonic general, was victorious at Mascara (4 December 1835) and Tlemcen (13 January 1836), although he failed at Constantine in 1836. On 6 July 1836 Bugeaud defeated el-Kader at Sikkak and the following year the French were able to advance into the interior, storming Constantine on 12–13 October after a long siege. Tlemcen fell in 1842. The French faced political as well as military problems in extending their rule. Colonialism by incorporation, in which existing power structures were adopted and accommodated by the imperial state, was made far more difficult by the seizure of land for French settlement; although the French did benefit from divisions within Algerian society and the support of some Algerians.

The Algerian war forced the French to change their strategy and tactics. At the outset, the French commanders of the Army of Africa sought to employ familiar tactics: those of Napoleonic conflict, namely mass manoeuvre and large columns, and the holding of territory by posts creating a front. This policy was changed by Bugeaud in 1840–47, as the French came to emphasize a more fluid strategy, in order to deal with an elusive opponent who only risked battle in the harsh terrain when it suited them. Many posts were abandoned in order to free troops for a more aggressive strategy in which rapidly moving columns and cavalry units attacked the Algerians, threatening their agricultural base. The *razzia* (raid) became a devastating instrument designed to terrorize the population. It depended on fast-moving columns and threw much responsibility on to unit commanders, for example, the defeat by the Duke of Aumale's cavalry column of Abd el-Kader at Smala on 14 May 1843. These flexible tactics were supported by overwhelming force. By 1846, the French had 108,000 effectives, one-third of their regular army, in Algeria. This was one soldier for every 25 to 30 Algerians and a force that greatly outnumbered that of Abd el-Kader: his army consisted of a core of about 10,000 well armed regulars and about 40,000 less well armed irregulars. He surrendered in 1847. Meanwhile, accusing Sultan Abd el-Rahman of helping opposition in Algeria, Bugeaud had invaded Morocco in 1844, defeating the Sultan's forces at Isly on 14 August.[4]

The Spaniards devoted their efforts first to an unsuccessful attempt to retain their empire in Latin America and then, in the Carlist Wars, to civil conflict. Portugal was no longer able to maintain a successful imperial impetus. The Gaza Nguni of southern Mozambique destroyed a Portuguese army in 1834 and the Zulus sacked Lourenço Marques the previous year.

The Dutch also failed to resume their eighteenth-century pace of expansion after the disruption of the Revolutionary and Napoleonic Wars. Expeditions against Palembang in Sumatra were defeated in 1819 and, initially, in 1821, but they were eventually victorious that year. Also on Sumatra, the Dutch only won the Padri War (1821–38) after defeats, including a serious one at Lintau in 1823. The Java War, which began in 1825, was only brought to a successful conclusion by the Dutch after five years of hard fighting. The Dutch were short of troops, but they benefited from Indonesian allies, including the Sultan of Yogyakarta. Initially, the Dutch were thwarted by the mobility and guerrilla tactics of their opponents, but they developed a network of fortified bases from which they sent out mobile columns that policed the local population, prevented the consolidation of rebel positions and attacked the rebels.[5]

On the land frontiers of European powers the principal shift occurred as a result of Russian expansion. Austria did not advance into the Balkans, although the Turks were affected by the success of insurrectionary movements there. The most important of these was in Greece. Greatly assisted by the Anglo-French-Russian naval victory over the Turks at Cape Navarino in 1827, the Greeks won their independence. The Russian advance in this period was not directed into the Balkans; the acquisition of Bessarabia in 1812 was not followed up immediately. Instead, the Russians focused their landward expansion on the area between the Black and Caspian Seas and also to the east of the latter. In the Russo-Persian War of 1825–28, the Russians under Paskievich won the battle of Ganja, captured Erivan, and forced the Persians to sign the Treaty of Turkomanchi. This led to the Russian acquisition of the Khanates of Erivan and Nakhichevan.

In the Russo-Turkish War of 1828–29, the Russians advanced into the Balkans again. Tsar Nicholas I personally directed the successful siege of Varna in 1828. The Russians had advanced through Moldavia and Wallachia, crossing the Danube near Ruszczuk, which they captured. The following year, they advanced as far as Adrianople, which fell on 29 August. Farther east, they captured Anapa, Akshaltsikhe, Kars and Erzurum,[6] and by the Treaty of Adrianople (1829) forced the Turks to abandon their position on the Circassian coast on the north-eastern shore of the Black Sea. Nevertheless, the subsequent Russian effort to subdue Circassia proved very costly, despite ethnic and religious divisions among the Circassian peoples, as well as major commitments of Russian troops, naval blockade, fort construction, and attempts both to pursue pacification and to adopt more brutal tactics. Chechnya and Daghestan were not conquered until 1859, Circassia until 1864.[7]

To the east of the Caspian Sea, the Russians made major advances. In 1822, they annexed the lands of the Middle Kazak Horde, restructuring its organization and leadership and introducing Russian administrative control based on a number of forts built in 1824–31. New fortified lands – the Ilek and the New Line – brought much of the best pasture land under Russian control. The Kazaks revolted, capturing the Russian fort of Akmolinsk (1838), but their opposition was weakened by divisions: the rebels had to help the Elder Horde fight off the Khanate of Kokand, while the Russians subsequently gained the allegiance of the Elder Horde (1846) and allied with Kokand. Kirgiz, loyal to Kokand, then destroyed the rebels. Meanwhile, the inexorable advance of Russian forts and farmers continued. As elsewhere, the advance of a Western power reflected the weakness of other imperial systems. The Chinese, who had largely controlled the Elder Horde and had a considerable impact on the Middle Horde the previous century, were no longer strong enough to intervene in the region.[8] The Russians also advanced in Turkestan. A campaign launched in 1839 against the Khanate of Khiva for robbing Russian caravans was unsuccessful, but, thereafter, fortresses were constructed, beginning with Aleksandrovskiy in 1840.

In the New World, the major dynamic power was the United States, although newly independent Latin American states, such as Mexico, also deployed their forces against Native Americans. In the Seminole wars (1817–18, 1835–43), Florida was brought under American control. In the first war, Andrew Jackson was helped in his 1818 invasion by a force of Lower Creeks. In the second war, the government deployed over 40,000 troops, especially after the Seminoles, about 5,000 strong, won several battles in the initial stages. A three-pronged encirclement planned by Winfield Scott in 1836 miscarried. The Americans were affected by the great difficulties of fighting in the waterlogged and humid terrain. The Seminoles generally avoided fighting in the open and preferred guerrilla tactics; they eventually took shelter in the more inaccessible parts of the Everglades. Having driven them to these refuges, the government wound down the war.[9] The frontier of European American settlement also moved west of the Mississippi, a move helped by the defeat of Black Hawk and the Sauk and Fox peoples in the Black Hawk War in Illinois and Wisconsin in 1832. This war ended rapidly with the crushing defeat of Black Hawk at Bad Axe River (2 August). Newly independent Texas was more exposed to Native American raids. This led to campaigns against the Plains Indians, and in August 1840, the Great Comanche Raid was ended at the Battle of Plum Creek.

The situation changed greatly in scale in 1848 when success in the Mexican War left the American state in control of very extensive new territories in which Native Americans dominated. Furthermore, white settlers now began to enter the territories in substantial numbers. As a result, the US army found itself forced to take up armed constabulary duties in the 1850s on an hitherto unprecedented scale.[10] The Native Americans suffered from a lack of unity, and from the replacement of the weak presence of Mexican control (and the accommodating views of the British in the Oregon Territory), by the more insistent territorial demands and military activity of the burgeoning American state. Nevertheless, it was the demographic weight of the European-Americans that was crucial, combined with their willingness to migrate and force their way into regions already occupied by Native Americans.

An evaluation of Western warfare with non-Western powers in 1815-50 reveals a faster pace of expansion than in the previous 35-year period. The decisive decade was the 1840s, although it would be misleading to underrate the importance of earlier moves. For example, once Java had been brought under control, it came to serve as the basis for an expansion of Dutch power comparable to, although on a smaller scale than, that of Indian-based British power. The French capture of Algiers in 1830 was also important as a commitment to an overseas expansionism that was to be far greater in scale than any hitherto.

Nevertheless, the 1840s were of particular importance because they saw bitter struggles with non-Western forces, success in each of which cleared the way for consolidation, new commitments and further expansion. This was true both of the French in Algeria and of the Anglo-Sikh wars. In addition, the Opium War was the first time a West European state had waged war on China, the first European victory over the Chinese and one achieved in China itself. Combined with the British action against Egyptian forces in 1840, an impressive demonstration of Western power against a modernizing and empire-building non-Western power, this suggests that a "tipping point" had indeed occurred. In 1807, British forces in Egypt had been defeated at Rosetta, while in 1809 the Chinese had rejected the suggestion of a British presence in Macao to protect the Portuguese colony against possible French attack. By the 1840s, the situation was very different. In part, this reflected the extent to which military resources in the 1800s had been devoted to conflict between the Western powers, but there had also been an important enhancement in Western military capability both in absolute terms and relative to that of leading non-Western powers.

This process continued in the years from mid-century to the British occupation of Egypt in 1882. This was a period of major conflict within the Western world, but expansion at the expense of non-Westerners continued, not least because the Western powers best placed to gain territory, Britain, Russia and the USA, were not involved in conflict within the West, with the exception of the short-lived Crimean War of 1854–56 and the American Civil War of 1861–65.

Whereas Russian pressure on Turkey led to Anglo-French intervention, the British were able to fight Persia unmolested in 1856–57. Again, the British used their amphibious capability, staging a successful landing. Persian positions were seized, a Persian force defeated at Khush-āb (8 February 1857), and Persia intimidated into evacuating Herat.

India again served as the basis of British expansion. Lower Burma was annexed by the British in 1852, although it was not "pacified" until 1857. Within India, Nagpur, Jhansi and Berar followed in 1853 and Awadh (Oudh) in 1856. The Indian Mutiny of 1857–59 was violently suppressed by British and loyal Indian troops, especially Sikhs and Gurkhas, in the largest deployment of British forces between the Napoleonic Wars and the Boer War of 1899–1902. Victory in this lengthy conflict was seen as crucial to British prestige and power in India. The challenge was exacerbated by the presence of numerous trained artillery men among the rebels. Lieutenant Hugh Pearce Pearson wrote from Cawnpore in 1857, that the rebels did not dare "charge our little squares with their clouds of cavalry. They had most magnificent gunners". The rebels also had new Enfield rifles. The important role of Indian military manpower was indicated by the trigger of the mutiny: the British demand that their Indian soldiers use a new cartridge for their new Enfield rifles greased in animal tallow, a measure that was unacceptable to Muslims and Hindus for religious reasons. This was doubly significant because of the low level of confidence between British officers and Indian subordinates, both officers and soldiers. Both of the latter groups felt neglected. The British military presence had also been weakened by the movement of units to the Crimea. Already in 1850 there had been problems over conditions of service, which had led Napier to write "seeing the great peril to which the Indian Government was exposed, by the mutinous spirit which has appeared among the troops, it seemed to me that the greatest caution and the promptest decision on my part was necessary".

The Indian troops at Meerut mutinied on 10 May 1857 and, the next day, mutineers took over Delhi, proclaiming the Mughal Bahadur Shah sovereign.

Fortunately for the British, much of the Indian army remained loyal, includ-ing the Madras army in the south and most of the Bombay army. The Punjab remained under control, and the rulers of Hyderabad, Kashmir and Nepal provided assistance. However, most of the Bengal Army in the Ganges Valley mutinied. British failures to regain control – Delhi was not retaken and on 29 June an attack on mutineers near Chinhat was defeated – helped the mutiny to gather momentum.

The movement of troops and cannon from outside the rebellious area helped the British regain the initiative. On 14 September 1857, Delhi was stormed and, although there were heavy losses in street fighting, the city was cleared by 20 September. In November, Lucknow was relieved and then the British made a safe withdrawal from it. Mutineers defeated a British force at Cawnpore on 27–8 November, but were, in turn, routed there by Colin Campbell on 6 December. The following spring, the British were able to overrun the rebellious area. On 21 March, Lucknow was recaptured, and, in May and June, Awadh (Oudh) was cleared. Sir Hugh Rose regained control of central India, defeating the Rani of Jhansi and Tantia Topi. The latter's defeat at and near Gwalior (19–22 June 1858) was the last major battle of the mutiny, although there were still clashes the following year; Tantia Topi was not killed until 18 April 1859.[11]

The fighting in the Indian Mutiny was very hard. Pearson wrote on 1 August 1857 that the British forces had taken very heavy casualties, adding "village fighting . . . desperate . . . we took two sepoy prisoners the other day and they were blown away from the guns: the stink of fresh flesh was sicken-ing in the extreme, but I have seen so many disgusting sights and so much bloodshed that I have grown quite callous". The following May, Pearson reported that the rebels were elusive "owing to the intense thickness of the jungle".[12] The storming of fortified positions, such as Delhi, Jhansi and Gwalior, played a major role in the fighting. So also did sieges. As a result, although battles were important, comparatively they were less so than in many other conflicts in the period.

After the mopping up operations that followed the Indian Mutiny, the British were involved in a series of mountain wars on the "North-West Frontier". These posed serious problems of hill warfare, not least of pinning down their opponent. The pacification of Baluchistan by Sir Robert Sandeman in the 1870s offered a model for other frontier regions; winning local allies played a crucial role, but so also, as the Punjab Irregular Force repeatedly showed, did an ability to adapt to local conditions and to devise specialized tactics.[13]

Elsewhere, indigenous resistance was overcome in Australia and, although less easily and completely, in New Zealand. In Australia, the Aborigines were hit hard by Western diseases, especially smallpox and influenza. These not only killed many but also hit social patterns and morale. Aborigine resistance was also affected by the very fragmented nature of the Aboriginal "nation", which greatly lessened the prospect of cooperation. The extent to which a failure to adopt firearms on any scale lessened Aborigine chances is controversial. It can be seen as a sign of inflexibility, but also as a response to the limitations of early nineteenth-century firearms and to the difficulty of obtaining supplies. By the second half of the century, the settlers enjoyed an important technological advantage thanks to the spread of breech-loading rifles and were able to make rapid advances, especially in Queensland.[14]

The course of the conflict in New Zealand indicated the extent to which Western power projection spanned the globe, but also that its progress was far from easy. The Maoris used well sited trench and *pa* (fort) systems that were difficult to bombard or storm, and inflicted serious defeats on the British. In 1860, in the First Taranaki War, Te Āti Awa Maoris were able to inflict heavy casualties on British troops at the *pa* at Puketakauere and Onukwkaitara. Elsewhere the British were more successful in using artillery bombardment to get the Maoris to abandon *pa* at Te Kohia and Ōrongomāihangi, but the Maoris were able to do so without heavy losses. Without either side winning a decisive victory, a ceasefire was negotiated in 1861. Further north, conflict broke out in 1863 as the British sought to expand their control over land to the south of Auckland. This involved road and fort construction. The British deployed up to 9,000 men, as well as local colonists. The major clash at Rangiriri (20 November 1863) saw the outnumbered Maori surrender mobility in order to defend a position in which they were battered by artillery fire from land and sea. The Maori inflicted heavy losses on attacking infantry staging frontal attacks before leaving their fortifications at night. The following spring another position was attacked at Orākau. Again, the Maori broke out after heavy attack. At Pukehinahina, on 29 April, the Maori lured British forces into a *pa* before inflicting heavy losses on them and then retreating. In 1865, conflict spread. The British responded by constructing forts at river mouths on the contested west coast of North Island. The following year, Maori *pa* were captured at Ōkōtuku and Pūtahi, but, in 1868, Maori forces under Titokowaru defeated colonial forces twice at Te Ngutu-o-te-Manu and once at Moturoa. However, Titokowaru's support ebbed in 1869 and the colonists were able to regain ground.

Also on North Island in 1868, another Maori leader, Te Kooti, launched a vigorous attack on colonial settlements. The response was mostly by colonial and Maori forces as most regular units had now left. A siege of the *pa* at Ngā Tapa in January 1869 went wrong for the besieged Te Kooti and he found less Maori support than he had anticipated. Hostilities continued, but by 1872 Te Kooti had clearly lost. Militarily, the mobility of the colonial forces, including the Arawa Flying Comumn was combined with a process of steady entrenchment. Roads, telegraph lines and armed constabulary stations were all constructed. As more generally with Western imperialism, local cooperation was crucial to success, and in military terms entrenchment and battle were two mutually supporting sides of the same coin.[15]

In West Africa, Lagos was annexed in 1861, although an expedition against the Asante in 1864 was wrecked by disease. The Asante (Ashanti) were one of the more militarily powerful of all African people. In 1873–74, the British mounted another expedition, under Sir Garnet Wolseley, in which they used Gatling guns and seven-pounder artillery. The Asante were also outgunned by the British breech-loading rifles – shots from their muskets could only inflict minor wounds – and defeated at Amoafu (January 1874), the advancing British square firing repeatedly into the surrounding vegetation. The Asante capital, Kumasi, was seized and burned down on 4 February. The well prepared British force also benefited from the assistance of other African peoples, especially the Fante.[16]

Other European powers also made important transoceanic advances. The French expanded their control in Algeria, repressing an uprising in 1871, and began a territorial presence in Indo-China, Somaliland and the Ivory Coast. In the Pacific, they annexed New Caledonia in 1853. In the Senegal Valley, the French expanded their strength from 1854, developing an effective chain of riverine forts linked by steamboats. General Louis Faidherbe, Governor of Senegal 1854–65, developed the somewhat dormant economy and infrastructure of French Senegal, and launched a policy of expansion into the interior. This brought him into conflict with Moors and with the fervently Islamic Tukolor empire of al-Hajj Umar Tal. The French benefited from the firepower of their trained African regulars, from their ability to win local allies, and from their mobility, especially their use of armed river steamers. These were used to relieve the besieged fortress of Médine in 1857, a serious defeat for Umar Tal. The same year, Faidherbe had formed the first units of the *Tirailleurs Sénégalais*, local light infantry, who provided vital manpower.[17]

The Dutch made gains in the East Indies – in Borneo, the Celebes, Bali, Sumatra and New Guinea – although the process was a slow one. This owed much to the problems of campaigning – logistics, disease and native opposition, but the limited nature of the resources and political will devoted to Dutch expansion were also important.[18] The Dutch devoted fewer troops and less attention to imperial expansion than did the British and French: there was certainly nothing to compare with the British in India or the French in Algeria. Nevertheless, they made important gains. Aceh in Sumatra, a historic centre of resistance to European power, fell in 1873–74, although bitter guerrilla resistance continued in the hinterland.

Across the land-boundaries of the European powers the major gains were again made by Russia. Once it had sold Alaska to the USA, the Russian empire was an extension of its frontier, rather than, as with Britain and France, the creation of an overseas empire. Although the Crimean War checked Russian ambitions on the Turkish empire in Europe, elsewhere the Russian frontier expanded greatly. The Crimean War arose from a Russo-Turkish war that began in 1853. The Russians were beaten when they tried to cross the Danube in late 1853, but in 1854 they advanced again, crossed the Danube and besieged Silistria. However, thanks to Turkish success in resisting bombardment and assaults, Silistria did not fall rapidly. Austrian diplomatic pressure forced the Russians to raise the siege in June 1854 and to withdraw to Russia, but, further east, the main Turkish army in the Caucasus was defeated at Kurudere on 7 August 1854. The following year, after repeated attempts to storm it had failed, the Russians took the city of Kars, when, without supplies or relief, the garrison surrendered. The Austrians were opposed to Russian gains in the Balkans, because they were a potential threat to the Habsburg empire. The Austrian role is a reminder of the importance of political factors in the strategy and course of campaigns.

In Central Asia, the Russians made important advances. A line of fortresses against Turkestan was constructed in 1864–65, and Kazakstan, now isolated from outside intervention, was brought under increased Russian administrative control and opened to further settlement. A revolt by the Younger Horde in 1869 was put down. In Turkestan, the Russians made gains at the expense of Kokand in the 1850s. In the early 1860s, extensive conquests were made in what was organized in 1865 as Turkestan. Tashkent was gained in 1865, and Samarkand in 1868. Kokand (1866) and Bukhara were defeated, as was Khiva (1873), the latter two becoming Russian protectorates. Russian expansion owed much to the disunity of the Khanates. Bukhara itself was weakened by rebellion. Further east, the shifting balance of advantage between Russia and China enabled the former to gain the Amur region in 1858 and the Ussuri region in 1860. The Treaty of Beijing of 1860 delimited the new frontier. Vladivostok was founded in the Ussuri region in 1860, providing Russia with a warm-water Pacific port.

In North America, regular troops were withdrawn from the Far West during the American Civil War. They were replaced by local volunteers who reacted very violently to Native American actions. The pace of expansion at the expense of Native Americans resumed after the disruption of the Civil War. The railway played a major role, not only in speeding American troops but also in developing economic links between coastal and hinterland America and integrating the frontiers of settlement with the exigencies of the world economy. This was important both in the spread of ranching, with the cattle being driven to railheads, and of mining, for example for silver. Thus, as with the Russians in the Ukraine in the eighteenth century, the spread of politico-military control has to be seen alongside that of settlement and economic exploitation. Not all Native American tribes fought the European-Americans. The Utes, Crow and Pawnees, for example, were generally friendly, and, indeed, provided the army with scouts. Nelson Miles, a veteran of the Civil War, used Crow assistance when he attacked the Sioux and northern Cheyenne after Custer's defeat by the Sioux at Little Bighorn on 25 June 1876; eight days earlier, the Sioux under Crazy Horse had defeated George Crook at Rosebud Creek.

The Civil War had badly disrupted the continuity in army experience of fighting Native Americans. Many commanders from the 1850s were dead or had lost their commissions by serving the Confederacy. Trained in, and from, the Civil War, with its emphasis on commanding and fighting large numbers of regulars, their replacements were not adept at dealing with the very mobile Native Americans, although Custer did defeat the Plains tribes at the Washita River in 1868, Crook forced some of the Arizona Apaches to surrender in 1871–73, and Ranald Mackenzie won successive victories, against the Comanches at Palo Duro Canyon (1874) and over Dull Knife's Cheyennes at Crazy Woman Creek (1876). The sharp reduction of the army in the aftermath of the Civil War, ensured that there were few troops available for frontier warfare. When, in 1867, Philip Sheridan took command of the Department of the Missouri, which covered much of the frontier, he had only 6,000 troops. It proved difficult to force the mobile Native Americans to battle: they knew the terrain and were adept at surprise. The Sioux showed this in 1866 in their successful campaigning against the army in Montana and Wyoming in the Bozeman Trail War.

As a consequence, the army developed techniques that focused on winter campaigning, and the coordination of independently operating columns advancing from different directions. The former were used in late 1868 in attacks in north Texas, the latter, successfully, in the Red River War of 1874–75 with the Southern Cheyenne. Native American villages were attacked, their crops and food stores destroyed, and their horses seized, which crippled their mobility. Settlements were particularly vulnerable in the winter as those who escaped risked starvation and death by exposure. The killing of bison was seen as a way to weaken the Natives. Mackenzie destroyed Native camps at both Palo Duro Canyon and at Crazy Woman Creek. Similarly, in 1876, Crook destroyed the Sioux village at Slim Buttes, while the following year Miles destroyed Crazy Horse's village at Wolf Mountains. The totality of such methods can be compared to the devastation of parts of the Confederacy in 1864–5, but the wholesale destruction and persecution of the Native Americans was further justified by depicting them as pagan savages. The shortage of troops and the precedent of the assault on enemy civilian life in the Civil War encouraged a preference for quick and brutal campaigns, directed at crippling resources and maintaining the tempo of attack. In the Nez Percé War of 1877, pursuing federal cavalry were defeated at White Bird Canyon (17 June), Clearwater (11–12 July), Big Hole River (9–10 August) and Canyon Creek (13 September), but ultimately a far larger force under Miles forced the surrounded Nez Percé to surrender at Eagle Rock (5 October).[19]

The European Americans were no longer interested in pushing the Native Americans back. They now sought total control of the whole of America. After 1877, there were still problems with Native Americans, especially the Apache, but Native American resistance had been largely broken and a successful military methodology had been evolved. Its focus on wrecking civil society, or rather on the notion that there was no civil sphere separate to the military, had been seen in the latter stages of the American Civil War and in counter-insurgency operations in Europe. In the American West, this system was made especially effective thanks to the mobility of the regulars and their ability through a superior logistical service to stage winter campaigns.

In the last quarter of the century, the pace of Western expansion worldwide increased. There were defeats, sometimes due to poor generalship, but also to being greatly outnumbered. At Isandlwana, on 22 January 1879, a multi-column British advance failed because the columns were unable to offer mutual support and the Zulus brought overwhelming force against one of the columns. A 20,000 strong Zulu army defeated a British force of 1,800, of whom only 581 were regulars. The British had only two seven-pounder guns and their camp was not entrenched. The Zulus enveloped the British flanks and benefited from their opponents running out of ammunition, but, thanks to the British Martini-Henry rifles, Zulu casualties were very high. The Zulus, who did not want rifles, referred to the British as cowards because they would not fight hand-to-hand.[20]

The following year, at Maiwand (27 July), an 11,000-strong Afghan force under Ayub Khan, armed with British Enfield rifles and 30 well handled cannon, including three rifled 14-pounder Armstrong guns, defeated a 2,500 strong British brigade, killing 962: the British artillery was outgunned and part of the infantry gave way after five hours, leading to a harrowing defeat.[21]

These defeats, however, were against the pattern. The British went on to defeat both the Zulus and the Afghans, the former at Gingindlovu, Khambula and, decisively, Ulundi (4 July) in 1879. At each, heavy defensive infantry fire from prepared positions, supported by artillery, stopped Zulu attacks before the Zulus could reach the British lines, and British cavalry then inflicted heavy losses as the Zulus retreated. In the Second Afghan War (1878–80), the British succeeded in increasing their influence in Afghanistan in an effort to block that of Russia. It proved possible to advance to both Kabul and Kandahar from India, but positions there were vulnerable. In 1878, a force advanced on Kabul and defeated the Afghans at Peiwar Kotal (2 December). The following year, the newly installed British Resident was killed and a fresh advance proved necessary. The British were victorious at Charasia Ridge (6 October 1879), but it was difficult to win a lasting success, not least because of the fractured nature of Afghan politics, which made it difficult to find a central authority with whom to make peace. The British position outside Kabul was soon embattled, and the garrison at Kandahar was invested after Maiwand. It proved necessary to send a relief expedition from Kabul, and this was successfully accomplished by Sir Frederick Roberts; his crushing of Ayub Khan outside Kandahar (1 September 1880) proved the last major action of the war. Nevertheless, the political and logistical problems of operating in Afghanistan, challenged the efficacy of the forward policy which the government of India had been pursuing, and encouraged the British to draw back and, instead, seek to stabilize their position to the east, on the "North-West Frontier".

More generally, in both Africa and Asia, major and/or expanding non-Western states were checked or defeated, ensuring that power and success were increasingly associated with Western states and models. The occupation of Beijing by an Anglo-French force in 1860 was an important symbolic step. It did not lead to any lasting occupation and followed an unsuccessful British landing at Taku in 1859, but it was a blow at the heart of Chinese prestige. The Chinese were forced to open their country to trade and missionaries. In the conflict, Anglo-French forces had also occupied Canton in January 1858.

In Africa, another long-lasting empire, that of Ethiopia, was also brought low by British power. Emperor Tewodros II committed suicide in 1868 after he failed to repel a force under Lieutenant-General Robert Napier. In a methodically planned campaign, Napier led his 13,000-strong force into the mountains from the Red Sea, defeated the Ethiopians at Arogee (10 April), and stormed the fortress of Magdala, rescuing the British hostages he had been instructed to free. The Ethiopians were outgunned, their matchlocks and smooth-bore shotguns less effective than the British rifles, whether muzzle-loading or the more recent breech-loaders. British volley fire proved devastating.[22]

The Russians demonstrated the weakness of the Turks in 1877–78, to a greater extent than in previous wars. The Russian army advanced to within 15 kilometres of Constantinople, though the Turks fought hard and well. They were helped by Russian deficiencies, including poor organization, training and weaponry. The Russians lacked breech-loaders and had no corps structure to match the Prussians. They had been influenced by Moltke's successes, which affected Russian strategy in 1877, but, as so often, it proved difficult to copy a victorious system. Although they successfully besieged Kars and Plevna, the siege of Plevna (19 July–10 December 1877) proved both long and costly and the Russians were unable to capture Erzurum and Batumi.[23] While the Turks had been able to defeat the Serbs in 1876, it was clear that, in the face of Russian power and ambitions, the Eastern Question had now become a matter of the fate of the Turkish empire.

Egypt was a tougher challenge than Ethiopia had been in 1868 (although the Italians were to fail in Ethiopia in 1896). The Egyptian army was 60,000 strong in 1875 and equipped with modern weaponry, including Remington rifles, Gatling machine-guns and 80 mm Krupp artillery. British forces came up against them in pursuit of protecting European, particularly British, interests in Egypt and gaining physical control of the Suez Canal. The Egyptians were distracted by political instability in 1879–81 and their army was routed by the British under Wolseley at Tel el Kebir on 13 September 1882. After a night march, the British attacked the Egyptian earthworks at dawn without any preliminary bombardment. Wolseley preferred to try to gain the advantage of surprise, and his infantry attacked using their bayonets. Gaining the initiative was worthwhile, because Wolseley retained control of his manoeuvrable force, while in combat they displayed cohesion, discipline and high morale. Earlier in the campaign, a British squadron had silenced the forts near Alexandria, although the battle was not particularly illustrative of the state of naval warfare at the time: the central battery ships forcing the harbour did not have to face mines or torpedoes, and the guns of the shore batteries were not particularly well handled by the Egyptians. As a sequel to the battle, a rapid cavalry advance seized Cairo, and a British quasi-protectorate over Egypt was established.

The French, meanwhile, had made Tunisia a protectorate in 1881. The French advance reflected the multiple capacity of European military power. A force invaded from Algeria, while other units were landed at Bizerta. The navy subsequently shelled Sfax, which had rejected French control, and covered a successful landing.

Military achievements have to be set in a wider context. This is not easy in a book devoted to military history, for there is neither the space nor the intention to write a history of everything else. Nevertheless, Western expansion was about more than the military progress of the West against much of the rest of the world. Military success was an enabler but by no means the sole one. Demographic, economic, cultural-ideological, and political factors were also all very important. Demographic factors were particularly important where the indigenous population was sparse. Western demographic growth in this period was rapid and this led to significant levels of migration. Imperial struggles provided both opportunity and encouragement for migration. Thus, Russians went to Kazakstan, the French to Algeria, and the British to Australasia and Canada, and many different kinds of Europeans went to the USA. Migration within large states with internal frontiers of control, such as Argentina, Brazil and the USA, was also very important.

The economic value of colonies diversified as states looked for sources of raw materials and for markets, and as steamships and railways aided continental and global economic integration; as they also did migration. Furthermore, economic growth within the West greatly increased the available investment capital for the world outside. Cultural-ideological factors focused on the attraction of empire. Imperialism became normative. This drew on a sense of mission, as well as triumphalism, racialism and cultural arrogance, all supporting a belief that the West was unbeatable and was bringing civilization to a benighted world. The net result was a commitment that encouraged persistence in the face of adversity.

These factors did not dictate any particular tactics or strategy. Nor is it appropriate to see one strategy or set of tactics as characteristic of Western versus non-Western conflict as there were a wide variety of environments and circumstances. The standard image of Western ordered fire-power formations against non-Western fluidity and, in particular, shock tactics, was not without some basis, but it was not a valid description of the wide variety referred to. Nevertheless, such an image accorded with the cultural requirements of many Western commentators. Military observers shared these values. Major-

General Stockley Warren felt that the battle of Mazina in 1880 showed that "the immense superiority of controlled volley firing, over independent blazing away, was clearly demonstrated". He noted that the Afghans had effective Snider rifles, but felt that the bayonet charges, artillery and "heavy volleys" of the British were crucial to the outcome.[24]

The British (and other Western forces) tended to rely in battle on massed formations that provided controlled fire-power. Volley firing, hollow squares and close-packed lines were all employed. At the same time, such tactics were made more effective by a strategy that emphasized mobility and flexibility, especially mobile columns of light infantry with only light artillery support. The latter, for example, was seen in French campaigns, including Bugeaud's in Algeria in the 1840s and Louis Faidherbe's in Senegal in the 1850s and 1860s, and also in rapidly moving British columns. Such movement provided a key to overcoming the factors of distance and force–space ratios that were very different to those of the European warfare of the 1840s–70s or of the crucial Virginia campaigning zone in the American Civil War.

The principal value of a chapter devoted to these conflicts outside the West is twofold. First, individually and collectively, they were very important to the history of the world. Control over large tracts of the world and a significant portion of its population changed hands. Furthermore, areas that did not experience such a change in control, most obviously Japan, were, nevertheless, affected by processes of modernization that hinged on the need to respond to the challenge of Western imperialism. Secondly, the range and variety of these conflicts underlines the hazard of thinking of Western warfare largely in terms of a paradigm; most famously for this period the Prussian army that won the Wars of German Unification. Instead, it is possible to stress a multiplicity of challenges and the need to be flexible in response.

Commanders trained in colonial wars came to play a large role in warfare within Europe. This was particularly so with the French army. The three successive French commanders in chief in the Crimea in 1854–56 had all served in Algeria, as had Achille Baragucy, commander of the French force in Rome in 1849–50 and subsequently of the French expeditionary force to the Baltic in 1854 and of I corps in Italy in 1859. Bazaine and MacMahon, the leading commanders in the war with Prussia in 1870, had both served extensively in Algeria. Faidherbe went on from Senegal to Algeria and in late 1870 brought new energy to the Republican cause as commander of the Army of the North. From colonial service, commanders generally acquired a belief in the importance of seizing the initiative and of rapid attack in order to fix their often elusive opponents. This took precedence over manoeuvres designed to lead to an attack in flank or rear, and reflected the lesser threat of non-Western defensive fire-power to frontal attack. Such tactics were of limited value and very expensive in lives when used against Prussian infantry. More generally, operations in Algeria and elsewhere in the colonies provided little training for coping with the high tempo Prussian offensive.

It is important not to see conflict with non-Europeans as in some fashion backward looking or redundant. Instead, it could be all too predictive of the impact of improving weaponry on modern warfare. In the defence of Plevna in 1877, entrenched Turks using American-manufactured Peabody rifles inflicted heavy casualties on Russian frontal attacks. In the second assault on Plevna, Russian casualties amounted to 23 per cent of their rank and file.[25] Similarly, the Turks lost heavily in their unsuccessful assault on Russian positions covered by integrated fire zones in Shipka Pass in 1877. The successive attempts to storm Plevna also prefigured other aspects of the First World War, including the difficulties of destroying trenches by artillery fire, the employment of machine guns, and the heavy use of munitions, both rifle rounds and shells, i.e. the increasing dominance of fire-power on the battle-field.

Looking ahead, the conflicts with non-Western powers in this period did not prefigure to any great degree the problems that were to be encountered in holding down colonies in the face of insurrectionary movements in the twentieth century. However, there were signs of the limitation of the "exposed" character of nineteenth-century punitive expeditions and battle formations. These were seen, for example, in the British defeat by the Boers at the battle of Majuba Hill on 26–7 February 1881, a battle that led the British temporarily to accept Boer independence (for the time being). The report on a punitive expedition into "Luchye country" in East Bengal in January 1850, threw light on the difficulties that could be encountered. Lieutenant Colonel Lister wrote "It is not their muskets or other offensive weapons that are to be dreaded, but their expertness in the use of the dow, and the facilities which their jungles afford, both in materials and position, for throwing obstacles in the way of an advance or retreat".[26]

Despite defeats and failures, Western expansionism maintained a pace unprecedented in the seventeenth and eighteenth centuries. Furthermore, this was true of a variety of military environments. As victory and conquest became easier, so expansionism and a sense of superiority were encouraged. However, because it was not necessary to transform Western armies (or navies) to achieve these goals, this expansionism did not have an effect on Western military thought or practice comparable to that of conflict within the West. It is to that that we must now turn.

CHAPTER SIX

After Waterloo:
Conflict Within the West, 1815–60

The history of Western warfare in the nineteenth century is generally dominated by two periods, the Napoleonic Wars of the first fifteen years and the conflicts of 1854–71, especially the Crimean War, the Wars of German Unification and the American Civil War. This is understandable. Each of these was an important struggle, and they also affected ideas about warfare in the following decades. Yet such a focus also risks underrating developments in the "peaceful years" between these periods. This chapter seeks to give due weight to the decades after Waterloo. As with naval warfare in this period, the task of evaluation is made more difficult by the paucity of full-scale conflict, certainly prior to 1848.

Nevertheless, such a paucity did not mean that there were no military operations. Furthermore, it did not mean that speculation about military capability ceased or that military thought stood still. Much of the latter focused on the Napoleonic Wars because of their inherent interest and importance and also because many of the operations between 1815 and 1848 were counter-insurgency in character, and so not seen as informing the likely character of future wars between the great powers. Indeed, if the Spanish American Wars of Independence and the Texan rebellion against Mexico are also considered, then this becomes more generally true of Western conflict. These counter-insurgency conflicts have received insufficient attention, not least because military history places a premium on warfare between the regular forces of defined states. Yet such an emphasis is misleading not only as an account of 1816–47, but also, more generally, for military history that encompasses all forms of warfare. This chapter will begin by considering some of these wars, then turn to those of 1848–49, and then assess the warfare of the 1850s in light of changes in military technology and practice in the period as a whole.

Latin American Wars of Independence

The Latin American Wars of Independence barely feature in global military histories. They do not seem to be on the cutting edge in terms of weaponry, practice or doctrine, and cannot therefore be placed in the standard paradigm model of military development. Furthermore, they suffer from the general neglect that is accorded Mediterranean military history after the Turkish defeat at Lepanto in 1571. As far as the early nineteenth century is concerned, this can be seen not only with the neglect of Latin America, but also of military operations in Iberia itself. Yet as far as the former are concerned, the course and consequence of the wars were of considerable political importance. Not only was Spain (the imperial power, other than in Portuguese-ruled Brazil, in Latin America) defeated, despite major efforts on its part, but also there was now no hegemonic power in Latin America capable of matching the USA, but rather a number of states.

Political factors provided a crucial context for the Latin American wars. The Spaniards were weakened more by political than by military problems. The weaknesses of Spain itself were significant: alongside the disruption caused by the Peninsular War of 1808–13 there was serious post-Napoleonic disruption. Napoleon's seizure of power in Spain in 1808 had led to a breakdown of structures of authority and practices of power in the empire and to a struggle for control. With the exception of Peru, governing *juntas* in 1809 and 1810 assumed authority in Spanish America in the name of the imprisoned Ferdinand VII. However, the *juntas* found their authority contested, and the situation was made more difficult in 1814 when Ferdinand VII, having returned to power, chose to use force in order to restore royal authority in Spanish America. As a consequence, the royal authorities there suppressed the autonomy movements, although not that in the distant Plate estuary.[1]

However, the cause of Ferdinand VII faced many difficulties. The royalists (Spanish supporters) in Latin America were badly divided, and their divisions interacted with contradictions within Spain's incoherent policies. Civil and military authorities clashed frequently, as did metropolitan and provincial administrations. For example, in New Granada (now Colombia), the Viceroy and the Commander in Chief were bitter rivals. Furthermore, financial shortages forced the royalist army to rely on the local economy, which proved a heavy burden on the population and antagonised them from Spanish rule. This was exacerbated by the use of forced loans and seizures. The royalist forces sent from Spain were also hit by disease, especially yellow fever and dysentery, and they were forced to recruit locally, leading to fresh political problems. New Granada had largely welcomed the royal army from Spain under Pablo Morillo at first in 1815, but by 1819 there was widespread support for an independent Colombia.[2]

Spain did not possess any technological advantages akin to those enjoyed by the *conquistadores* in the early-sixteenth century. Indeed, it was regarded as militarily backward by other European powers. The insurgents, for their part, were partly supplied by arms dealers in the USA. Spanish governments sent relatively few weapons to their troops in the Americas. Most of the weapons used by the royalists were acquired locally. If anything, the insurgents had a slight advantage in weaponry.[3]

Nevertheless, the course of the conflict was not foreordained. As in other wars of liberation, the colonial power enjoyed more success than is frequently appreciated. This was true both of the degree of local support for the Spaniards and of conflict in the field. Victories at Huaqui (1811) and Sipe Sipe (1815) led to Spanish reconquests of Upper Peru (Bolivia), and that of Rancagua (1814) led to the reconquest of Chile. In 1806 and 1812, the Spaniards suppressed rebellions in Venezuela led by Francisco Miranda; the second had begun in 1811. The Spaniards were helped by the limited support enjoyed by the revolutionaries and by their lack of funds. Although there was revolutionary enthusiasm among the rebel officers, the same was not true of the bulk of the peasant conscripts. Furthermore, there was no compensation in the shape of reliable payment. Venezuelan revolutionary forces were also poorly supplied and armed and inadequately trained.

The conflict swayed back and forth. Simon Bolivár, who had fought under Miranda, escaped to New Granada, raised a volunteer force and invaded Venezuela in 1813. Successful in battle, especially at Tagaunes on 28 July, he captured Caracas that August, but the royalists mounted a strong resistance. Bolivár won a number of battles including Araure (5 December 1813), La Vitoria (1814), San Mateo (25 March 1814) and Carabobo (1814), but the Venezuelan republic lacked widespread support, and its forces were short of funds and arms. Bolivár was heavily defeated at La Puerta (15 June 1814) and again fled to New Granada. There he seized Bogota, but was defeated at Santa Maria.

Having fled to Jamaica, Bolivár returned yet again to Venezuela, but his expedition, mounted from Haiti in May 1816, failed to win support and was abandoned. A second expedition was launched that December. Bolivár won a battle near Barcelona (16 February 1817), but was defeated by Morillo the following spring, and retreated into the Orinoco region. The morale of his troops was low, desertion was rife and supply problems had not been solved. Furthermore, the revolutionary cause was divided. In contrast, the discipline and fighting quality of the Spanish infantry was high: they were better able to stand up under fire and to maintain fire discipline. There were also Spanish victories elsewhere. At Cancha-Rayada in Chile on 16 March 1818, a Spanish army under Mariano Osorio defeated José de San Martin, while at Bombino in Ecuador on 7 April 1822 royalist forces were able to delay Bolivár's invasion of Ecuador.

However, the Spaniards suffered from the debilitating impact of weaknesses in Spain, especially the revolution of 1820, and from the willingness of independence forces in South America to travel great distances in order to affect the struggle elsewhere. After Argentina had gained independence in 1816, forces under San Martin and Bernard O'Higgins crossed the Andes and defeated the royalists in Chile at the battles of Chacabuco (12 February 1817) and Maipo (5 April 1818), before moving north into Peru. Peru was invaded in 1820 and Lima was captured in 1821, but the Spaniards were not crushed. Further north, Bolívar invaded New Granada from Venezuela in the summer of 1819, crossing the Andes via the allegedly impassable Pisba pass. This was a bold step, but one that was made necessary by difficult conditions in Venezuela. Losses on the crossing were high. Having gained the element of surprise, Bolívar still suffered heavy losses at Vargas (25 July), but out-manoeuvred and defeated the Spaniards under José Barreiro at Boyacá (7 August). This enabled him to seize Bogotá and create a republic. As President, Bolívar the following year moved on to found the state of Grán Colombia, comprising what is now Colombia, Venezuela and Ecuador, although much remained in Spanish hands.

The Spanish effort was weakened by revolution in Spain in 1820, which had led to the cancellation of a 20,000 strong expeditionary force, the first major reinforcement for the royalists in Latin America since 1815, and one that was much needed. In addition, Morillo was ordered to negotiate a truce, which gave Bolívar a breathing space and made Spain appear weak. Further-more, the new liberal political system in Spain failed to fulfil Latin American expectations. The Spanish majority in the Cortes rejected the idea of home rule.

When war resumed, the royalists in Venezuela were demoralized. Their local levies deserted and Bolívar was able to outnumber Miguel de La Torre at the second battle of Carabobo (25 June 1821). The royalists were defeated in large part thanks to British mercenaries and to mounted spear-wielding *llaneros*. Having captured Caracas, Bolívar invaded what is now Ecuador. Bolívar and Sucre freed Ecuador in 1822, especially thanks to Sucre's victory at Pichincha (22 May), before advancing into Peru in 1823.

In 1824, a pro-Spanish/royalist rising in Peru was supported by the dispatch of Spanish troops. However, Bolívar defeated the Spaniards in the Peruvian Andes at Junín (6 August), essentially a cavalry fight, and Sucre followed suit at Ayacucho (9 December). This was a more serious encounter. The royalists dissipated their superiority in manpower, artillery and position with an unsuccessful initial attack. Morale had been low from the beginning, but sank lower when the war appeared lost.[4] The following year, Sucre over-ran Upper Peru, which was renamed Bolivia. In 1826, the fortress of Ancud on the island of Chiloé off south Chile, the last Spanish stronghold in South America, surrendered.

Further north, in Central America, rebellion against Spanish rule began in 1810. Led by Father Miguel Hidalgo, this was defeated by General Calleja, outside Mexico City (6 November 1811) and at the Battle of the Bridge of Calderón (17 January 1812). The royalists used local militias against the rebels. Insurgents who had captured Texas in 1812–13 were overthrown later in 1813. In Mexico, the rebellion was continued by Father José María Morelos, but he was defeated in 1815 by Calleja, now Viceroy of New Spain. Guerrilla action continued, led by Vicente Guerrero. The strengths and limitations of such action were amply illustrated. For example in the Papantla region near Veracruz, which had rebelled in 1812, the royalist reconquest of the towns by 1818 did not end the rebellion. Instead, it changed it into a guerrilla war with royalist garrisons in the towns unable to control rural hinterlands. In the summer of 1820, a change of strategy under a new royalist commander, José Rincón, altered the tempo of the war. Whereas, previously, the rainy season had served as a break in campaigning, providing the rebels with an opportunity to recover, Rincón planned no such break. In a campaign against the rebel stronghold of Coyusquihui, he circled the area with forts and kept campaigning. This hit the rebels, but the royalists were badly affected by disease. Both sides accepted a settlement in December 1820.[5] This conflict is a reminder of the extent to which the defeat of Morelos in 1815 did not lead to an end of the insurgency, but rather to more fighting. However, affected by the regionalism that made it difficult to establish a common front, the insurgency fragmented, as indeed did the army as units engaged in counter-insurgency operations with little central supervision, while their commanders tried to build up local power bases. By 1820, helped by numerous pardons, the guerrilla war was nearly over.[6]

Rebellion had been largely overcome, but Spanish rule collapsed, because the liberal constitutional revolution in Spain of 1820 was not welcome to those who wielded power in Mexico. In November 1820, the Viceroy had ordered Augustín de Iturbide to destroy what was left of the rebellion, but, instead, in early 1821, he agreed with the rebels on a declaration of independence. As this was widely acceptable, the new regime gained power with very little fighting, and none at all in the provinces from California to Texas: a situation very different to that in much of Spanish South America. The new Junta was dominated by army officers. Liberalism in Spain encouraged conservatives in Mexico to support independence. Iturbide declared himself Emperor Augustin I in 1822, but he was forced to abdicate in 1823 after the army turned against him.[7] Spanish forces seeking to regain Mexico were defeated by the Mexican general Santa Anna at Tampico in 1829.

In Brazil, the Regent, Dom Pedro, rebelled against his father, King John of Portugal, in 1822. However, the northern provinces and the coastal cities south of Rio remained loyal and had to be conquered. This was done in large part thanks to the successful use of naval force, which gave Pedro's forces long-range capability: the Brazilians hired British officers and men. In 1823, the Portuguese were forced to leave Sálvador da Bahia and the Brazilian squadron also captured Maranhão (São Luis), Belém do Pará and Montevideo. In the case of the last, the squadron supported the blockade of the city by Brazilian forces. The garrison, which had already held out against the land blockade for many months, quickly surrendered. The following year, a rising in the province of Pernambuco was suppressed after Recife had been block-aded into surrender.[8] Other risings in the north were also suppressed. As a consequence, Brazil (Portuguese Latin America) retained a coherence that Spanish Latin America lacked.

Whereas the defeated generals in the North American and European wars of 1861–71, for example Lee, Benedek, Bazaine and McMahon, are well known and their generalship often discussed, their counterparts in the Latin American wars of independence, such as Monteverde, San Mateo and Morillo, are neglected. Yet the generalship on both sides was often impressive. The force–space ratios of conflict in Latin America were very different to those in western and central Europe during the Revolutionary and Napo-leonic Wars. This ensured that logistics were a greater problem. In addition, the need that both the revolutionaries and the royalists faced to create new armies put a premium on overcoming problems in recruitment and in resist-ing desertion. The creation and legitimization of government structures were important in providing the context for harnessing resources. Remedies were often brutal. Recruitment was enforced with violence and the threat of violence, desertion punished savagely, frequently with executions and supplies raised through force. There was much burning and destruction – of crops, haciendas, towns –in order both to deny resources and to punish. A shortage of arms put a premium on foreign supplies, but also ensured that weapons other than firearms were used. In Mexico in 1810–11, there was much use of bows and arrows, clubs and knives.

The character of the wars as civil conflicts put a premium on political factors in strategy. Furthermore, the time-scale of conflict was long. This was less the case if some individual areas were considered, but in, for example, Venezuela and Peru, fighting lasted for a considerable period. In addition, the interaction of different areas was such that success in one did not pre-empt countervailing action originating from another. This underlined the difficulty of ensuring a lasting military-political verdict.

These issues might seem to have been of little relevance to Western warfare as a whole if it is understood as a story from say Austerlitz (1805) to Sadowa (1866), in other words the climactic battles of large, well provided regular forces. However, if the full range of conflict is considered, then the Latin American wars are of wider interest, although it is not easy to demonstrate that their lessons were widely considered, let alone absorbed. The wars attracted very few foreign observers and most of the foreign troops who fought in them on land were not units from regular Western armies. Never-theless, the wars suggested the difficulty both of sustaining a revolutionary struggle and of mounting effective counter-insurgency action. The problems of creating new governmental structures, including an army, that faced the Latin American revolutionaries were to be faced anew by the American Confederacy in 1861, but it was more successful in maintaining unity.

106

Latin America after independence

However, prior to that, the history of the West had shown numerous examples of the problems of creating new governments and armies in a series of revolutionary conflicts. Those in Europe attract most attention, but it is also important to note the creation of new states in Latin America. The turbulence of Latin American politics did not end with the severing of Portuguese and Spanish metropolitan control. There were outbreaks of war within and between the successor states. Several of the polities that had been produced by the Wars of Liberation fractured. Thus, for example, Venezuela, under General José María Córdoba, successfully rebelled against the state of Grán Colombia in 1829–30, and Texas against Mexico in 1835–36; while the Peru-Bolivian Confederation of 1836–39 failed. However, rebellions in Brazil, the "Cabanos" in Pernambuco in 1832–35 and in Pará in 1835–36, the "Sabinada" in Bahia in 1837–38, the "Balaida" in Maranhá in 1839–40 and the "Farrapos" in Rio Grande do Sul and Santa Catarina in 1835–45, did not lead to a similar fragmentation, and independence movements in the Yucatán that were fired by peasant resentment were suppressed by Mexico in 1843 and 1848.[9] In contrast, General Santa Anna was unsuccessful in suppressing the Texan revolt. He stormed the Alamo at San Antonio, but was defeated by Sam Houston at San Jacinto and, once captured, had to sign a treaty recognizing Texan independence.

Other civil wars included that between federalists in the provinces and *unitarios* in Buenos Aires in Argentina in 1828–29. This issue went on to cause fresh conflict, especially in the 1850s. Juan Manuel de Rosas, the powerful Governor of Buenos Aires, was overthrown in 1852: his domestic opponents in Entre Rios were supported by Brazil and Uruguay and Rosas was defeated at Caseros. The Brazilian navy also played a major role in the conflict. However, another Governor of Buenos Aires, Bartolomé Mitre, defeated the Argentine Confederation at Pavon in 1861.

In Mexico, there was a civil war in 1832, when General Anastasio Bustamante was overthrown. More generally in Mexico, federalist tendencies competed with local forces. Bustamante's federalist government overcame and disbanded several state based militias in 1830. Several states, however, including Zacatecas, retained their militias, which helped overthrow Bustamente. In 1835, the government under Santa Anna sought to restrict the size of the surviving civic militia. Francisco García, Governor of Zacatecas, opposed the decree, but was defeated in May 1835 by an expedition commanded by Santa Anna. Based on the military commandancies (regions) created in 1823, regional *caudillos* (strong men) subsequently emerged to challenge the centre.[10] There was civil war in Uruguay from 1838 to 1851, including a nine-year siege of Montevideo.

The independent American states also clashed with each other. Thus, in 1825–28, Argentina and Brazil fought over Uruguay. This Spanish-speaking province had been annexed to Brazil in 1816, and the resistance was suppressed. The war in 1825 began with an invasion by Juan Lavalleja, a Uruguay patriot. Initially with 33 supporters, he sailed from Buenos Aires and touched off a rebellion. Gaining support, including from General Fructuoso Rivera, who abandoned the Brazilian army, Lavalleja defeated the Brazilians at Rincon de las Gallinas and Sarandí, overrunning the bulk of the province of Banda Oriental, although not the garrison towns. Lavalleja declared the Banda Oriental independent and sought union with the United Provinces, the modern Argentina. This was accepted and by the end of the year Argentina and Brazil were at war.

This was a wide-ranging conflict waged on land and sea. The scale can be gauged from the invasion of southern Brazil in 1827: 10,000 Argentinian and Uruguayan troops defeated 7,000 Brazilians at Ituzaingú on 20 February. There were also significant naval battles such as the Argentinian victory at Juncal on 9 February 1827. Neither side was able to gain a decisive advantage. The Brazilians held on to their major positions throughout the war and only evacuated Colonia and Montevideo after peace was agreed. The settlement left Uruguay independent as a buffer between Brazil and Argentina.

Uruguay itself fought Argentina in 1843–47. Elsewhere, Peruvian support for an attempt to overthrow the conservative regime in Chile in 1836 helped to lead the latter to declare war, although that also owed much to concern about the Peru-Bolivian Confederation and to tariff conflicts. José Ballivan's victory at Ingavi (20 November 1841) over a Peruvian invasion brought the Peruvian-Bolivian war of 1840–41 to an end with Bolivia free of Peruvian attempts to dominate her through a federation.[11] As with the Wars of Independence, European interest was limited. However, Giuseppe Garibaldi, an Italian revolutionary who had been condemned to death in Europe, fought for Rio Grande do Sul against Brazil, and, from 1843, for Uruguay against Argentina, winning his first battle at Sant' Antonio in 1846.

Mexican-American War of 1846–48

The most-extensively covered conflict is the Mexican-American war of 1846–8. This far-flung conflict arose as a result of Mexican opposition to the admission of Texas, independent since 1836, into the Union. Had the Mexicans accepted this step, then war between the two countries might have been avoided until Mexico was in a stronger state relative to America. It is interesting to speculate whether a conflict in the 1850s or early 1860s over the territory between Texas and the Pacific would have averted or accentuated divisive territories within America.

However, news of the American annexation of Texas led in 1845 to strong pressure within Mexico for war. American forces were sent into disputed territory on the Texas/Mexico border along the Rio Grande/Rio Del Norte, and in April 1846 an American patrol was ambushed. An expeditionary force was ordered into northern Mexico. Its commander, Zachary Taylor, won the battle of Palo Alto against an advancing Mexican force (8 May 1846) and captured the stronghold of Monterrey (24 September 1846). The following year, Taylor lost many of his regulars to support Scott's attack on Vera Cruz. This was exploited by the Mexicans under Santa Anna, who had returned from exile in Cuba to take charge. Santa Anna advanced to attack Taylor, but the latter took up a good defensive position at Buena Vista, and defeated the Mexican attack on 22–3 February 1847, although with heavy losses.

However, successes in 1846 had not led the Mexicans to negotiate, and a strike at the Mexican centre was deemed necessary. Winfield Scott conducted the bold stroke of an amphibious expedition followed by an advance on Mexico City. He staged an uncontested landing near Vera Cruz on 9 March 1847 and captured it on 29 March after a short siege. Scott then advanced inland, defeating the Mexicans at Cerro Gordo, occupying Puebla, and, in a struggle for the capital, defeating the Mexicans at Contreras, Churusbusco, Molino del Rey, Chapultepec, and Mexico City itself. Mexico City fell on 14 September 1847, just over six months after Scott had landed.

Further afield, American forces had advanced into Mexico's northern possessions. Troops moved overland into Santa Fé (18 August 1846) and then to San Diego. Meanwhile, the Pacific Squadron, under first John Sloat and then John Frémont, occupied Monterey, the capital of California (7 July), Santa Barbara and Los Angeles. However, the Mexican inhabitants in southern California rebelled. They were defeated by Stockton and by the overland troops under Stephen Kearny at San Gabriel (8 January 1847) and Mesa (9 January). There were also uprisings in New Mexico, which led to anti-insurgency operations, although there was nothing in Mexico to match the Spanish popular response to Napoleon. This was a testimony to the far more skilful management of the situation by the Americans, especially Scott. They avoided relying on logistics of depredation or turning to a politics of brutality. The eventual peace treaty of Guadalupe Hidalgo, signed on 2 February 1848, left the USA with what were to become California, Nevada and Utah, as well as most of Arizona and parts of New Mexico, Colorado and Wyoming.

American campaigning was what would be subsequently described as "high tempo". Its aggressive and fast-moving character was necessary for political as well as military reasons. The Americans were helped by naval superiority, as well as better artillery, which made a major difference in battle. In addition, Scott's effective generalship displayed strategic insight, a skilful transfer of this insight into effective operational direction, and an ability to gain and retain the initiative. He always favoured the attack. Rather than relying on lines of infantry, Scott advocated looser formations, especially clouds of skirmishers. He also tended to turn Mexican flanks as at Cerro Gordo. Molino del Rey was unusual in involving a frontal assault, and the result was heavy American casualties. In 1847, he showed strategic daring when, in his advance on Mexico City, he cut away from his lines of communication and pressed on despite being in hostile country. This boldness horrified Welling-ton. It was more characteristic of the advances of Western forces outside the West, for example the march of a British force 785 miles from Bengal to Surat in 1778–79, or French campaigns in West Africa in the late nineteenth century, than of those of armies in Europe. Size–supply ratios were one factor. Smaller forces could take their supplies with them and/or seize them en route. Scott had fewer than 20,000 men, and only 10,700 effectives for his final advance on Mexico City in August–September. The situation was very different with larger forces. Other issues also played a part. The American conviction of superiority encouraged boldness. So also did fighting a mobile opponent who could be difficult to fix.

The Mexicans benefited from numbers, especially against Taylor at Buena Vista, but also against Scott, and from the fighting quality of their troops, for example at Churusbusco and Molino del Rey. American advances encoun-tered serious problems, as in Taylor's attack on Monterrey in September 1846. Nevertheless, the Mexican army was poorly armed and supplied, affected by the unpopularity of military service and by flaws in command and equipment. No master-strategist, and lacking skill at the operational level, Santa Anna was out-generalled and the Mexicans were outfought.[12] The American invasion of Mexico offered no comparison with the disastrous British advance to Kabul in 1842.

The war provides an opportunity for probing the impact of politics on conflict. The Mexican army and war effort suffered from many of the consequences of post-independence Mexican politics and political culture, including economic decline and regional, social and political divisions. Given that the USA was soon to face a major civil war, it is paradoxical that it faced no such problems in the Mexican-American war. There was factionalism in the military leadership, but the American military effort was not affected by debilitating domestic problems. The Americans did suffer difficulties in recruitment and logistics, but these did not reflect deep divisions in society. Thus, there was no equivalent in America to the dictatorial policies of Santa Anna and to the opposition this inspired, nor to the rift between army and civil militia that had played an important role in politics from independence on. The civic militia played a major role in the overthrow of Santa Anna's government in 1844–45. In turn, the new government was overthrown the following winter. There were major disturbances within Mexico during the war including in June and October 1846 and February 1847, the last a civil war. These seriously affected the Mexican war effort.[13]

Warfare in Iberia

In Spain and Portugal in the 1820s and 1830s there were a series of rebellions and civil conflicts that amounted to the most sustained warfare in western Europe in the period. Attempted coups by liberal military figures had been defeated in Galicia in 1815 and Catalonia in 1817. In 1820, troops outside Cadiz, ready to go to Latin America, rebelled and won support across much of Spain, forcing Ferdinand VII to restore the liberal constitution of 1812. This stimulated the Oporto garrison to mount a successful liberal *coup d'état* in Portugal. However, in turn, these led to counter-revolutions in both countries in 1823. In Portugal a reactionary rising led to the repudiation of the constitution, while in Madrid, the previous July, the National Militia had defeated four Guards battalions that had tried to seize power from the Constitutionalists.

In 1823, civil conflict between liberals and supporters of the king was resolved by an invasion of Spain by 56,000 French and 35,000 Spanish troops in support of Ferdinand VII that began in April. Assisted by liberal division and weakness, the French made rapid progress. Short of supplies and unpaid, the Spanish army was affected by extensive desertion and retreated. There was some resistance in Catalonia, which was conquered by IV Corps under Moncey, who had been made a Marshal by Napoleon. At Barcelona, which was blockaded for several months, he found himself in conflict with Francisco Mina who had been a prominent guerrilla leader in the Peninsular War. The main French drive was on Madrid, which they entered on 23 May, and then, via Cordoba, to Cadiz, where the liberal Cortes had fled. It was successfully besieged by land and blockaded by sea, surrendering on 1 October. There was fighting elsewhere, but Morillo capitulated in Galicia on 10 July and Ballesteros in Andalusia on 4 August. Resistance ended when Alicante surrendered on 5 November. The 1823 operation was a successful example of how foreign intervention could tip the balance in a domestically divided state.

Four years later, the "Revolt of the Aggrieved" in the Catalan mountains was directed against those who were seen as Ferdinand's evil advisers: support came from purged officers, but the uprising was swiftly suppressed. From the liberal camp there were a series of unsuccessful invasions which culminated when General José Torrijos invaded Malága in December 1831; an attempt that was rapidly crushed.

Full-scale civil wars broke out over the royal successions in Portugal in 1828 and Spain in 1833. Miguelism and Carlism, respectively, were counter-revolutionary movements that drew on peasant anger against government. From 1828, Dom Miguel controlled Portugal, but in 1832 his brother Pedro IV invaded. He was besieged in Oporto, but sent an expedition to the Algarve. This turned to Pedro, whose forces then captured Lisbon. Miguelist attempts to storm Oporto and Lisbon on 25 July 1833 and 5 September 1833 respectively were repulsed with heavy losses. The Miguelists were beaten in a series

111

of battles, including Piedade (23 July 1833), Almoster (18 February 1834) and Asseirceira (16 May 1834). The last was decisive. Eight days later, Miguel surrendered at Evora.

Both sides had been very short of funds, and, compared to the campaigning in Portugal during the Peninsular War, the war was under-resourced. The manpower, matériel and funds that the British and French had been able to provide were lacking. Nevertheless, that did not mean that skill was lacking (as Saldanha showed at Almoster and Asseirceira), but rather that judgements of military capability in a given period have to be sensitive to circumstances.

In Spain, in the First Carlist War (1833–40), Don Carlos resisted the bequest of the Spanish throne to his niece Isabel by her father, Ferdinand VII. Opposition to a female monarch was combined with hostility to the constitutional reform backed by Isabel's supporters, and, more generally, to liberalism. As the government and army stayed loyal to Isabel, Carlos had to create his own forces. Initial success owed much to Tomás Zumalacárregui, a Basque veteran of the struggle against Napoleon who became commander of the Carlist forces in the Basque-Navarre region. He brought coherence to Carlist operations and created a successful guerrilla army that made full use of the difficult terrain in order to seize the initiative. This army overran much of the mountainous north, the centre of Carlist support, where regular troops were few, but was less successful when it left the mountains and sought to capture cities, although Córdoba was briefly occupied in 1836. The cities, including Bilbao and Pamplona, were dominated by the liberals and Isabel also benefited from the backing of Britain, France and, once Pedro had succeeded, Portugal. This solid political strength combined with the weakness of the Carlists when they sought to embark on conventional warfare led to their eventual defeat. Zumalacárregui died in an unsuccessful siege of Bilbao, a liberal centre, in 1835, and the advance of the Carlists on Madrid in 1837 failed to topple the regime.

The battles of these conflicts, such as Piedade, Almoster and Asseiceira in Portugal, and Laveaga Pass (1835), Descarga (1835), Mendigorría (1835), Luchana (1836), Chiva (1837), Villar de los Navarros (1837), Aranzueque (1837) and Morella (1838) in Spain, are scarcely known, but they, and the military operations in general, throw light on the factors that were crucial to success. In battle, morale, experience, surprise, terrain and numbers were crucial, and all were as important as effective tactics, if not more so: these were not campaigns that left much room for a complex strategy or for sophisticated tactics by complex formations. At Laveaga Pass (19 May) and Descarga (2 June) larger government forces were surprised and routed. Surprise was also important in the Carlist defeat at Aranzueque, the end of their operations in central Spain in 1837. Mendigorría (16 July) was a pitched battle that arose from the determination of Zumalacárregui's successor, Moreno, to inflict a decisive defeat on the government forces. However, Moreno chose his position badly, and the Carlists, not used to resting on

112

the defensive, had to withdraw under the pressure of government attacks. The Carlist losses, about 2,000, were a major blow, as was the end of Zumalacárregui's string of victories. Government forces, however, were affected by a shortage of pay and supplies.

In addition, as with other civil wars, strategy, morale and generalship were shot through with political considerations. For example, Carlist divisions weakened the movement and helped lead to the end of the First Carlist War. In early 1839, General Maroto, the Carlist Commander-in-Chief, arrested and shot five generals from a rival faction. He then negotiated the Convention of Vergara (31 August 1839) with the government's General Espartero; the Carlists who fought on under Ramón Cabrera in Aragon and Catalonia were defeated and fled to France in the summer of 1840. Cabrera returned to lead Carlist guerrillas in Catalonia in 1846–49.[14]

The Carlist War helped both to politicize the army and to militarize politics. Generals came to play a major role in government, while, in turn, political support was necessary in order to obtain backing both within the army and in operations against the Carlists. Aside from the Carlist challenge, there was also pressure from urban radicalism in Spain. This led to a successful liberal revolution in 1836, the same year in which radicals also seized power in Portugal. This politics pushed the military into the centre of government. In 1841, Espartero became regent in Spain. He was overthrown by a military rising commanded by General Narváez, leader of the Moderates, in 1843 after Narváez had successfully marched from Valencia to defeat loyal forces at Torrejón de Ardoz outside Madrid.

Civil conflicts in Europe

There is not the space to devote to the other civil conflicts of the period, but similar comments could be made about them. They serve as a reminder of the role of counter-insurgency operations in the military history of the period. These were enhanced by the ideological legacy of the French Revolutionary period, and the sense among most of the powers that developments in the domestic politics of other states could be a threat and had to be suppressed. This was not new, and, irrespective of ideological factors, there had earlier been invasions in response to domestic political developments, for example the Russian invasion of Poland in 1733 in order to secure the election of a pliant king and the Prussian invasion of the United Provinces (Netherlands) in 1787 in order to secure the position of the House of Orange. The ideological character of the revolutionary crisis of the 1780s and 1790s had encouraged interventionism. In 1782, when the ruling oligarchy of Geneva was overthrown, forces from Berne, France, and Savoy-Piedmont (the kingdom of Sardinia), which had guaranteed the constitution, besieged the city and reestablished the old constitution. In Liège, where the bourgeoisie had seized power in 1789 during an economic depression, Prussian troops restored the old constitution in 1790. In 1792, the Prussians had similarly sought to restore the old order in France.

For the period of the French Revolutionary and Napoleonic Wars, it is not easy to distinguish between invasions and external interventions designed to ensure a favourable internal situation. Both tended to be subsumed in a blanket treatment of warfare, as with the Napoleonic invasion of Spain in 1808. Such interventionism became more common from 1815 as the leading Continental powers sought to maintain the internal political, as well as the international, order left by the Congress of Vienna of 1814–15. This was to be enshrined in a number of agreements, including the Protocol of Troppau of 1820 by which Austria, Prussia and Russia agreed on intervention to reverse the overthrow of a government by revolution, and the Austro-Russian Treaty of Münchengrätz in 1834.

Some commentators have seen the post-1815 collective security system as reflecting a new-found understanding of the value of mutual awareness and restraint in international relations,[15] but this was not incompatible with the search for advantage seen at the Congress of Vienna. Rather than focusing on a new standard of conduct, it is possible to stress the role of intelligent self-interest, and a desire for stability in order to ensure survival and security, the latter an attitude that could encourage war if circumstances changed. Fear of France, Bonapartism and revolution were the prime causes of unity among the major powers, and financial exhaustion after the warfare of 1792–1815 was important.

The leading powers had demobilized much of the forces deployed in 1815, but were still left with sizeable forces. One of Napoleon's marshals, Marmont, who had backed Louis XVIII in 1815, was sent by the king to suppress disturbances in Lyons in 1817. More widely, Liberal uprisings in 1820–21 led to a military response. Advancing to Naples and Turin, Austrian forces crushed rebel forces in Naples and the kingdom of Sardinia (often known as Piedmont) in 1821 and restored the previous system of government. Austrian victories included Rieti in the Papal States and Novara in Sardinia. At Rieti (7 March 1821), the Austrians defeated Neapolitan *Carbonari* under Guglielmo Pepe. The untrained and poorly disciplined Neapolitans broke quickly before the trained regulars. The decision to fight a battle had exposed the *Carbonari* in unsuitable circumstances. The Austrian success was decisive: on 23 March, Austrian forces entered Naples. The Austrians were fortunate that the crisis did not exactly coincide with that in Piedmont. On 10 March 1821, the garrison of Alessandria had rebelled, demanding liberty; two days later, the Turin garrison followed. This divided Piedmont, and at Novara, Austria and Piedmontese loyalist troops successfully defeated the rebels.

There was no comparable foreign support for the Turks against the Greek rising that broke out in 1821, because the classical educational background of the European élites and the religious sympathies of the Tsar led them to favour the Greeks. However, the Turks were able to turn to another power, Mehmet Ali, the semi-independent Pasha of Egypt, who crushed the rising on Crete in 1824 and had initial success when he landed troops in the Peloponnese the following year. Independence (although only for a portion of modern Greece) was only secured in 1830 as a result of naval intervention by Britain, France and Russia. Once independent, the Greek government, in turn, faced a rebellion in 1831 which was put down with Russian naval support.

The failure of the French regular troops to prevent the armed rising in Paris in July 1830 was in part a matter of the deficiencies of regulars in street fighting, but it has to be set in the wider context of a very unpopular government and its attempt to reverse the verdict of recent elections. Much of the army was disaffected with the policies of Charles X, and there were only 12,000 troops near Paris. Many deserted. In Paris, the lack of training, equipment and discipline that characterized most rebel forces did not lead to failure. Four years later, however, the new government was more successful: Bugeaud suppressed riots in Paris with great brutality, and others in Lyon were also suppressed.[16]

In August 1830, a rising broke out in Brussels directed against rule by the Dutch William I: Belgium had become part of the United Netherlands in the post-Napoleonic peace settlement. The garrison of only just over 2,000 troops was taken by surprise and initially the Dutch forces in Belgium failed to respond effectively. In September, however, a stronger attempt was made to suppress the rising, which had become more radical. On 23 September, 10,000 troops entered Brussels, but street fighting in the face of determined opponents who employed the cover of barricades and fire from windows and housetops proved difficult. The troops withdrew on 26 September, and the Dutch retreated to Antwerp.

In October, the Belgians declared independence. In some respects, the crisis mirrored that which had overthrown rule of the Austrian Netherlands (Belgium) by the Habsburg Emperor Joseph II in 1789. The Dutch were determined to fight on and still held the powerful citadel at Antwerp from which they bombarded the city in October 1830. International efforts to settle the crisis failed and on 2 August 1831 the Dutch invaded Belgium. A force of 36,000 troops and 72 cannon under the Prince of Orange met poorly organized defenders. Invading from a different direction than Napoleon in 1815, the Prince also faced two opposing forces, but he was able to exploit the gap between them and drive them back. On 12 August, the Prince defeated Nicolas Daine at Louvain. However, eight days later, the Dutch stopped their advance in the face of Anglo-French pressure including an invasion of Belgium by French forces under Marshal Gérard, a corps commander under Napoleon. An armistice led both sides to pull their troops back. The Dutch still held the citadel of Antwerp, but an Anglo-French blockade and siege forced them out in December 1832: the 62,000 strong besieging French army, which had advanced that November, was led by Gérard. The siege indicated the continued importance of fortified positions in warfare and in the politics of confrontation.[17]

Elsewhere, 1830 was also a year of serious revolutions. An uprising in Bologna spread to all of Emilia-Romagna, the Marches and Umbria, and was ended only by Austrian occupation on behalf of their rulers, the Dukes of Modena and Parma and the Papacy . The French took part by sending an amphibious expedition to Ancona; a successful example of the deployment of troops by sea.

In Poland, an uprising on 29 November against Russian rule benefited from an initially weak Russian response, but, once independence had been declared, the Russians moved in force, deploying over 100,000 troops. The Tsar demanded unconditional surrender. As with the Polish uprising of 1794, the Russians suffered initial checks. They met strong resistance at the battle of Grothów (25 February 1831), although the Russians won the battle, and hopes of a speedy capture of Warsaw had to be abandoned. In the spring of 1831, the Poles won a number of encounters, including at Siedlce (10 April), but were defeated by Diebitsch in a major clash at Ostroleka (26 May). Diebitsch died in the same cholera outbreak that killed Gneisenau and Clausewitz. The new Russian commander, Field Marshal Paskievich, shifted the direction of Russian attack. Instead of approaching Warsaw directly from the east, as had happened earlier in the year, he circled north of Warsaw, crossed the Vistula at Osiek near the Prussian border, and advanced on Warsaw from the west. The Polish defensive lines were breached on 6–7 September, and Warsaw capitulated on 8 September. This was the end of the uprising, although isolated positions surrendered later, Zamosc on 21 October. Elsewhere, Polish units crossed into Austria, Prussia and the republic of Cracow and were disarmed. The Poles suffered from the difficulties of creating a war-winning government, but, more seriously, from the absence of any important diversion of Russian strength. In contrast, much of the French army had been sent to Algiers, and was thus unavailable to suppress the rising in Paris.[18]

On a far smaller scale, troops in Wales suppressed the Merthyr Tydfil uprising in 1831. Eight years later, a Chartist rising of over 5,000, in which many colliers sought to seize Newport as part of a revolutionary uprising, was stopped when a small group of soldiers opened fire and the rioters dispersed. Also within the British world, far-flung uprisings in Canada in 1837–38, supported by American sympathizers, were suppressed by regulars and loyalists.[19]

In 1846, a revolt in the then independent city of Cracow was followed by Austrian occupation; the clashes of that year, such as Chrzanow, Jaworzno and Krzeszowice, do not feature in the works on military history, but serve as a reminder of the widespread nature of conflict in a period sometimes misleadingly described as peaceful, and the need to remember the role of small-scale engagements, alongside the Austerlitzs of the age, in setting the functions and goals of the military. In 1846, Austrian troops were also deployed in response to class warfare in Galicia; part of Poland annexed by Austria in the Partitions in the previous century. In the "Rabacja", Ruthenian peasants had rebelled against their Polish landlords.

The following year, tensions between Catholic and Protestant cantons in Switzerland led to a 25-day war between a secessionist league of Catholic cantons, the *Sonderbund*, and the Protestant-dominated Swiss Confederacy. The short conflict was swiftly won by the latter; the major battle was at Gislikon. The secessionists lacked determination and military resources. This helped lead to total casualties in the war of only 93 killed. The Confederate forces were commanded by Guillaume Dufour, who had received his military education in France. He was not only able, but also determined to keep casualties down.[20]

1848: the year of revolutions

Warfare again flared up in Europe in 1848, another year of revolutions. Tensions within a number of states, some of them nationalist in character, became a spreading crisis of governance across much of Europe. The crisis began in Naples, where revolution broke out in January. Pressure for liberal reform then spread in France, Italy, Germany and the Habsburg lands. In Italy, for example, there were uprisings in Bologna, Florence, Livorno, Messina, Modena, Naples, Parma, Rome and Venice. Nationalist tensions, especially Italian hostility to Austrian rule, German opposition to Danish rule of Schleswig and Holstein, and Hungarian disquiet about Austrian rule, lent particular energy to the rejection of authority in some states. There was a rebellion in Neuchâtel, then still Prussian (it did not become part of Switzerland until 1857). In addition, some nationalist tensions ensured that domestic struggles interacted with international divisions. For example, the *Risorgimento*, the movement against foreign rule in Italy, became inseparable from the disputes in north Italy between the kingdom of Sardinia and Austria. German sympathy for the cause of compatriots in Schleswig exacerbated that crisis.

The warfare of 1848–49 involved both the widespread deployment of troops in suppressing insurgency and also more conventional operations. Josef Radetzky was the most prominent commander. A veteran of the French Revolutionary and Napoleonic Wars who was recalled to service, he restored the Austrian position in northern Italy, which had been overthrown thanks to rebellions in Milan and Venice and the intervention of Charles Albert of Sardinia. Radetzky responded to the escalating crisis by retreating from Milan into the fortresses of the "Quadrilateral": Legnano, Mantua, Peschiera and Verona. Charles Albert advanced as commander of the united Italian patriotic forces, but was outmanoeuvred and outfought by Radetzky, who employed interior lines to achieve a concentration of strength against a strung out Sardinian "cordon". His crushing victory at Custoza near Verona on 24–5 July 1848 was followed by the recapture of Milan and most of Lombardy. The following year, his heavy defeat of Charles Albert at Novara (21–3 March) forced the latter to abdicate. As with Custoza and Santa Lucia, this was a victory for column attacks and bayonet tactics. Radetzky then blockaded Venice. After starvation and cholera had led to its surrender on 22 August 1849, the war was over, although in 1850 Radetzky had to prevent a rebellion in Milan. The role of force in securing the settlement was made abundantly clear when Radetzky became Governor of Lombardy and Venezia in 1850–57.

The Austrians also faced opposition further north. The Hungarians rebelled in 1848, declaring a republic and creating a national army. There were also uprisings in Austria and in Bohemia. An uprising in Prague was put down in June 1848 only after the city had been bombarded. The victor, Count Windischgrätz, also suppressed uprisings in Vienna (October 1848) and Budapest (1849), and defeated a (rebel) Hungarian army at Kapolna (26–7 February 1849). At Vienna, the Habsburgs used Croatian *Grenzer*, long habituated by their border status to conflict, to defeat the urban defenders of the revolution. Another Austrian force fought with success against Hungarian insurgents in Transylvania. However, under Artur Georgey, the Hungarians defeated Windischgrätz at Gödöllö/Isaszeg (6 April 1849): having pushed back the Austrian centre the Hungarians were able to take their left in front and rear. They recaptured Budapest the following month after a short siege.

Keen to stop the spread of nationalism, the Russians intervened to help restore order. They invaded Hungary via Galicia, Moldavia and Wallachia, and inflicted a number of defeats on the Hungarians, including at Losonc (2 July). With their situation elsewhere improving, the Austrians were able to maintain their pressure. Julius Haynau, who had put down an uprising in Italy in Brescia, was given command of the Austrian forces in western Hungary. Having defeated the Hungarians there in a series of battles in June, he advanced to Budapest, then Szeged, near which he beat the Hungarians at Szoreg (5 August) and finally to Temesvár, where he defeated Georgey on 9 August. Haynau's rapid and successful advance was an impressive feat that restored momentum to the Austrian effort.[21] Repeated defeats were followed by Hungarian capitulation. The Russians also crushed an uprising in Poland.

More conventional operations included a war over Schleswig-Holstein between the Danes and German forces in 1848. Invading on behalf of rebels in Schleswig-Holstein, the Germans had successes and in 1848 pushed their opponents back into Jutland, but there was no decisive victory, in part because of poor tactics. Frontal attacks, a lack of tempo and a failure to exploit successes on the part of the Germans gave the Danes opportunities and the war ended in a stalemate. The Germans failed to achieve their goals.

The Parisian workers' uprising of February 1848 that had forced out King Louis-Philippe was crushed that June by Cavaignac. There was a clear geographical-social edge to the struggle, with Cavaignac using peasant regular troops and National Guardsmen to fight his way through the city's barricades. 1,600 troops and over 10,000 insurgents were killed. This division among the working class was more apparent than Karl Marx's claim that it was "the first great battle . . . between the two classes that split modern society". The monarchy was not restored, but radicalism had been crushed, and the beneficiary was Napoleon's nephew, Louis-Napoleon Bonaparte, who was elected president that December. He used an army-backed coup to strengthen his grip on power in 1851, replacing an elected presidency by the Second Empire. Anti-Napoleonic demonstrations after his coup were met by troops firing on the crowd, and Hausmann later redesigned parts of Paris to give the artillery a clearer field of fire against future rebellious mobs, which did not deter the Communards in 1871.

Elsewhere, regular troops were also deployed against popular uprisings. In Germany, Prussian forces put down uprisings in Saxony, Baden and Hesse, winning a victory in Baden at Rastatt; while in 1849 the Sardinians suppressed a revolt in Genoa.[22]

The status quo was also enforced elsewhere in Italy. Pope Gregory XVI (1830–46) had been reliant on Austrian troops. The crisis of 1848 led to the withdrawal of these troops and, in 1849, to the overthrow of Pius IX (1846–78) by the Roman Republic, and his flight to Gaeta. In 1849, however, the French restored traditional authority in the Papal States. The revolutionary government in Rome had turned to Giuseppe Garibaldi, a radical supporter of the *Risorgimento*. He repulsed a French attack on the city (30 April), as well as Neapolitan forces (9, 19 May), but finally, that summer, overwhelming French forces, brought by rail, besieged and captured the city. Spanish forces had also been sent to help the Pope. Austrian forces restored Papal control east of the Apennines, capturing Ancona, and also restored the old order in Tuscany.[23] Neapolitan forces marched to Palermo to restore order in Sicily.

The effectiveness and strength of the Austrian military[24] was underlined the following year in a confrontation with Prussia over the German constitution. Both Austria and Prussia mobilized their armies, but Austrian mobilization was more effective, and the Austrians also had Russian diplomatic support. The Prussians backed down. This was one of the "non-wars" that are too often overlooked in military history. The crisis showed the importance of non-German powers in any confrontation between Prussia and Austria, a lesson that eighteenth-century Prussian rulers had fully appreciated. It also indicated the importance of effective mobilization. The lessons of 1850 were to be well learned by Prussian planners over the following decade.

Although the fighting in Italy and Hungary was on a different scale to that in Iberia earlier, again there was a complex interaction of warfare and policing, politics and campaigning, as both sides sought military and political advantage. The conflicts of the 1830s and 1840s also saw the continued impact of the Napoleonic period. Radetzky used Napoleonic tactics in his envelopments of the Sardinians in 1849. Tactics at the battle of the Alma in the Crimean War in 1854 would also not have been out of place on the Napoleonic battlefield.

Senior commanders were veterans of the Napoleonic Wars. Thus Karl Philip Schwarzenberg was President of the Austrian Higher War Council in 1814–20, while Radetzky, born in 1766, was Chief of the Austrian General Staff in 1809–12 and 1815–29. Marshal Bourmont (1773–1846), who had fought with the Vendean rebels in 1794, rejoined the French army in 1807 and became a Napoleonic general in 1814, went on to be Minister of War in 1829 and to command the expedition to Algiers in 1830. He lost his position as a result of the fall of Charles X in 1830, but went on to command the unsuccessful Miguelist attacks on Oporto and Lisbon in 1833. Marshal Soult was Minister for War in France in 1830–34 and 1840–45, and, in Britain, Wellington was Commander-in-Chief in 1827 and from 1842 until his death in 1852. Lord Raglan, who had acted as aide-de-camp to Wellington and had lost an arm at Waterloo, was Secretary at the Horse Guards, the headquarters of the British army, from 1827 to 1852, before succeeding Wellington as Commander-in-Chief.[25] In September 1833, Bourmont was succeeded as commander of the Miguelist forces by Sir James Macdonnell, who had entered the British army in 1794, and served in Calabria (1806), Egypt (1807), the Peninsular War and Waterloo. The role of commanders such as Bourmont and Macdonnell helps to explain how military techniques spread. At a more junior level, Field Marshal Hugh Gough (1779–1869) entered the army in 1794 and served in the French Revolutionary and Napoleonic Wars. Subsequently, he commanded British forces in China (1840–42) and India (1843–49), defeating the Sikhs. Similarly, in the USA, Winfield Scott was a hero of the war of 1812, and had first become a general in 1814.

This reliance on experience was in part a response to the lack of large-scale conflict within Europe for most European states between 1815 and 1854. The experience of such conflict was thus very much a monopoly of an earlier generation. Nevertheless, it would be mistaken to exaggerate the conservatism of military thought and practice in all countries. Partly as a consequence of the experience of Algeria, which was neither a distant nor an "easy" colonial war, the French showed an interest in new military techniques and ideas. Their military schools worked, and were certainly better than their British equivalents, and the French were more open to experimentation with new weaponry on land and sea.[26]

It was not only a question of veterans in command. Veterans of the Napoleonic Wars had also played an important role in the lower ranks in campaigning, especially in the Latin American Wars of Independence and in the wars in Iberia; in each case, they served on both sides. In Latin America, the revolutionaries recruited British and other veterans, while the royalists used Spaniards who had served against Napoleon. This serves as a reminder of the value placed on military experience. Rather than seeking large numbers of untrained conscript troops – the cannon-fodder of big formations – commanders preferred experienced men. They were of value both for the more irregular operations seen in Latin America and Iberia and for the more formalized battlefields of Italy in 1848–49. In Europe, long-service regulars were also seen as more politically reliable, especially, but not only, in France.

The 1850s were dominated by struggles between conventional forces: the Crimean War (1853–6) and the Franco-Austrian War of 1859. These were widely reported and helped to encourage a sense that the Napoleonic era was past. The Crimean War was extensively followed by the public thanks to newspaper reports and also to military observers. Thus, the American War Department drew up a *Report on the Art of War in Europe, 1854, 1855, and 1856* (3 vols, Washington, 1857–61) based on the reports of American army officers, including George B. McClellan, who was to become Union General-in-Chief in 1861. One of his generals, Philip Cooke, had been an observer in the war of 1859. Henry Halleck updated his *Elements of Military Art and Science* (1846), the first major American textbook on war, with *Critical Notes on the Mexican and Crimean Wars* for the second (1859) and third (1862) editions.

New weaponry

The conflicts of the 1850s saw the use of improved weaponry, for both infantry and artillery. Innovations had improved the reliability and rate of fire. In 1807, Alexander Forsyth, a Scottish cleric, patented the use of fulminates of mercury in place of gunpowder as a primer for firearms. Mercury fulminates ignited when struck: there was no need for external fire and thus detonation. The resulting use of the percussion cap, coated with fulminates of mercury, produced a reliable, all-weather ignition system; although a lack of government support delayed the use and development of Forsyth's invention, and its impact was minor until after 1815. Joshua Shaw developed the mass-produced metal percussion cap in 1822. Positioned over the fire hole, it ignited the main charge, replacing the flintlock mechanism. Percussion muskets were introduced into European armies, the Austrian from 1836. The dramatic reduction of misfires resulted in a great increase in fire-power. In the 1840s, percussion-lock rifles followed. Their rifled barrel gave bullets a spin, which led to a more stable and thus reliable trajectory and, therefore, far greater accuracy and effectiveness than the balls fired by smooth-bore muskets. They were also less expensive to manufacture than earlier rifles and, unlike them, could be fitted with bayonets, an important increase in the capability of the rifle as opposed to the musket.

Yet, before any simple teleological model of weaponry development is adopted, it is worth noting that there was considerable hesitation about switching to new weapons. This was not based on an anachronistic preference for old methods, but rather on an informed concern about new weapons and on careful comparisons with the old. In 1849, Sir Charles Napier, the Commander-in-Chief in India, sent a memorandum to the Governor General about the respective merits of rifles and muskets explaining his preference for the latter. It is worth quoting as it shows the factors believed important in combat. "As an old rifleman myself I cannot be supposed to have any prejudice against the rifle, but as a weapon of war . . . it is inferior to the musket". Several reasons were given. First, the rifle took longer to load,

> Secondly, It does not range much farther, but if it does (which I doubt) the musket ranges quite as far as any man should fire, for those long shots waste powder and rarely kill any body.
>
> Third, After much firing the barrel becomes foul; and the firing slackens, when it is required to be heaviest.
>
> Fourth, It is not so *handy* as a musket and bayonet; the length is important especially against cavalry.
>
> Fifthly, The bore has been increased to the same calibre as that of the musket, because of the very great inconvenience of having two kinds of ammunition to carry.
>
> . . . the supposed great merit of the rifle is the thread or groove which acts on balls having no "windage" that is to say balls which fit tight (hence the invention of the belt to give a rotatory motion) now the small smooth ball reduces the rifle to a level with the musket in point of firing.

Napier continued to argue that the musket/bayonet combination was more effective than the rifle at close quarters and that the rifle was at a disadvantage because it was heavier. It was also more expensive.[27] Napier's memorandum is valuable both because it reflected the experience of a commander who saw active service (in India) in the 1840s and because it indicates what was believed important in a period of fire-power that was coming to a close. The lack of emphasis on range and the stress, instead, on an ability to use the weapon at close quarters were both rapidly to become dated. Instead, new parameters for assessing the capability of individual weapons were soon to be in place.

The percussion cap was followed by Captain Claude-Etienne Minié's cylindro-conoidal lead bullet (1848) which expanded when fired to create a tight seal within the rifle, thus obtaining a high muzzle velocity, and by Johann von Dreyse's "needle" rifle, invented in 1835. The Minié bullet replaced the musket ball. It contained an iron plug in its base and was cast with a diameter slightly less than that of the gun bore. When fitted in the muzzle, it slid easily down the bore. When the gun was fired, the charge pushed the iron plug into the base of the bullet, causing it to expand and grip the rifling of the bore. Thus it was fired on an accurate trajectory. The combination of ease of loading and accuracy was a major advance that encouraged the mass-use of rifled small arms. A later form of the Minié bullet had a hollow base, which had the same effect of expanding when the charge went off and sealing the bore. This did away with the need for the iron plug. The charge was fired by an external percussion cap, and this system married up the reliability of fire of the latter with the greater accuracy of the Minié bullet. Thanks to its easy loading, the Minié bullet made for rapid fire and accuracy, and the Minié rifle was adopted by the British army in 1851, the Enfield rifle following two years later. Minié bullets fired by percussion-lock rifles offered a much greater accuracy than balls from smooth-bore muskets, especially as the range increased.

The Minié bullet had an effect in the 1850s, especially in the Crimean War; but the potential of the breech-loading Prussian Dreyse *Zündnadelgewehr* or "needle" rifle (named after its needle-shaped firing pin), a rifle with a hitherto unprecedented high rate of fire, was not fully realized until the 1860s. Although it was first used, with great effect, by the Prussians against German revolutionaries in Baden and Hesse in 1849, Prussia was not a combatant in the 1850s. Furthermore, early versions of the Dreyse rifle suffered from design faults, including a brittle firing pin, a bolt action that was liable to jam, and a weak seal around the breech. These discouraged a borrowing of the breech-loading technology comparable to the rapid diffusion of percussion-lock rifles. More generally, the problems encountered by the Prussians in improving their infantry fire-power in the first half of the century offer a warning against any sense of easy or clear-cut technological development.[28]

Rifled steel artillery was difficult to produce because it was necessary to find ways to cool barrels evenly in order to prevent them cracking. Alfred Krupp's improvements in casting methods opened the way in the 1840s and in 1851 he showed an all-steel cannon at the London Great Exhibition. Stronger, and thus more durable than bronze guns, steel guns were able to take larger charges and thus offered greater range.

For the 1850s, the combination of the percussion-lock rifle and the Minié bullet was deadly. The effective range of infantry fire-power increased and the casualty rates inflicted on close-packed infantry rose dramatically. Attacking Russian columns, seeking to close to bayonet point, took major losses from the Enfield rifles of the British at the battle of Inkerman (5 November 1854). The formations and tactics of Napoleonic warfare were no longer possible except at the cost of heavy casualties. This posed serious problems for deciding how best to achieve an offensive victory. To adopt less dense formations, especially a development of the French Revolutionary skirmishing line, cut across tradition and training and seemed to threaten the cohesion of units. In addition, the battlefield value of cavalry decreased; although this was not a new process. Cavalry remained most important in reconnaissance and in action against other cavalry, as well as in long-range movements away from rail links. While important in all these spheres, cavalry had thus been marginalized from battle.

A similar process of marginalization had occurred with fortresses. They played a relatively minor role in the French Revolutionary and Napoleonic Wars, certainly in comparison with the situation during the wars of Louis XIV. Instead, there was an emphasis on the decisiveness of battle, with control over territory, including fortresses, being seen as an adjunct. This remained the case in the decades after Waterloo, for example in Latin American warfare or in the fighting in the 1830s and 1840s. It would be unwise to minimize the role of fortresses, however. Antwerp played a key role in the campaigning in Belgium. Much of the Crimean War revolved around operations against Sevastopol, while Vicksburg played a key role in the campaign in the Missis-sippi valley in 1863. However, aside from a degree of strategic irrelevance in many spheres of conflict, there was also to be a new-found vulnerability to rifled artillery. Fortification patterns had to change in order to restore strength to fixed defences.

The Crimean War

Begun between Russia and the Turks in 1853, the Crimean War widened when Britain and France came to the support of the latter in 1854 in order to prevent Russia from dominating the Black Sea and the Balkans, and thus apparently threatening the overland route to India. Napoleon III sought prestige in order both to strengthen his domestic position and to enhance France's diplomatic situation. French interests in the Near East led to support for demands by Catholic priests for access to the Holy Places. Turkish conces-sions led to matching demands from Russia, the protector of the Orthodox clergy, but Russian pressure was resented by the Turks. Nicholas I sought to continue earlier Russian expansion at the expense of the vulnerable Turkish empire; in the past, other powers had not come to the help of the Turks. He, however, mishandled relations with these powers. The British exaggerated the threat from Russia. The Sardinians joined in on the Allied side in 1855, to get a seat at the peace table and raise Italian issues, sending 15,500 troops to the Crimea.[29]

Despite French suggestions of a march on Moscow, this was to be no 1812: the Allies lacked the land resources of Napoleon, but, conversely, were far more powerful at sea; the Russian navy was capable of beating the Turks but not the British. Instead, the war focused on naval and amphibious action against the Russians. Naval operations in the Baltic, which threatened St. Petersburg, were matched by a full-scale expedition to the Crimea in order to take the Russian naval base of Sevastopol. This seemed an appropriate response to the Russian naval victory over the Turks off Sinope. However, the difficulty of the task had not been properly assessed. In addition, the Allies lacked the necessary manpower.

The Allies started the campaign late in the season. Landing to the north of Sevastopol, the 55,000 strong Anglo-French force faced a contested passage of the river Alma (20 September 1854). In the end, more effective fire-power broke down the strong defence; the poorly trained Russians suffered heavily from an absence of rifles and rifled artillery. Anglo-French superiority in weaponry ensured that this frontal attack was successful; had there been no such superiority it would certainly have led to very heavy casualties on the Allied side.

The Allies then surrendered mobility and besieged Sevastopol, although the siege was not fully effective as road links to the north stayed open. The Allies also had to face both particularly bad weather, which hit supply links across the Black Sea, and attempts by the Russian army in the Crimea to disrupt the siege. This led to unsuccessful Russian attacks on the ports through which the Allies were landing all their supplies, the cause of the battles of Balaclava and Inkerman. The Russian failure to breach the supply links was an Allied defensive success matched by that of the Russians at Sevastopol: despite heavy artillery support, Anglo-French land assaults in 1855 initially failed, as had a naval attack by Admiral James Dundas the previous year, for Sevastopol was well defended. In 1855, the attacking Allied armies lacked adequate experience in siege-craft; and had to face a type of trench warfare that was different to earlier sieges. The Russian army was strongly entrenched outside the town, making able use of earth defences, and supported by over 1,000 cannon. The Allies fired 1,350,000 rounds of artillery ammunition during the siege.[30] In the end, Sevastopol fell after a successful French surprise attack on the Malakov redoubt, a major position in its defences, on 8 September.

The Treaty of Paris of 30 March 1856 achieved Allied war goals: Russian naval forces in the Black Sea were severely limited. The long-term effects, however, were not those that had been anticipated. The war breached the Austro-Russian alignment that, albeit with important breaks, had been so important in European power politics since 1726, and this weakening of Austria provided the opportunities for Italian and German unification.

Victory had been won at a heavy cost; although more to disease, hunger and the winter than to weaponry. The Crimean War offers an interesting parallel with World War One (1914–18). Both are generally seen in terms of folly, futility and horror. In the case of the Crimean War, attention thus focuses on the heavy casualties and mismanaged heroism of the charge of the British Light Brigade at Balaclava on 25 October 1854, and on the horrific conditions in the winter siege of Sevastopol.[31] The terrible conditions of the troops, especially a lack of adequate food, clean water, shelter and clothing, helped lead to very heavy losses from disease. For World War One, the equivalents are the Somme and the horrors of trench warfare, which were indeed also seen at Sevastopol. In both wars, there has been criticism of the calibre of the generalship. In the Crimean War, the British commanders had seen action, but in the Napoleonic Wars, and most of them proved wanting, not least in professionalism. Their French counterparts had mostly seen action in Algeria, and showed greater diligence and skill in running an army.[32] Saint-Arnaud, Canrobert, and Pélissier, the successive commanders, had all supported the 1851 coup. In both wars, only a brief conflict had been anticipated, and there were no adequate preparations, not least in strategic and tactical doctrine, for the struggle that was to arise. In the Crimean War, strategy occurred almost by accident. There was a lack of purposeful planning. The British and French were fortunate that the Russians lacked modern rifles and artillery: they were still reliant on smooth-bore muskets.

Yet in both cases it is possible to underrate the achievement of deploying, supplying and controlling large forces and also the extent to which each war ended with victory for one side. In each case, the struggle had lasted longer and taken more lives than had been anticipated, but that is apt to be a characteristic of war. In the Crimean War, the Allies successfully deployed forces into Russia and kept them there until they had achieved their task, a goal that had eluded Napoleon. The contrast was instructive: the Allies did not strike at the heart of Russian power, St. Petersburg, but, instead, at a peripheral target. Britain and France combined lacked the forces that Napoleon I had commanded at the height of his power. Distance–movement of force ratios had been altered by the greater allied success in embracing new technology, in the form of steamships; as opposed to the lack of Russian rail links to the Crimea. The French were short of boats, but the British provided most of the necessary "lift". Once ashore, the Allies preserved this advantage by making a port their target; there was no deep deployment into the interior comparable to the attacks on Russia in 1812 and 1941–42. The British war effort became more effective in 1855, especially after the death of Raglan from cholera. Better transport, medical and supply provisions helped improve the health of the army.[33]

The Franco-Austrian War of 1859

In intervening to support Piedmont/Sardinia against Austria in 1859, Napoleon III sought both to unravel the 1815 peace settlement and to assert French superiority over Austria.[34] The hard-fought battles of the war, especially the Franco-Sardinian victory over the Austrians at Solferino on 24

June, saw very heavy casualties and the impact of improved artillery. The Austrians lost 22,000 men at Solferino; their opponents lost 17, 200. Rifled artillery allowed the cannon to move back out of the range of accurate infantry fire, without losing their own accuracy. It had showed its range and effectiveness at the expense of the Russians at the Alma in 1854 and at Traktir on the river Tchernaya on 16 August 1855. In the latter, explosive shells fired by French rifled cannon caused heavy Russian casualties among the force that unsuccessfully sought to dislodge the attackers of Sevastopol. In 1859, the new French rifled cannon were superior to their Austrian smooth-bore counterparts and destroyed most of them with highly accurate counter-battery fire, before devastating the Austrian infantry, as at Magenta (4 May) and Montebello (20 May). At Magenta, MacMahon pushed forward his guns to provide vital cover for the advancing French infantry. Although developed in the mid-seventeenth century, optical sights on cannon only became common in the mid-nineteenth century.

In another sign of change, in 1859, both sides employed railways in the mobilization and deployment of their forces; in the opening stage of the war, the French moved 50,000 men to Italy by rail, thus helping to gain the initiative. The total forces deployed were substantial. At Solferino, there were 160,000 on each side. This created major problems for command and control. Indeed the high commands of both sides largely lost control of the course of battles, as at Magenta and Solferino. These battles were not to be the masterpieces of Napoleonic envelopment that were held up as an ideal. Instead, they were more attritional in character.

The command ethos and practice shown by both sides in 1859 did not match that which Moltke developed in Prussia. Instead, as with both sides in the Crimean War, there was a lack of planning and of command coherence. The basis for a systematic process of effective and rapid decision making was absent, as was one for the implementation of strategic plans in terms of timed operational decisions and interrelated tactical actions. Put differently, "the mid nineteenth century was the heyday of loose command arrangements".[35] This encouraged not only incoherent strategies and piecemeal tactics, that led to battles without overall direction, such as Inkerman, but also command "structures" and decisions that were heavily influenced by the politics of possibility. Professionalism did not carry the disciplined meaning that it did in the Prussian army, although even there standards were a continual battle and senior commands were sometimes given to well born individuals who did not merit them. Nevertheless, in the Prussian army there was nothing to match the vicious command rivalries that lay behind the Charge of the Light Brigade, nor the acute differences within the Confederate and Union armies and the weaknesses of many of the commanders. Specific problems included the difficulty of getting subordinate commanders to carry out their orders. This can be seen as bringing a welcome flexibility to the implementation of plans, but wilfulness was as much the issue.[36] This was seen for example with

Braxton Bragg's invasion of Kentucky in 1862, which was wrecked in part because of the failure to cooperate by his senior corps commander, Leonidas Polk, and the theatre commander, Edmund Kirby Smith.

In 1859, the French suffered from the poor military leadership of Napoleon III, who did not match his famous namesake in strategic or tactical skill. In addition, there were problems with transporting, supplying and controlling the numbers deployed. The French were fortunate that their battlefield determination in what turned out to be a short war enabled them to overcome the effects of these deficiencies.

Solferino is known as a "soldiers' battle", although that underrates the role of French corps commanders and of the successful Austrian rearguard action by Benedek. At Magenta and Solferino, French infantry advances with the bayonet were successful against poorly trained and led Austrian infantry who were unable to draw much benefit from their technically advanced (although still muzzle-loading) rifles; there had been inadequate training in range-finding and sighting, and, as a consequence, the French were able to close and use their bayonets. Tactics were similar to those under Napoleon I.[37] These battles were a success for dense deployments and column formations. The French gained both ground and the battle.

However, there was to be no exploitation of victory and far-reaching advance comparable to that of Napoleon I in 1796–97. The heavy casualties at Solferino, the lack of French reserves, and concern about Prussian views, led Napoleon to negotiate the Armistice of Villafranca in July. Unlike in 1796–97, Napoleon III did not run a war state, whose military sought continual conflict, and whose civilian population had been terrorized. Furthermore, in 1796–97, the French had benefited from the earlier defeat, and departure from the war, of important powers, especially Prussia and Spain.

In 1859, rather than press on to attack the powerful Austrian fortresses of the Quadrilateral and conquer the Venetia, it was left to Austria, while Sardinia gained Lombardy and Parma, although it soon had to cede Savoy and Nice to France. Unlike Algeria, these were gains in Europe and this brought Napoleon III some of the prestige that he felt to be so important to the domestic position of his regime. Thus France had gained a direct territorial benefit from the defeat of Austria, which then appeared her leading continental European rival.

Conclusions

Solferino encouraged commanders to think about how best to ensure coordination during combat. The Prussians were to show themselves particularly effective in this in the 1860s, and this helped ensure successive triumphs. Prussian observers also noted both the value of railway deployment and France's lack of reserves. Reliant not on a large short-service conscript army, but on smaller, long-service regular forces, the French did not have the numbers able to respond to (and recover after) heavy casualties. French politics and public culture was very different to the situation in 1792–1815, and this undercut many of Napoleon III's bombastic plans. The relatively small size of the French army was a problem on the offensive in 1859, and was to be one on the defensive in 1870: reserves were necessary for defence in depth. Yet larger numbers on their own were scant solution. They posed serious problems in training, supplies and command as the American Civil War was to show.[38] Another consequence of Solferino was the formation, in response to the plight of the wounded, of the International Red Cross in 1864. Prussian expansionism was to give it plenty of work.

Yet, before focusing solely on big battles and their consequences, it is important to note a major theme of this chapter, namely the wide-ranging nature of rebellions and the importance of counter-insurgency warfare. This was true not only in 1830 and 1848, but on many other occasions. Furthermore, such warfare affected all the major armies, and they all had to be aware that rebellions might break out at any moment. The character of these operations varied greatly. At times, they involved the suppression of semi-sovereign bodies, as when the Turks restored their authority in Montenegro by successfully invading in 1852–53 and 1860. At other times, the challenge came from peasant or worker opposition, as in Galicia in 1846. Furthermore, the scale of the challenge varied enormously: Poland in 1831 or Hungary in 1849 posed formidable problems in terms of both the territory in dispute and the number, armaments and organization of the opponents. The political importance of these struggles was also far greater than colonial conflicts, which were generally easier to contain.

Rebellions at the centre of power were scarcely novel. Indeed in the 1640s, there had been a series of them, and royal governments had lost control of London and Paris. Thereafter, however, they had become less frequent and serious. The riots in Madrid in 1766 and in London in 1780 were expressions of opposition towards particular ministers and policies, rather than attempts to overthrow the state, comparable to successive episodes in Paris during the Revolutionary period. This situation changed with the 1790s, in part because of the politicization of social tensions as a consequence of the French Revolution, but also because of a greater sense of national self-determination. This was particularly focused in Poland as a consequence of the partitioning of the state out of existence, which culminated in 1795. The successive uprisings in Poland from 1794 to 1863–64, have generally received insufficient attention, partly because they were unsuccessful, but, more generally, because the history of eastern Europe has not received its due in general military history. Indeed, a parallel can be drawn with Latin America.

In the specific case of Poland, one can see the use of force to maintain an unpopular foreign rule, as well as the continued ability of regular military forces to suppress rebellions. The latter is an important part of the "subtext" of the military history of the period. Because the regimes of central and eastern Europe saw off challenges, their militaries maintained a degree of continuity that was far less apparent than in those affected by major political discontinuities. They were political, in the sense that they reflected the social politics of their societies, but not politicized to the degree seen in France, Spain and Portugal. There careers were made and broken by major changes in regime, understandably so as the army was the principal force that could be used to resist coups as well as rebellions. The resulting danger to military cohesion and efficiency can be exaggerated. The French army proved itself effective in the 1850s, and was more successful in its operations against Sevastopol than the British. Nevertheless, this factor can be noted as a long-term problem with the French military machine, and one that contributed to command failings in 1870 in the Franco-Prussian War.

Although used to suppress rebellions in Paris in 1834, 1848, 1851 and 1871, the French army lacked any equivalent task to that facing the Austrians in Hungary, and, to a lesser extent, Austrian Italy, or that facing the Russians in Poland. It was possible to extend the army's mission by helping to suppress liberal regimes and rebellions elsewhere, as the French did in Spain in 1823 and Rome in 1849, the Prussians did in Saxony, Baden and Hesse, and the Russians in Hungary. These were more containable operations, as it was possible to cut them short, but the very willingness of states to take part in such activities helped to widen the importance of counter-insurgency warfare, and thus to lessen the value of analyses that neglect it.

After 1849, such intervention in foreign states became less common, and did not play a major role in military planning. Instead, there was a greater tendency to treat states as cohesive. Democratization incorporated most of the politically active and interested into peaceful political processes, democratic methods appeared to offer a way to change governments in several states, and states appeared more stable than they had done earlier in the century. The revolutions of 1848 had been overcome and subsequent territorial changes occurred as a consequence of the intervention of other states: Italy was unified round the kingdom of Sardinia and with the support of France. Revolutionary movements throughout the century suffered from the conservatism of much of the European peasantry and from the marginality of revolutionary views, a point that has wider resonance for post-1945 "liberation" movements.

The contrast with the situation in the New World, where revolutions succeeded, cannot be explained by strength of fervour: Poles sought independence more clearly than Anglo or Latin-Americans because they had a tradition of statehood, were different to Russians and had suffered authoritarian rule. Instead, circumstances were crucial; as also with explaining why the American War of Independence was a successful revolution, while the Jacobite risings of 1715 and 1745 were not.

In the New World, the colonial power did not benefit from foreign intervention. Instead it suffered from it. More significantly, the factor of distance not only gave a time advantage to rebels by hindering the response, but also increased the cost, in terms of military resources, of suppression. It also produced the political factor of distancing, leading the colonial power not to follow the conflict as closely, or be as concerned, as it would have been had a war been occurring on its European frontier.

An emphasis on the suppression of rebellions looks forward as well as back. The American Civil War of 1861–65 and the Polish rising of 1863, which was finally suppressed in 1865, can both be placed in this context. The appropriateness of the use of force to suppress popular rebellions stands out, and forms an interesting contrast with modern constraints on its use for such purposes in the Western world. Both these struggles involved large casualties on both sides, and the acceptance of these was an important dimension to the political-cultural context of conflict.

As with French forces used against rebellions in 1834, 1848 and 1871, so more generally, generals and units that had gained experience in combat outside the West were then employed to suppress uprisings. This encouraged both a brutal response and more generally an attitude of seeing the two tasks as similar, certainly in military terms. Thus, Diebitsch, the Prussian-born Russian Field Marshal who led the army sent to suppress the rising in Poland in 1830–31, had served extensively against Napoleon and also in the Russo-Turkish war of 1828–29. As Chief of Staff, he had also been responsible for suppressing the Decembrist rising in 1825. His successor in Poland, Paskievich, had also served against Napoleon, as well as against the Persians. After his success in Poland, Paskievich went on to command against the Hungarians in 1849, and in 1854 invaded Turkish-ruled Bulgaria as part of the Crimean War.

Such a career is a reminder of the danger of segregating tasks and aspects of military history. In particular, a focus in military history on symmetrical warfare, state-to-state warfare between similarly armed forces, has led us to misunderstand the subject, not least by underrating the range of tasks and by simplifying the challenge-response processes that occurred.[39] This is linked to the general preference for a linear account of military history. Such an explanatory device requires a simplification both of the circumstances that are described and of the processes of change that are discerned. Such a simplification encourages judgements about appropriate responses that can be both ahistorical and misleading. This analysis is linked to a hierarchization of military capability that is also of dubious value. If power X was more successful at state-to-state conflict than power Y within Europe in a particular war, that did not imply that it had a greater all-round capability. The complex nature of relationships between this capability and individual wars also repays attention.

A reminder of complexity returns us to the circumstances of the period. Furthermore, even for those who saw a single path of linear development, it was not clear what it should be. This was understandable given the rapid changes of the period and the different lessons that could be, and were, drawn from individual conflicts. It is worth bearing this complexity in mind before making easy and/or critical judgements about the war-making and generalship covered both in this chapter and in the next.

CHAPTER SEVEN

Conflict Within the West, 1861–82

To begin a discussion of this section with an account of warfare in Latin America or Iberia would be considered truly bizarre. There were, of course, conflicts in both, including the Second Carlist War in Spain, and they will be briefly discussed. However, the Wars of German Unification and the American Civil War easily dominate the scene, both for their inherent importance, and because they subsequently transfixed the military imagination and military thought as the Napoleonic Wars had earlier done. To begin with the Wars of German Unification rather than the earlier American Civil War might appear surprising, but the American Civil War had little impact on conflict elsewhere. There were foreign military observers, as well as newspaper reports, but the reports of the former did not receive great attention. This reflected a sense that the methods of fighting were scarcely an advance on those in Europe, especially in the Franco-Austrian War of 1859. There was also an unjustified condescension towards American generalship and staff work, unjustified not in the sense that these were particularly good, but rather, as the Crimean War and that of 1859 revealed, that their European counterparts were scarcely better. Instead, the focus here will be on the Wars of German Unification. They had a greater impact on contemporaries, both politically and militarily, revealed the importance of staff work, and also, in sum, provide examples of conflict between four armies.

Prussia as a military power

If Frederick the Great had grasped the military imagination of Europe in the mid-eighteenth century, Prussia's reputation had rapidly fallen in the 1790s and, even more, in 1806. Thereafter, it was Russia that gained most renown for defeating Napoleon. After 1815, there were very few opportunities for the Prussian military to regain their laurels or to acquire operational experience. Prussia was more powerful in the German Confederation, founded in 1815, than it had been in the Holy Roman Empire abolished in 1806, but it was still subordinate to Austria. When Frederick William IV of Prussia sought a Prussian-directed union of German states in 1849–50, the other major German states instead backed Austria and Prussia had to back down. It had been found wanting militarily as well as politically: the Prussian mobilization of 1850 was singularly unsuccessful and had Prussia and Austria come to blows the auguries were not good for the former.

In the 1850s, the Prussians sought to overhaul their military system. They also benefited from the international volatility encouraged by the ambitions of Napoleon III. However, as yet, the strength of their military system was not obvious to contemporaries.

System was the key word. The Prussians planned for war and sought to control conflict as a process, in which the systematized application of planned pressure led to predicted results. A series of wars – in 1864, 1866 and 1870–71 – led to sweeping victories over Denmark, Austria and France. Helmuth von Moltke, the Chief of the Prussian General Staff, adapted Napoleonic ideas of the continuous offensive to the practicalities of the industrial age, including railways. In place of frontal attack, he sought to envelop opposing forces and to oblige them to mount such attacks themselves in an effort to regain freedom of manoeuvre. Thus he sought by strategic advantage to counter the benefits that rifled weapons and the scale of conflict had given the defence. He was able to do so with great effect against Austria and France.

In tactical terms, the Prussians benefited from the adaptability with which they responded to new weaponry. The Dreyse "needle" rifle could be loaded lying down and fired four to seven times a minute: in practice, it was fired largely from the hip because of the problem of escaping gases. The Prussians used these rifles to deadly effect against Denmark in 1864 and Austria in 1866. The accuracy rate was 65 per cent at 300 feet, 43 per cent at 700 feet. In particular, Prussian infantry fire devastated successive Austrian advances, for example the attacks at Burkersdorf, Rudersdorf and Skalice on 29 June. The Austrians had drawn the wrong conclusions from the success of French bayonet attacks in 1859. Conversely, Prussian fire-power training was superior to that of the Austrians in 1859 and 1866. At the decisive battle – Sadowa/Königgrätz – on 3 July, the Austrians had 64,000 casualties (dead, wounded or captured); the Prussians only 9,000. Conversely, where a Prussian force, against Moltke's orders, had launched a frontal attack on well entrenched infantry – at Langensalza – it had taken heavy casualties; although in that battle the Hanoverians were ultimately defeated by the convergence of more numerous Prussian forces.

More generally, the volume of fire, rather than its accuracy, was important; none the less, the Prussians trained all their soldiers to be skirmishers, able to fire their rifles accurately. Soldiers who could load and fire their rifles lying down were more readily able to benefit from cover, and this encouraged the digging of trenches.

Sadowa was decisive in the outcome of the Austro-Prussian War, not the seizure of any particular position or piece of territory. The emphasis on large battles that characterized the wars of 1854-71 was linked to a situation in which battle, not conquest, was crucial. This was not new, as, for example, Saratoga, Yorktown and Austerlitz all showed, but this feature was accentuated by Moltke, who very much sought a rapid close to the war through decisive victory in battle, which destroyed the ability of the enemy forces to continue effective resistance. Moltke noted the dominance of battle over conquest in his "Instructions for Large Unit Commanders" of 1869. This also stressed the value of seizing the initiative. His Prussia was heavily militarized, but not a war state like Napoleon I's France: Napoleon had had a marked inability to accept any long peace, but Prussia's aims, as inspired and directed by Otto von Bismarck, the Chancellor, and Moltke, were focused specifically on the creation of a Prussian-dominated Germany.

The Danish war of 1864 developed out of the continuing crisis over Schleswig-Holstein. In 1863, Christian IX of Denmark issued a new constitution that incorporated Schleswig into Denmark. The following January, an Austro-Prussian ultimatum required the abrogation of this constitution. Danish refusal led to the outbreak of fighting on 1 February and to an Austro-Prussian invasion of Schleswig. Moltke wanted a quick victory before other powers intervened, a defeat of the Danes before they could retreat into Jutland, and a reliance on flanking attacks. The commander in chief, the elderly Field Marshal von Wrangel, was less than perfect from an orderly General Staff perspective. He also retained a preference for frontal storming attacks. These led to heavy losses when used against the fortified position of Dybbol. However, the Prussians benefited from better rifles and training. The Danes were still reliant on muzzle loaders, which were slower and had a shorter range than the Prussian "needle" rifle. The merits of the weapons on both sides were clearly shown at encounters where Danish losses were far higher, such as the battle of Lundby (1 July). The Danes also lacked rifled cannon. The Prussians failed to destroy the Danish army at the Danewerk, their southerly defensive line, but subsequently inflicted heavy blows. The outnumbered Danes were driven to accept an armistice on 20 July and then peace terms – the Treaty of Vienna of October 1864 – that gave Schleswig-Holstein to joint Austro-Prussian control.

Prussia's success against the outnumbered Danes had less of an impact on contemporaries than the defeat of Austria two years later. Domestic problems encouraged Wilhelm I of Prussia to press for war in 1866, and had the same effect on Franz Joseph of Austria, although the unsettled nature both of the Austro-Prussian condominium of Schleswig-Holstein and of the political situation within Germany were themselves a cause of serious dispute. Success in war had encouraged a more authoritarian politics in Austria in 1849 and 1865. War in 1866 seemed the only solution to the domestic political and financial problems of the Habsburg state, and the sole way to tackle fissiparous nationalism, most obviously in Venetia. Austria was still also widely regarded as the strongest German state.

Austro-Prussian War, 1866

The Seven Weeks' War (June–August 1866) saw a speedy triumph not only over the Austrians but also over their German allies. The Hanoverians, under Arentschildt, were defeated by Falkenstein at the battle of Langensalza (27–9 June), and the Prussians overran Hanover, Hesse-Cassel and Saxony. The allied forces did not combine. In contrast, the Prussian victory in 1864 had been won in cooperation with Austria. In 1866, Prussia, instead, benefited from an alliance with Italy. This both drew off 100,000 Austrian troops and also provided Prussia with the pretext for war.

Prussia and Austria faced each other with comparable numbers, providing an opportunity for Prussia to demonstrate the superior quality of her army. The Prussians gained the initiative thanks in part to their more effective mobilization and deployment plans. They were able to benefit from the rail system, which was both better in Prussia and Saxony than in the Habsburg dominions as a whole, and also far better organized for wartime deployment. The Austrians were taken by surprise by the speed of the main Prussian advance into Bohemia in June, while the Prussian right advanced through Saxony, occupying Dresden on 19 June.

Once engaged in a series of frontier battles, Prussian fire-power inflicted casualties in a 4:1 ratio on larger Austrian attacking forces at Trautenau. The massed Austrian columns proved less flexible than the more mobile Prussian companies which had been trained to move independently, albeit within the confines of a plan. These companies found and fired on the flanks of slower moving enemy columns. The Prussians also benefited from the low morale that existed in much of the multi-ethnic Habsburg army; Hungarian, Italian, Czech, Polish and Croat support for the Habsburgs was limited, and the effect could be seen in the numbers who surrendered unwounded.

Each side deployed a quarter of a million men at Sadowa, the decisive battle on 3 July. Benedek was in a reasonable defensive position, had better artillery and had the possibility of using interior lines to defeat the separate Prussian armies in detail, but, in practice, due in large part to his irresolution, the Austrian situation was less favourable. Benedek was unable to take advantage of his interior position. As a result, prior to the battle, he had been outmanoeuvred by the three Prussian armies, which were operating Moltke's strategy of exterior lines, and his line of retreat was threatened. Whereas

Napoleon had used separately operating corps within his army, Moltke employed independently operating armies, i.e. much larger forces. Further-more, unlike Napoleon who concentrated his forces prior to the battle, Moltke aimed for a concentration of his armies in the battle.

In 1866, Moltke failed to realize his ideal aim of closing the trap by driving in the Austrian flanks completely and most of Benedek's troops escaped, but the Prussians had shown themselves superior not only in manoeuvre but also on the battlefield. Prussian units in attack possessed a flexibility their opponents lacked, ensuring that the Austrian positions were caught in the flank and hit by cross-fire. Massed Austrian attacks led to heavy losses. The Austrians did best with their artillery, which out-shot the Prussians and hit Prussian infantry advances, although their small-unit character minimized casualties.

Sadowa ended with the flight of the Austrians and the loss of their artillery. Most of the Austrians had escaped, but the coherence and morale of the army were gone. The Prussians pressed on, into Moravia and towards Vienna. Archduke Albert, who had defeated the Italians at Custoza on 24 June, with a column attack and shock tactics, had then to move most of his army north and prepare to defend Vienna. However, the regime had been devastated by Sadowa, while the Prussians wanted a speedy end to the war, not least to forestall French entry; so there was no final battle, no siege of Vienna to prefigure that of Paris in 1870-71. Despite victory over the Italians, Austrian civilian determination had collapsed and Franz Joseph sued for peace. He paid an indemnity, withdrew from the German Confederation, which was dissolved, and recognized the annexation of his allies in North Germany. The two-power system in Germany, with Austria the senior, had gone.

Prussia gained no territory from Austria, but annexed Hanover, Hesse-Cassel, Nassau, Frankfurt and Schleswig-Holstein. This left it dominant in northern Germany, and this dominance was underlined in 1867 when the North German Confederation was formed: it incorporated the rest of north Germany into a federal state that was very much controlled by Prussia.

This took place in the aftermath of one of the important and underrated building blocks in military history, wars that did not take place. Such conflicts are crucial in affecting military planning; they also register senses of relative capability. In 1866, France sought revenge for 1859, for Prussian mobilization and talk of armed mediation in the Franco-Austrian war had helped pressurize France into accepting terms that were less than had been anticipated. In 1865-66, both Austria and Prussia had tempted Napoleon III with hopes of a favour-able (to him) settlement in the Rhineland, and when war broke out between the German states he hoped to impose a profitable mediation. In fact, Prussian success led Napoleon to consider armed mediation and he demanded territo-rial gains on the left bank of the Rhine, only to be outfaced by Bismarck. Napoleon was not willing to risk war in 1866, in part because his army was not thought ready, and in part because Bismarck outmanoeuvred him.[1]

The Seven Weeks' War led other powers to adopt or seek to better Prussian weaponry and tactical formations. Breech-loading rifles were now seen as far better than the slower muzzle-loaders. In 1866, the French adopted the *chassepot* rifle, which had a more gas-tight breech and a far greater range than the Prussian "needle" rifle, which no longer represented cutting-edge military technology. The Prussian tactic of concentrating strength on the skirmishing line, and adopting more extended formations that were less dense than columns or lines, and thus less exposed to fire, commanded attention. The redundancy of cavalry on the battlefield was another lesson from the recent war, but one that many cavalry officers were reluctant to accept. Similarly, for infantry, there was less need for the bayonet: reliance on a more effective fire-power decreased the frequency with which units clashed in hand-to-hand fighting. This led Charles Ardant du Picq, a French officer, to argue in his posthumously published *Études sur le Combat: Combat Antique et Moderne* (1880) that shock action had become redundant. His stress on unit cohesion, morale and discipline was designed to provide an explanation for how best to win in the face of effective fire-power on both sides.[2]

Franco-Prussian War, 1870–71

Relations between France and Prussia remained tense after 1866. Napoleon III was fearful of Prussian strength and determined to prevent Prussia from taking over the southern German states – Bavaria, Baden, Württemberg and the Palatinate – by leading them into the Confederation, as they had been brought into a new customs union in 1869. Bismarck felt that war with France might be necessary in order to secure such a union.

Public opinion in France and Germany played a role in creating an atmosphere favourable for war. This opinion was manipulated when Bismarck edited a telegram recording a meeting between Wilhelm I of Prussia and the French ambassador Count Benedetti at Bad Ems, in order to make their discussion over a Hohenzollern candidature for the vacant Spanish throne appear acrimonious and threatening. Certain leading figures in Paris, notably the foreign minister, Gramont, were easily provoked, or simply lost all sense of proportion. Hostile to growing Prussian power, Napoleon III brought matters to a head by declaring war, and did so without allies.

The Prussian/German victory was in part due to weaponry. Prussian artillery, which in 1866 had been out-ranged by the effective Austrian rifled artillery, introduced after exposure to the French in 1859, was superior to its muzzle-loading French counterpart. After 1866, the Prussians improved their artillery tactics and organization, and pushed their guns to the front to make them more effective. Ironically, the French had turned down an approach from Krupp to sell them the breech-loading steel artillery he made for the

Prussian government. The deployment of weaponry was also important. In the *mitrailleuse*, the French had the first effective machine gun, a hand-cranked ring of 25 gun tubes that could fire 100–150 rounds per minute, but they were used neither extensively nor intelligently; this was one of the many occasions in which a failure to develop an appropriate tactical doctrine reduced the impact of new technology.

The Prussians were fortunate that their planning left them with little need for large-scale frontal attacks; strategy was as, if not more, important than tactics. The Prussian use of dispersed forces outmanoeuvred the more concentrated and slower moving French armies. In part, this reflected Prussian superiority in command and control, but a fixity of purpose and a clearly planned strategy were as important. Furthermore there were also important tactical differences. The French responded to the Austro-Prussian War by adopting tight defensive formations designed to shoot down Prussian attackers. However, the resulting positions were vulnerable to flank attack and the more dispersed formations favoured by the Prussians reduced the target for the French. In an essay of 1864, "Remarks on the Influence of Improved Rifles on the Attack", Moltke decried closely packed frontal assaults.

In addition, the Prussians benefited from the respective size of the armed forces. The French had no equivalent to the reserves of the Prussian *Landwehr*, in part because political opposition in the *Corps Législatif* had hamstrung the attempt in the 1868 Military Law to create a 400,000 strong reserve of *Garde Nationale Mobiles*. For political and military reasons, there was to be no well trained second army like the *Landwehr*. Distrustful of his adventurism, Republican opponents of Napoleon III were dubious about the value of a larger army. Military spending was actually cut in January 1870. The regular army was not keen on expansion because it feared that a large number of conscripts would dilute military quality. Nevertheless, a smaller population (and lower growth rate) than that of Germany reduced the pool for the army and underlined the damage done to France by Prussia's success in unifying Germany other than Austria in 1866. In light of the relative potential numbers, it would have been sensible for the French to take the initiative, before the Prussians could call up the reserves and link their forces with those from southern Germany. As France had declared war (on 16 July), she also had the initiative.

However, there was no adequate plan for war with Prussia. The improvisation that had worked against the slower-moving (and more distant) Russians in 1854 and Austrians in 1859 was no longer appropriate. Experience in Algeria, Mexico and the Papal States in the 1860s was no preparation for a conflict in which a powerful Prussia was to seize and retain the initiative. None of these three conflicts provided experience in mass mobilization and warfare, or in manoeuvring against large numbers of well trained, led, equipped and gunned forces. Colonial expeditions were not the best preparation for coordinating corps on a European battlefield.

Napoleon III decided to mass troops at Metz and Strasbourg before invading the Prussian Rhineland and Baden. This was designed to win the initiative and ensure that the Prussians (as the forces of the German states are referred to for ease of convenience) would be put at a strategic disadvantage before the crucial clash. In practice, mobilization was very poorly handled, and when the French invaded on 1 August, there were only 140,000 troops at Metz and Strasbourg, not the planned 300,000. More effective operational plans had been drawn up by General Frossard and Marshal Niel but they were overturned by Napoleon III's wilful confidence in his own judgement.

In contrast, Moltke had rapidly deployed a force capable of regaining the initiative and taking the war into France. Rail mobilization worked as never before, and the French were outnumbered. In response, Napoleon III ordered the retreat of the units that had captured Saarbrücken on 2 August. Most of the war was to be fought on French soil, which was a damaging blow for French resources and morale. Four days later, the Prussian Third Army invaded Alsace and defeated the greatly outnumbered I Corps under MacMahon at Fröschwiller and Wörth. The *chassepot* showed its value against frontal attacks, but the Prussians benefited from greater numbers, which also enabled them to outflank the defenders, and from their superior artillery. The French entrenchments provided an easy target, and the use of percussion, rather than time-fused, shells made it easier to ensure accurate fire.

Defeat at Wörth exposed the flank of the French position at Metz, but, far worse, let Moltke further gain the initiative. Napoleon III lost confidence, and his maladroit choice of commander of the Army of the Rhine, Marshal Achille Bazaine, retreated into the extensive fortifications at Metz, thus surrendering both mobility and an opportunity first to block the Prussians and later to prevent envelopment. The Prussian Second Army crossed the Moselle unopposed before Metz and cut the roads to the west of the city. The vulnerability of the Prussian communication lines gave Bazaine opportunities that he squandered. At Mars-la-Tour on 16 August, Prussian artillery repeated the decisive role it played at Wörth. At Gravelotte-Saint Privat on 18 August, 188,000 Prussians under Moltke attacked 113,000 French troops under Bazaine in good defensive positions. With their effective *chassepots*, and some use of the *mitrailleuse*, the French inflicted heavy casualties, 20,163 Prussians to 12,273 French, but they failed to take advantage of checked attacks in order to mount counter-attacks. Instead, the initiative was retained by the Prussians, who were able to use their more numerous and superior artillery with great effect. Repeated pressure finally led Bazaine to fall back on Metz. The road to Paris had not been reopened.

Bazaine made no real attempt to break out and he did not take a dynamic stance capable of distracting Moltke. The planned breakout on 31 August was never launched. This provided Moltke with an opportunity to destroy the Army of Châlons being assembled under MacMahon. This was to be a victory of manoeuvre, not the attritional pounding with which Grant defeated Lee in 1864–65. Moltke was able to think through the options offered by the possible positions of Bazaine and MacMahon and rapidly to execute a plan that allowed the Prussians to defeat them separately.

MacMahon advanced from Châlons on 22 August towards Metz, a risky manoeuvre, because Napoleon III assured him that Bazaine was pushing towards him from Metz. When it became clear that this was not true and that Moltke was preparing to encircle him, MacMahon tried to retreat to safety, but was trapped at Sedan by the rapidly advancing Prussians: forced marches, day and night, were one key to Moltke's victory. In the valley of the Meuse, Sedan was surrounded by hills. MacMahon lacked the forces and foresight to hold them, but once they had been seized by the Prussians they gave their artillery a strong position. On 1 September, MacMahon tried to gain the hills, but his men were driven back by accurate and heavy artillery fire. Unlike at Gravelotte, there was no need for Prussian infantry assaults, and, as a result, Prussian casualties were far lower than at Gravelotte. In contrast, the French, now on the attack, lost more than the Prussians.

Having lost so heavily on 1 September, the French surrendered on 2 September. Aside from Napoleon III, 83,000 troops were taken prisoner: 21,000 had already been captured in the battle. The French emissary, Wimpfen, had argued that generosity was the sole possible base for a lasting peace, only for Bismarck to reply that it was particularly difficult to rely on the gratitude of a people. Metz surrendered on 28 October.

The Prussians had developed a system of General Staff work and training at a General Staff academy that was given much of the credit for victory in 1866 and 1870. Training of staff officers gave the Prussian army a coherence its opponents lacked: the Austrian commander Benedek scorned the staff system, while the French staff was out of touch with combat conditions and recent developments. The French system of muddling through had, to no avail, been criticized in *L'Armée française en 1867*, by General Louis Trochu, a member of an investigative commission of that year.

Prussian staff officers were given an assured place in a coordinated command system. Officers from the General Staff were expected to advise commanders and the latter were also expected to heed their chiefs of staff. This led to a system of joint responsibility in which either the commander or his first General Staff officer could issue orders. Such a system rested on the reputation of the staff system. It also made predictable planning possible, which encouraged forward planning. From 1857, there was an emphasis on preparing for a whole campaign rather than simply for battle. This led to a stress on war plans.

Prussian preparedness and staff work ensured that its large numbers of troops and reserves could be mobilized successfully. This was achieved in 1866 and 1870, in part thanks to an effective exploitation of the railway network in order to achieve rapidly the desired initial deployment and thus gain the strategic initiative. The Crimean and Franco-Austrian Wars had led to an understanding of the need for good rail links. Through use of *planned* rail movements, the Prussians made mobilization a predictable sequence and greatly eased the concentration of forces. This was of particular value in a short conflict. Uniform speed by all trains was employed in order to maximize their use. Military trains were also of uniform length. Train use was planned and controlled by a Railroad Commission and by Line Commands, creating an integrated system linked and made responsive by the telegraph. Trains and the telegraph had been adapted for military ends in the 1850s. The number of locomotives was kept high in order to cope with a wartime rise in demand.[3] The efficiency, and thus capability, of the rail system was greatly enhanced between 1866 and 1870. After 1866, the Austrians understood these advantages. Archduke Albert, who became Inspector-General of the Austrian Army, improved both the general staff and rail transport.

The French failed to match Prussian advances in war-preparation capability. Their commanders lacked recent practice in handling armies in European conflict. They made more mistakes than their Prussian counterparts. Napoleon III was a poor overall commander; a meddler who failed to coordinate his marshals; a Napoleon only in name. Bazaine had experience of campaigning in Algeria, the Crimea, Piedmont and Mexico, but these had not involved large forces in battle. He also lacked a staff in any way comparable to that of the Prussians. Bazaine was to show indecision and a low level of competence. The French had no organizational system comparable to that of Prussia: their planning was inadequate and they had no effective General Staff.[4] The 1869 report of the Railroad Commission was not implemented. The British also lacked a General Staff.

The Prussian command system was not without problems; it could not prevent Prince Frederick Charles, nephew of Wilhelm I of Prussia, an army commander, from failing to observe strategic and tactical plans in 1866, while in 1870 Steinmetz, Commander of the First Army, also disobeyed the strategic plan. Aside from straightforward departure from plans there was also a range of factors causing the "friction" that Clausewitz had seen as the prime inhibitor of plans. Even so, the effective Prussian General Staff system ensured that the Prussians were better able to contain mistakes and to prevent them from overthrowing their plans. The Prussians managed risk and error; the French experienced it. Moltke was Napoleon I with system. Combined with the quantity and flexibility of military resources, their operational culture and structure also meant that the Prussians were better able than before to fight major battles, with their attendant casualties and disruption, and press on to new tasks.

The Prussians were also more effective at the micro-level. Thanks both to an ethos of commitment and training, there was an emphasis on a professionalism on the part of officers, NCOs and soldiers that was more consistent than in the French army. More particularly, the Prussians trained officers to take their own decisions at all levels within the constraints of the command plan. This was important because defensive fire-power, by encouraging a "lower density" battlefield with spread-out units and dispersed formations, accentuated problems of command and communication. This put a premium on coordination and on morale. The use of *Auftrags*, orders that explained the situation and goal of a force and left a degree of flexibility, was particularly important. This ensured a dynamic interaction between hierarchy and devolved decision-making, one mediated by training, that meant that small unit operations supported and harmonized with those of large forces.

The uncertainty of war contributed to Prussian success, rather than undermining it, because of their superior ability to cope with it through better field staff work. Partly as a consequence, Moltke's 1866 and 1870 campaigns worked out very differently to Napoleon's of 1815. There were, of course, major contrasts, not least Napoleon's need to attack with a scratch army and his opponents' generalship and numbers, but, nevertheless, it is still valuable to focus on particular differences. One such was staff work and campaign coordination. In 1815, Soult did not operate as an effective Chief of Staff. Instead, crucial orders were unclear and slow. This affected Ney at Quatre Bas, but, in addition, the marshal did not show the responsiveness and promptness expected of a Prussian corps commander under Moltke. Grouchy failed to keep contact with Blücher in 1815, and thus Napoleon lost knowledge, let alone control, of the movement of the pieces. Moltke encountered problems with opponents failing to move as anticipated, but, in the circumstances of 1866 and 1870, was better able to understand, think through and control the consequences. His nephew was to be far less successful in 1914, a reminder of the need to keep relative capability in mind and to avoid assuming progressive or linear improvement.

Prussia's victory led to her gaining Alsace-Lorraine and a substantial indemnity from France. It also enabled her to transform her hegemony within Germany into a German empire ruled from Berlin, an achievement greater than any aimed at by Frederick the Great.

Prussian success led to the conclusion that offensive operations that were carefully planned by an effective and professional General Staff and that drew on the logistical possibilities provided by railways could, indeed would, lead to swift and decisive victories. This encouraged emulation of German military systems, both within and outside Europe. A similar stress on extended order, and initiative in battle was to be seen in the American Infantry Drill Regulations of 1891.[5]

Yet Moltke himself warned of the hazards of extrapolating from his victories. While arguing that it was preferable to fight on the territory of one's opponent, he was increasingly sceptical about the potential of the strategic offensive, because of increases in defensive fire-power and the size of armies. Furthermore, in 1866 and 1870, deficiencies in leadership and strategy on the part of Austria and France played into Prussian hands, enabling the Prussians to outmanoeuvre their opponents. Benedek failed to make adequate preparations for attack or defence, and responded incompetently to the Prussian advance into Bohemia. No help was offered to Austria's German allies. French failures included a reluctance to benefit from the strategic possibilities of a rail system considerably better than Austria's and an unwillingness to strengthen the defensive by using both a flexible defence and entrenchments comparable to those employed by Lee in Virginia. Had the French had artillery to compare with that of the Prussians then the attacks of the latter, especially at Wörth and Gravelotte, would have been devastated. The difference was to be seen in 1914 and 1916, although, in both offensives, the Germans also suffered from their failure to keep or create an "open" campaign zone with room for manoeuvre and a tempo permitting the retention of the initiative as Moltke had done: the strategy of envelopment failed in 1914, and in 1916 the strength of the defence compensated for the exposed nature of the Verdun position. More generally, in World War One the expanded range of modern weaponry limited the possibilities of flank movements and attacks. This made envelopment more difficult and thus made it more likely that defeated forces would be able to retreat, avoiding both destruction and a speedy enforced peace. Nevertheless, on the eastern front in 1914, the Germans showed that their strategic concepts were not without merit, although their decisiveness was shown in a defensive success rather than an offensive triumph.

The campaigns of 1866 and 1870 did not demonstrate that the Prussians were bound to win, although they did show the value of winning the initial attack in a short war. This looked forward towards the danger of assuming that German successes in 1939 and 1940 demonstrated the ineluctable superiority of *Blitzkrieg*. A past parallel was that of Frederick the Great in 1740–42, 1744–45 and 1756–63. His successes did not imply that his methods were in some way a paradigm of military perfection or his army the best in the West. Instead, they showed that it was appropriate for the tasks it was expected to undertake; and that these were carefully kept in line with Prussian capability. Even so, Prussian failures in offensive operations, as in 1744 and 1778, suggested that the Prussian military system had deficiencies. These were in addition to the limitations of its restricted "tasking", namely its inappropriateness for amphibious and colonial operations.

In neither 1866 nor 1870 did Prussia have to conquer its opponents. To that extent, the wars more closely approximated to Napoleon's attacks on Austria than to his invasions of Spain and Russia. Indeed, Prussia and the Prussian army were not really up to the task of conquering their opponents. After successes in the decisive battles fought near the frontier in 1870, the Prussians encountered difficulties as they advanced further, not least supply problems and opposition from a hostile population. Dennis Showalter has referred to Germany coming close to "conquering itself to death".

More generally, the resources for the total conquest of Austria and, later, France, including, for example, possibly resisting a war of *revanche* mounted from Algeria were simply not present. This was not the option the government or Moltke sought; they wanted a swift and popular conflict, with relatively low casualties. The rate at which resources were used up militated against a long war. In 36 hours at Sedan, the Prussians fired 35,000 shells.

Yet it is important to note that the Prussians were not required to win only near the frontier. Due to political factors, the replacement of Napoleon III by the Third Republic, proclaimed at Paris on 4 September, the war continued: Sedan was not a Sadowa. Determined not to surrender territory as the price of peace, Léon Gambetta's Government of National Defence raised new forces. After the French surrender at Sedan on 2 September, the Prussians advanced on Paris which they had surrounded by 19 September. Moltke relied on starvation and Bismarck persuaded Wilhelm I to add bombardment; Moltke had not been keen. There was no attempt to storm the city which indeed had a garrison of 300,000 troops, spread out over a 60-kilometre long fortified defensive perimeter. Relying on new draftees, troops from Algeria, *Gardes Mobiles* and American arms shipments, the French assembled armies to relieve the city, leading to a series of battles from early October to late January 1871.

The Prussians, with the forces besieging Paris as their centre point, and now able to use the French railways, were in a strong position, although they suffered from wartime damage to the French railways and from their inadequacy for the task of keeping the massive force besieging Paris supplied. The Prussians also benefited from the prestige they had gained in victory, from the surrender, at Metz, of the last major professional French force, and from the disorientation of their opponents. Prussian morale was high due to their initial stunning victories.

In response, the new French Republic appealed to the tradition of French Revolutionary enthusiasm to repel the invader at all costs, only to be disabled by a different internal revolutionary force – the Paris Commune. None the less, helped by the superiority of the *chassepot* over the Dreyse rifle, the republican armies still won some small actions, for example Bourbaki's success at Villersexel on 9 January 1871, and showed themselves capable of defensive operations, especially if in fortified positions, although they lacked the ability to mount successful attacks. Instead, they proved vulnerable to Prussian artillery. The French also discovered, as the Americans had done in 1861, that rapidly raising large forces created serious problems of supply, training and command. These were made much worse because France was already experiencing defeat, division and dislocation. Numbers alone could not suffice: it was the way in which men were integrated into already existing military structures that was crucial, as the Prussians showed, and this could not be done quickly or easily given the demoralized state of the French army.

The forces in Paris failed in their attempts to break out of Paris: the confidence of Republican enthusiasts in a *sortie en masse* proved misplaced. To the north, Faidherbe, who had been successful in Senegal in the 1850s, was defeated by Manteuffel at Amiens on 27 November, and Rouen was occupied. Faidherbe was subsequently successful at Pont-Noyelles (3 December) and Bapaume (4 January 1871), but was defeated at Le Mans. The Army of the Loire was defeated by a smaller Prussian force at Orléans on 2–4 December. Prussian forces that had finished their successful siege of Strasbourg on 27 September, after heavy shelling had led to its surrender, advanced to besiege Belfort, although that was defended more successfully. Nevertheless, the Germans defeated a relief attempt by the Army of the East under Bourbaki on the Lisaine (Battle of Belfort or Héricourt, 15–17 January 1871), and pushed into Franche Comté, driving poorly supplied and demoralized French forces there over the Swiss border. This led to an armistice signed on 28 January and to the French National Assembly, which had taken refuge in Bordeaux, accepting Prussian terms. German troops remained in France until an indemnity was paid in 1873.[6]

Wars of Italian Unification

Within Europe, the Wars of German Unification engaged most military attention and stimulated most military change, but the conflict in Italy in 1860 also had an impact. After the end of the war between France/Sardinia and Austria in 1859, Victor Emmanuel II of Sardinia had forbidden Garibaldi from advancing the liberal cause by attacking the Papal States. Resigning his Major Generalship in the Sardinian army, Garibaldi and 1,000 red-shirted volunteers in 1860 sailed from Genoa to Marsala in order to help a revolt in Sicily against the Kingdom of the Two Sicilies of the Neapolitan Bourbons (Sicily and southern Italy). After defeating a Neapolitan force at Calatafimi (15 May), Garibaldi captured Palermo, the capital of Sicily, after three days of street fighting. He defeated the remaining Neapolitan forces on the island at Milazzo (20 July) and, having crossed the Straits of Messina, marched north to defeat the Neapolitans at the Volturno and to capture Naples. Meanwhile, a Sardinian army under Victor Emmanuel had marched south from Bologna, winning battles at Castelfiadardo (19 September 1860) and Macerone, against the small Papal army and the Neapolitans respectively. Garibaldi handed over his conquests to Victor Emmanuel, enabling the latter to create the kingdom of Italy. Gaeta continued to defy the invaders, but fell in February 1861 after a long siege.

The conquest of the Kingdom of the Two Sicilies was one of the most complete victories of the century 1815–1914. In place of a defeat of the main field army of an opponent, there was a conquest of much of the state. This was more complete than the defeat of Mexico by the Americans, although Mexico City had been captured, unlike St. Petersburg, Copenhagen and Vienna in the Crimean War, Danish War and Austro-Prussian War respectively. As a result, it is somewhat surprising that the overthrow of the kingdom has not attracted more attention from military historians. It was more rapid than the conquest of Austrian-ruled Naples and Sicily by the Spanish forces of Don Carlos during the War of the Polish Succession (1733–35). Then, the first blow had been an overland invasion of southern Italy and the Austrian cause had collapsed after defeat at Bitonto (1734). In 1860, in contrast, two independently operating forces had each successfully advanced. The ability of Garibaldi to invade Sicily denied the Neapolitan Bourbons the safe haven they had enjoyed when Napoleon I's forces had captured Naples. The Bourbon regime was anyway fairly weak, especially in Sicily, much of which was close to ungovernable as a result of widespread brigandage. The overthrow of the regime was partly a revolution by the Neapolitan people, rather than a straight conquest.

This was not the end of the Wars of Italian Unification. Although much of the Papal States were annexed in 1860, the area round Rome remained under Papal control and was guaranteed by France, while the Austrians still ruled the Venetia. In 1862, Garibaldi planned to seize Rome, but this was judged inopportune by Victor Amadeus and the Italian army under Enrico Ciadini attacked and broke up his force at Aspromonte (29 August).

Venetia was gained in 1866 as a consequence of the Austro-Prussian war. The Austrians tried to buy the Italians off with a promise of Venetia at the end of the war, but they wanted more and still attacked. However, the Austrians fought well in Italy, not least defeating Garibaldi at Bececca, and winning the major clash at Custoza (24 June): the Italians launched uncoordinated attacks in what was a poorly planned operation. On his own initiative, Garibaldi sought to capture Rome again in 1867, with a force of 7,000 men, but he was defeated by a Franco-Papal army at Mentena (3 November). Instead, the Italians under Raffaele Cadorna successfully invaded the Papal States and captured Rome on 20 September 1870 as a consequence of the withdrawal of French support during the Franco-Prussian War. The outnumbered Papal forces were easily brushed aside.

American Civil War, 1861–65

In some respects, the American Civil War looked back to a different pattern of military mobilization and tasking. This focused on civil conflict, the resultant need to create military and governmental structures, and the fight for total victory. Thus the American Civil War can be related to the War of American Independence, the French Revolutionary War, especially in its civil war aspects, the Latin American Wars of Liberation and the First Carlist War.

The context was thus different to contemporary conflict elsewhere in the Western world, even though the weaponry might be similar. This contrast cannot be pushed too far. In one sense the American Civil War was a nationalist struggle, as were the Wars of German and Italian Unification. The American Civil War involved a degree of mobilization of resources that was hitherto unprecedented in the history of the USA, and that certainly contrasted greatly both with the War of 1812 and with the Mexican-American War. This reflected the fundamental constitutional issue at stake, the length of the conflict and, in particular, the failure to negotiate a settlement or to maintain the conflict as a limited war. Instead, in 1862 it became an increasingly bitter and punitive struggle.[7]

Furthermore, the American Civil War also witnessed an intensity of loss that marked it out from contemporary international conflict, as well as from all other American wars. The Confederate Army of Northern Virginia suffered a casualty rate of 20 per cent or more at each of the battles of Seven Days, Second Bull Run, Antietam and Chancellorsville, leading to 90,000–100,000 battle casualties in Robert E. Lee's first year in command (1862–3). The Confederacy mobilized 80 per cent of its military-age whites but, by the spring of 1865, a quarter of the white Confederate manpower pool was dead and another quarter maimed.

High casualty rates reflected the intensity of the struggle, which began in 1861 as the Confederacy of newly seceded Southern states sought to take over federal military posts. The successful bombardment of Fort Sumter off Charleston on 12–13 April was followed by a proclamation from President Abraham Lincoln calling for volunteers to help suppress the rebellion. The two sides were differentiated geographically, but this made the fate of the borderland states particularly important. They went separate ways, but the Union was able to gain control of Kentucky, Missouri and West Virginia; and thus consolidate their superiority in resources, block invasion routes into the North, and expose the South to attack. Gaining control involved civil wars in microcosm: local struggles that were affected by outside intervention. As Maryland stayed in the Union, the central battleground of the war lay between Washington, which remained the capital of the union, and Richmond, Virginia, which became the capital of the Confederacy. Their proximity helped give a geographical focus to the conflict and also cut across the potential expansiveness derived from the area in rebellion.

The American Civil War saw both the creation of a new military structure, that of the Confederacy, and the massive expansion of that of the American state, the Union. As such, it was a most massive expansion in Western military capability. The Mexican War and policing operations against Native Americans were not effective training grounds for the American Civil War. Many officers cut their teeth in the Mexican War, but it was different, both politically and militarily, to the American Civil War. In 1861, the US army was only 16,000 strong and the navy had only about 40 vessels in commission. Neither the Union nor the Confederacy were prepared for a major war in 1861: this was as true of the attitudes of their commanders as of the resources available. Yet, having been defeated that year at First Manassas/Bull Run (21

July), the Union reorganized its forces into the Army of the Potomac, developing a well disciplined, well equipped and large army.

Further west, there was a very different force–space ratio, and this created both problems and opportunities for commanders. There was a greater need for mobility, and more opportunity for it. Grant was to create opportunities for mobility round Vicksburg, the crucial Confederate fortress on the Mississippi, and, once he had made the campaign there fluid, to gain opportunities to achieve concentrations of strength that enabled him to take successful initiatives and drive the Confederates in on the city where they could be besieged. Vicksburg surrendered on 4 July 1863. Confederate resources west of the Mississippi were now cut off.

Organizational developments on both sides can be understood in two lights: the limited success in "modernizing" the American military in order to be able to fight a total war, but, on the other hand, considerable achievement in mobilizing resources for war. In the former case, much of the command techniques were amateurish, specifically the limited ability to coordinate widely spread operations, and the absence of high-grade General Staff work. The armies found it difficult to assimilate new military techniques and adapt tactics to new weaponry. Rather than focusing on the modernity of the struggle, it can be argued that in important respects it more closely resembled Napoleonic warfare than it did World War One.[8] This has been attributed to the difficulty of assimilating new technologies, and also the character of the generalship. The generals have been criticized for a failure to appreciate the defensive strength of rifle fire-power, and for focusing on the acquisition of positions rather than the destruction of opposing armies. Thus, both tactics and strategy have been found wanting.

Conservatism can be seen in a number of respects, including the weaponry used. Muzzle- rather than breech-loading rifles predominated, and this ensured that Napoleonic-style loading routines predominated. This led to volley fire and the accompanying tactics of massing troops in the open in order to increase the weight of the fire. Artillery remained dominated by muzzle-loaders firing solid shot by direct fire. The rifles and cannon were more effective than those of the early 1800s. The Springfield rifle, for example, had a greater effective range than its predecessors, while the cannon used timed fuses, but in neither case did the weapon match the breech-loaders that were soon to dominate battle. In addition, use of the machine gun in the war was limited: the Union Repeating Rifle, or Ager Gun, was used, following on from the Colt machine gun in the Mexican War of 1846–48. However, machine guns made scant impact. Aside from mechanical problems, high rate of ammunition usage and expense, they suffered from being considered eccentric to battlefield dispositions and tactics. Rail brought mobility towards the battlefield, but not on it. The same was true of telegraph and command and control. In neither case had there been a leap forward: this had to wait for the internal combustion engine and radio. The absence of both limited tactical flexibility, affecting the tempo of battle.

Conversely, the organizational achievement of the two sides should be stressed.[9] This can be seen not only in the mobilization and support of large numbers of troops and masses of matériel, but also in the transport and control potential posed by railway, steamship and telegraph.[10] The railway made a major difference in strategy and logistics. It helped the Union mobilize and direct its greatly superior demographic and economic resources, and played a major role in particular battles, and did so from the outset. Reinforcements arriving by train helped the Confederates win at First Manassas/Bull Run (21 July 1861). The following year, Braxton Bragg was able to move his troops 776 miles by rail from Mississippi to Chattanooga and thus create the opportunity for an invasion of Kentucky. Rail junctions, such as Atlanta, Chattanooga, Corinth and Manassas, became strategically significant, and the object of operations. Man-made landscape features created for railways, such as embankments, played a part in battles. The North's dependence on railways led to the South raiding both them and the telegraph wires that attended and controlled them, as with John Morgan's raids in Tennessee and Kentucky in 1862. Similarly, in 1864, Union cavalry in the Atlanta campaign raided the Atlanta and West Point, and Georgia Railroads. After a raid on the Macon and Western Railroad failed, Sherman moved his army to cut it, and forced the Confederates to abandon Atlanta.[11]

The new potential for transport and control created the problem of a new standard of achievement. The difficulty of the task can be underlined, not least the contrast with that facing the Prussian military: the latter had had more time to prepare and had more compact zones of deployment and operations. The Union created US Military Railroads as a branch of the War Department, which did not fully exploit the powers of the President under the 1862 Act, which gave him the authority to take control of the railways. US Military Railroads also built and repaired track and bridges, providing a quickly responsive system to enhance transport links as the exigencies of the war required.

There were also important developments in the infrastructure of government. The Union created a National Bank and introduced income tax and paper currency. Combined with the greater buoyancy of the Northern economy, these measures helped stabilize the finances of the Union: unlike the Confederacy it could raise substantial loans without causing damaging inflation. More generally, Northern society coped better with the burden of supporting the war.

The ability of both sides rapidly to create battle-winning armies able to further strategic plans was critical. This culminated with the command of Ulysses Grant, who was appointed General-in-Chief of the Union Army in 1864. He added a strategic purposefulness and impetus to Union military policy, and subordinated the individual battle to the repeated pressure of campaigning against the Confederates. The near continuous nature of the conflict from his advance in May 1864, which led to the Battle of the Wilderness (5–6 May), combined with heavy casualties, gave the war in the Virginia theatre an attritional character, and ground down the outnumbered Confedarcy, which had a smaller army. The Union not only had a 2.5:1 edge in manpower, but also a formidable advantage in manufacturing plant, railway track and bullion resources. This made it easier to equip the large numbers that were raised. For example, nearly 1½ million Springfields were manufactured, a total that reflected the capability of contemporary industry and one that could not be matched in the Confederacy. The Union also had a far greater capacity to raise both tax revenue and loans, and thus finance what was for America a conflict of unprecedented expense. In his farewell address to his soldiers in April 1865, Lee argued that they had been "compelled to yield to overwhelming power".

Yet it is important not to overestimate the sophistication of the organization on either side. They cannot be described as war machines if that is intended to suggest predictable and regular operating systems that could be readily controlled and adapted. Furthermore, organization was not only a matter of raising and moving resources. It also involved their effective use on the battlefield. In this sphere, both sides experienced major limitations, with the Union lacking the advantage it had in overall resources. The problem of the effective use of resources was seen in particular, with infantry-artillery coordination, which was later to be regarded as very important in twentieth-century conflict, not least in the success of the British in 1918. By these later standards, there was woeful inadequacy in all armies in the mid-nineteenth century. More generally, there were serious deficiencies in the operational dimension of war. It proved difficult to secure adequate concentration and cooperation on the battlefield.

This was true both of the Union and of the Confederacy. Such concentration was required for success in attack and for turning battlefield advantage into victory. Too many assaults were uncoordinated between units and arms (infantry, cavalry and artillery), while a preference for linear formations made it harder to retain unit coherence in the advance and to switch from firepower to shock attack. Organization was made even more important by the lengthy character of individual battles. Gettysburg, for example, was fought over three days. The deficiencies of organization in part reflected the rapid expansion of the armies and the consequent lack of appropriate training on the part of soldiers and officers. The deficiencies of generals were not counteracted by effective staff structures for these were lacking. The nature of the terrain, often heavily wooded and with a low density of roads and tracks, did not help.

Superior resources alone were not enough to guarantee Union success. The Confederates had to be beaten in the field. Furthermore, the resource situation was not always so favourable for the Union as it might appear. Thus, superiority in manpower, did not readily translate into trained troops on the battlefield, let alone the right battlefield. Advancing into the Confederacy, the

Union had to detach steadily more troops to occupy territory and to protect steadily longer supply lines, which were harassed by Confederate guerrillas. This posed serious problems for Union strategists. It reflected the asymmetry of the grand strategic aims of each side: the Confederacy ultimately had only to fend off the Union, which did not require its conquest, whereas the Union had at least to crush Confederate military power and probably to occupy considerable swathes of its territory in order to force it back into the Union.[12]

The successful application of military power was Grant's achievement, and his remorseless and skilful determination had led him to win the Mississippi war by capturing Vicksburg in July 1863.[13] This can be underlined by a consideration of the failures in the east of his well resourced predecessors. These failures also show the role of contingency in determining the outcome of operations. McDowell's advance on Richmond from the north was blocked on 21 July 1861 at First Manassas/Bull Run, a clash in which neither commander behaved adroitly and in which the fate of the struggle hinged not on planning but on the arrival of fresh troops. McClellan's advance on Richmond along the James River in May 1862 after a landing to the east of the city could have been a decisive blow. However, McClellan was no Moltke; he organized for battle but could not win it. McClellan lacked Moltke's fixity of purpose and ability to give rapid operational effect to strategic planning, and also greatly overestimated Confederate strength. A different general might have ended the war by capturing Richmond. Nashville and New Orleans had already fallen in early 1862 and most of Tennessee had been overrun, Grant defeating a Confederate counterattack at Shiloh on 6–7 April.

Instead, Lee reversed the pattern of retreat set by his predecessor, Joseph Johnston, who was wounded on 31 May at the battle of Seven Pines. Lee succeeded in blocking McClellan's cautious advance in the Seven Days battles and went on to regain the initiative.[14] McClellan, who had advocated modest war goals,[15] was replaced in November 1862 and Union goals and methods became more radical. The Union became committed to the emancipation of the slaves and more willing to attack southern society in other respects as well. The high casualties in the repeated battles in the east from Seven Days (26 June–2 July 1862) to Gettysburg (1–3 July 1863) both reflected and encouraged a sense that the war would be a massive struggle that would require unprecedented determination and ruthlessness. The task of conquering the Confederacy, an area of ¾ million square miles, was formidable, and this posed questions for political and military goals, as well as strategy and operational effectiveness.

The last has been found wanting in numerous detailed studies of particular engagements. Poor planning, an inability to implement plans, especially the coordination of units and the interaction of moves with a planned time sequence, and command flaws repeatedly emerge. In many engagements, it is both sides that are found wanting. This was a reflection of the fact that the USA was an unmilitaristic society, which had hitherto not needed to create massive armies, especially in the heat of war. Poor planning had a particularly serious impact on offensive operations as it made it difficult for units to provide adequate levels of mutual support.[16]

In addition, due to defensive fire-power, massed frontal attacks on prepared positions became more costly and unsuccessful, as the Union, in particular, discovered at Second Manassas (29-30 August 1862) and Fredericksburg (13 December 1862), and the Confederates at Corinth (3-4 October 1862), Stones River (31 December 1862-3 January 1863), Gettysburg, and Franklin (30 November 1864). The effectiveness of the defence was increased by the manoeuvrability of riflemen within the relatively compact battlefields. This permitted the ready presentation of new defensive fronts. Most of the casualties inflicted by rifle fire in the war resulted from long-range, accurately aimed defensive fire from behind entrenchments and log breastworks. Both sides learned the necessity of throwing up entrenchments as a consequence of fighting each other to a costly draw at the battle of Antietam (17 September 1862). There the Confederate defenders had taken heavy casualties because they were not entrenched. Bayonets and rifled muskets were increasingly supplemented by, or even downplayed in favour of field fortifications and artillery; a sign of the future character of war between developed powers. The strength of entrenched troops through fire-power became greater as the war continued, not least because the artillery did not find an effectual way of suppressing it, arguably in fact not until the British did so on the Western Front in 1918. As a result, the Union assault on the Confederate lines at Cold Harbour on 3 June 1864 was a bloody disaster.[17]

The Seven Days battle began a series of Confederate advances and victories in the east that affected the political as well as the military development of the struggle. Lee was a figure around whom the Confederates could rally. He understood that Confederate public opinion had a preference for taking the initiative, not responding to Northern moves, and that it sought offensive victories. The way he fought and won was very important to public opinion.[18] Equally, it proved impossible to win lasting success from Lee's victories, not least because the Union army remained in being and because the heavy losses of the Army of Northern Virginia forced Lee to be cautious in exploitation. Furthermore, success in an individual battle was not going to bring the destruction of the opponent's military strength. Conversely, Lincoln also needed to build up Union morale, and, as a result, sought a decisive victory.

The role of counter-factual possibilities is also illustrated by the relationship between Lee's successes and Union war-weariness. The latter might have become stronger and this could have led to greater pressure for peace from within the Union. There was a particularly strong need in the early summer of 1864 for an appearance of success. The heavy casualties in Grant's unsuccessful "Overland" campaign and the initial failure to capture Atlanta hit civilian morale in July and August. Lincoln feared that he would not be re-elected. However, a series of Northern successes in the Petersburg and Atlanta campaigns and in the Shenandoah Valley let Lincoln back in; Atlanta fell to Sherman on 2 September.

The Franco-Prussian War was "total" in one extent, in that Moltke's systematized warfare offered a hitherto unprecedented degree of methodical effectiveness. However, the scale, duration and mobilization of resources of the American Civil War provided a different degree of totality. The willingness to seize and, even more, destroy civilian property was also very marked. Whereas McClellan had opposed attacks on private property, Grant pressed it from the spring of 1862 in order to hit Confederate supplies and, thus, warmaking. This was declaring war on an entire people. It was not novel, and had been employed in counter-insurgency warfare in Europe earlier in the century; but the Americans were certainly not used to it, and the combination of such techniques with the more conventional conflict of the war was arresting in a struggle on this scale. The technique also enabled Grant to live off the land. He used this in order to manoeuvre round Vicksburg, rather as Scott had done in order to capture Mexico City in 1847.

Sherman destroyed $100 million worth of property as he set out to destroy the will of Confederate civilians in1864 by making "Georgia howl". His march in November and December 1864 did indeed, in his words, "cut a swath through to the sea". This was ideological warfare. Sherman set out to punish the Confederates and to cripple their morale, as well as to destroy their infrastructure;[19] and, as a result, sought a decisive victory. His soldiers shared his objectives.[20] The Great Valley of Virginia was devastated by Philip Sheridan in 1864; South Carolina suffering similarly, at Sherman's hands, in February 1865. The ability to spread devastation unhindered across the Southern hinterland helped destroy Confederate civilian faith in the war, and also made the penalty and limitation of guerrilla warfare apparent. Sherman had also destroyed the strategic reserve and economic resources provided by the size of the Confederacy. Slavery was also badly hit: thousands of slaves used the opportunities of Sherman's advance to escape their masters. The movement of Sherman's army into North Carolina in March 1865 was an instance of the indirect approach that has been overshadowed by Grant's successes against Lee in Virginia: Sherman's advance threatened Lee's rear.

Another aspect of "totality" was suggested by the character of warfare round Petersburg in 1864–65, at once attritional and prefiguring the siege tactics of World War One. The first recorded battlefield appearance of barbed wire (originally devised to pen cattle in) occurred at Drewry's Bluff in May 1864. Edward Porter Alexander, a Confederate artillery general, recorded of the Union bombardment of the trenches defending Petersburg:

> Beside his 60 mortar, Abbot also manned a tremendous battery of forty 30 pr. rifles, and six 100 pr. rifles . . . we . . . only built up our parapets thicker and let his big guns shoot.

We soon got our lines at most places in such shape that we did not fear any assault, but meanwhile this mortar firing had commenced and that added immensely to the work in the trenches. Every man needed a little bombproof to sleep in at night, and to dodge into in the day when the mortar shells were coming. They soon honeycombed the rear side of the trenches with all sorts of little caves and cellars . . . We could see that the Federals too were working like beavers, and every morning there appeared fresh piles and lines of red dirt thrown up during the night all along their front.[21]

The direct legacy of the American Civil War was political rather than military. There was a swift return to civil peace, legitimacy, and unity. There was not only no powerful revanchist movement for Southern separatism, but also, in order to win, with the important exception of the emancipation of the slaves, the Union had not embarked on a radicalizing process akin to that which eventually affected England in the Civil War, or France in 1793–94. The USA remained a united state dominant in the Western hemisphere and without the source of division that an independent Confederacy would have provided. This was crucial to global history: the century was to close with Britain and the USA the two most powerful countries in the world. However, the disbanding of the forces raised for the American Civil War ensured a lack of continuity that meant that the military lessons learned were not retained. Furthermore, the USA did not embark for another 50 years on a great power war that might have kept such lessons pertinent. Instead, prior to the outbreak of war with Spain in 1898, the American military engaged in conflict with Native Americans, a very different experience in terms of practice and relevant doctrine.

In the 1860s, American politics and society were not stamped with the marks of a permanent militarization, and, in the short term, there was a lack of promotion in the much reduced army, and an emphasis on peacetime professionalism.[22] Not only did the Americans not invade Canada, as was feared, but the troops stationed in the former Confederacy to support Reconstruction left in 1877 (and by then there were very few). In addition, northern politicians and public opinion came to support reconciliation. Lee received good obituaries in the northern press, and in 1898 the surviving Confederate generals were made US generals. Although there were four Black regiments in the post-Civil War army, there was no Black presence in the reconciliast view, much to the anger of Black veterans and leaders.

Spain

The American Civil War was not the sole civil conflict of the period. In both Spain and Latin America there were civil wars. The Spanish revolution of

1868, in which Queen Isabel was overthrown by an army rebellion after loyalist troops were defeated at Alcolea on 28 September, led to an insurrection in Cuba that was only suppressed after ten years. It also led to the Second Carlist War of 1873–6. This was less serious than the First, because support for the Carlists was largely restricted to the north, especially Navarre and upland Catalonia. They were also affected by disunity, by the opposition of the major towns, and by the lack of an adequate supply base or administration. Again, there was a series of major clashes that do not feature in general military histories, for example La Junquera, Mañeru and Tolosa in 1873 and Mora in 1874. The same was true of the civil conflicts in Latin America, such as that in Uruguay in 1843–52. The last Carlist field army was crushed at Montejurra in 1876. Aside from the Second Carlist War, there was also in Spain a radical and anti-centralist Cantonalist uprising at a number of cities in 1873. The Cantonalists, however, suffered from disunity and a reliance on militia forces. They were quickly suppressed other than in Cartagena, which was blockaded by land and sea; the rebels surrendered in January 1874.

In the war in Cuba, the rebels concentrated on trying to take advantage of the rugged terrain by using ambushes. Taking advantage of cover, they were able to harry Spanish forces with rifle fire. This was especially so if the Spaniards formed squares as at Palo Seco in 1873. This enabled the Spaniards to provide disciplined volley fire, but that was not an appropriate response.[23] However, the Spaniards benefited greatly from ethnic, geographical and social divisions among the Cubans and the willingness of many to support Spain. From 1870, the Spaniards benefited in particular from ethnic tension as Whites increasingly rejected what they now saw as an Black-run rebellion.[24] Once the Carlists had been overcome, 25,000 troops were sent to Cuba and a combination of military action and conciliatory promises led to a settlement in 1878.

Latin America

The Mexican civil war of the 1860s attracts some non-specialist attention because of European intervention, although the earlier civil conflict between the liberal government of Benito Juárez and conservative opponents, the War of Reform (1857–60), is generally ignored. Instability and a default on international debts led to intervention by Britain, France and Spain in 1861. In 1862, however, the French sought to take this limited intervention further. French troops arrived, and, in the face of bold French imperialistic goals, the other powers withdrew. The following year, the French captured Mexico City and Puebla, and Napoleon III encouraged the offer of the Mexican throne by Juárez's opponents to Archduke Ferdinand Maximilian, the brother of the Austrian Emperor. However, the attempt of Emperor

Maximilian to take over Mexico was mishandled and met a strong national-ist response. There was a long guerrilla war led by Juárez, with few conven-tional battles, and French backing, although 40,000 troops at the peak, was both insufficient and not maintained. The French benefited from naval sup-port on both coastlines, and on land were able to seize positions, such as Oaxaca in 1865, but this did not stabilize the situation. Maximilian also had a 7,100-strong Austrian volunteer corps, but they were hit by yellow fever and only infrequently encountered the enemy. Yellow fever was a particular problem round Veracruz, Mexico's leading port and the key base for French intervention.

After the American Civil War, American pressure led Napoleon in Febru-ary 1866 to decide to withdraw his forces. Juárez had already received covert support from Union forces during the American Civil War. The last French troops left in March 1867, and Maximilian, who refused to leave, was defeated at Queretaro, and shot in June.[25] The French had been more success-ful in 1838 when they had staged a more limited intervention in order to punish the Mexicans for depredations against French citizens. The French had then bombarded Veracruz and seized a fort there.

Elsewhere in the Western world, there was a major national revolt in Poland in January 1863 that was suppressed in April 1864 by Russian forces supported by Prussia, although fighting continued until 1865. This was a prominent example of the more common process by which military forces were used to maintain order across the Western world. Thus troops were deployed against nationalist agitation, worker demands and rural opposition. In newly united Italy, for example, a large army and the use of terror subdued peasant opposition in the south, where there was widespread brigandage. Sicily rebelled in 1866.

As suggested in the previous chapter, these conflicts have been underrated, as indeed has been the internal political role of armed forces. In general, internal military operations, when they involved conflict, saw less of an emphasis on battle or siege than war between regular forces did. Instead, there was a greater stress on militarized policing, the maintenance of fortified positions and of cordons round areas where opponents were believed to operate, and the pursuit of rebel "bands". In this respect, there was a parallel with operations against non-Western peoples, for example hostile Native Americans, or Maoris, or the native tribes in Argentina.

Conventional wars involved a greater willingness to engage in operations that led to the risk of battle, although due weight should also be given to smaller-unit clashes. These were relatively unimportant when conflict was short, as with the Franco-Austrian war of 1859 and the high tempo Wars of German Unification, and where the field of hostilities was not too extensive, as in the Crimea. Conversely, in longer and more far-flung conflicts the dominance of the entire war by battles between armies was less pronounced. This was particularly so in civil conflicts. Thus, in the American Civil War, alongside the movements of the major armies, there was much raiding, as well as widespread guerrilla warfare across a large area.[26]

In South America, there were two major wars between 1864 and 1883, each arising from the conflation of territorial demands and nationalist pressures. The War of the Triple Alliance of 1864–70 opposed Argentina, Brazil and the Uruguayan to the expansionist Paraguay. This was a major conflict. 330,000 died, many in savage battles in 1866, and Paraguay was devastated. The allies occupied the capital Asunción on 1 January 1869, and the Paraguayan leader, Francisco Solano López, the Marshal-President, was killed in March 1870, bringing hostilities to a close. The inability to reach a negotiated end to the conflict was crucial to the character of the War of the Triple Alliance. López fought to the death; there was no Appomattox. His removal was one of the conditions of the Allies.

The war arose as a result of López's interest in expanding towards the Plate estuary, possibly by incorporating Uruguay. A Brazilian invasion of Uruguay in September 1864 had driven the Blanco party from power and instead put in the Colorados. This was unacceptable to López. In 1865, campaigning began with bold Paraguayan advances, first north into the Mato Grosso region of Brazil, and then south east towards Uruguay. The latter took the Paraguayans across Argentina, and, rather than limit his number of opponents, López declared war when access was refused. López captured Corrientes and advanced to the Uruguay frontier, but the advantage of beginning the war had not been translated into any defeat of his opponents in detail. Instead, the Brazilians regained the initiative and blocked López's advance, forcing about 5,500 Paraguayans to surrender at Uruguayana on 18 September and pushing López back onto the defensive.

As in the American Civil War, infantry tactics relied heavily on frontal attacks. Thus, the Argentinian attack on entrenched Paraguayan forces at Curupaity (22 September 1866) was repelled with very heavy losses. The Brazilians were more successful at Ytororó (6 December 1868), but the Paraguayan forces inflicted heavy casualties on their assailants before being pushed back. On 21 December 1868, the Brazilians launched another frontal attack, throwing two columns against a Paraguayan trench at Itá-Ybaté. The Brazilians did not use their artillery well, and, although their forces penetrated through the trench position, the defenders eventually fought them off. However, the defending force had been so worn down that on 27 December 1868 it succumbed to a far larger attacking army. Allied tactics were more sophisticated in 1869, enveloping the greatly outnumbered Paraguayan defenders near Piribebuy on 12 August and making a more effective use of artillery. However, in contrast to North America, where railroads and steamships eased logistical problems, the difficult terrain and the weakness of transport systems placed a very heavy burden on logistical capability. Nevertheless, the river Paraguay did provide a crucial route for the invaders. On 11 June 1865, in the battle of Riachuelo the Brazilian fleet beat off an attack by the outgunned Paraguayan fleet. In 1868, the Brazilian fleet pushed past Paraguayan forts to arrive off Asuncion. The major Paraguayan river fort of Humaita was soon after abandoned. The ability of the Brazilian fleet to gain control of the rivers was crucial to the fate of the struggle.[27]

In the War of the Pacific between Chile, Bolivia and Peru in 1879–83, sea routes offered better transport links, necessarily so as the world's driest desert was at stake. The conflict was waged over the rich deposits of nitrates in the Atacama Desert. In part this dispute reflected the demands of war, as nitrates were of great value for explosives as well as for fertilizers. Bolivia's demand for more revenue from an Anglo-Chilean company working the deposits triggered the crisis. Peru supported Bolivia, but in 1879 Chile overcame serious initial lack of preparation.[28] The Chileans landed an army at Antofagasta on 14 February and advanced to overrun the Bolivian Pacific coastline and then to press on to invade southern Peru: Tarapacá in 1879 and Arica and Tacna in 1880. After the Chilean naval success off Punta de Angamos on 8 October 1879, the Peruvian garrison of Iquique fell to blockade that November; that in Arica fell to a night-time storming (1880). The capture of Arica threw light on both the vulnerability and the importance of fortified positions. Exposed to attack as a result of Chilean naval strength, the strongly fortified port, nevertheless, successfully resisted a naval bombardment on 27 February–3 March. However, the Chilean troops landed and overran the remainder of the province, ensuring that the garrison was left isolated. Even so it had to be captured, and, as a land bombardment failed to force a capitulation, the Chileans had to be willing to suffer casualties in a storming.

In the autumn of 1880, the Chileans used their naval strength to range further north attacking the coast north of Callao in order to inflict material damage and underline a sense of vulnerability rather as Sherman had done. Railways and ports were destroyed or damaged and private property seized.

Having landed as Pisco just south of Callao, and defeated the Peruvians at Chorillos (13 January 1881) and Miraflores (15 January 1881), the Chileans captured Callao and Lima. Chile held Callao and Lima until after fighting ended in 1883. The Peruvians had lost their centres of population, but, as earlier in the War of Independence, resistance continued in the interior. It was not suppressed until July 1883.

Continued Bolivian opposition only ended when the Chileans invaded. The subsequent peace left Chile with Bolivia's Pacific coastline and with the provinces of Tarapacá, Arica and Tacna. Again, this was a war of neglected battles, such as Calama, Pisagua and Tarapaca in 1879 and Campo de la Alianza in 1880. The availability of European weaponry was important. So also was Chilean amphibious capability. As with colonial operations in Africa, this was a war of rapid advances, and where problems of supply encouraged the high-risk tactic of frontal assaults. In addition, there was not the time to bring up heavy artillery in order to attack fortified positions.[29] While Chile,

Bolivia and Peru fought this war, the Argentinian army was conquering Patagonia, an extension of the "Conquest of the Desert" in which native peoples had been brutally subjugated.[30]

Balkan warfare

Balkan conflicts focused on Turkey in this period. They are covered in Chapter 5, although the Turkish forces that resisted Balkan opponents, for example the rebellion on Crete that broke out in 1866, could be placed in the context of European military history. The rising, which followed earlier risings in 1841 and 1858, broadened out into a Greco-Turkish war in which naval superiority enabled the Turks to maintain their position.

The war of 1877–78 between Russia, Serbia and Montenegro and Turkey was a bitter struggle that led to the acceptance of the independence of Serbia, Romania and Montenegro, while Bulgaria became an autonomous principality within the Turkish Empire. Uprisings in Herzegovina and Bosnia in 1875 and in Bulgaria in 1876 were preludes to the conflict. In 1876, Serbia and Montenegro declared war on the Turks. Turkish victory over the Serbs at Aleksinac (1 September 1876) and Djunis (29 October) and the Turkish refusal to accept the proposals of an international conference led the Russians to declare war the following April. The intervention of Russian forces (1877–8), and the degree of development of the Serbian army, ensured that the military situation was very different to that in the first quarter of the century, when there had been revolts in, first, Serbia and, then, Moldavia and Wallachia. The same was true of Greece. Although her armed forces were routed by the Turks in 1897, they were different in organization and character to those that had fought in the war of liberation in the 1820s. Yet the Greeks had also sent irregulars into Thessaly, Epiros and Macedonia to attack the Turks both during the Crimean War and again in 1877–78.

Conclusions

The Greek use of irregulars is a reminder of the danger, even during the heyday of Prussian influence, of assuming that there was a European, let alone Western, paradigm of war. This becomes even more clear when social and political contexts are considered. A stress on multiplicity undermines attempts to draw unitary conclusions. For example, Russell Weigley, claimed that:

> the Peninsular War . . . signaled the imminent eclipse of the age of battles. Before the close of the next great war – the American Civil

War – rival military chieftains would have abandoned the quest for rapid strategic decision through the climactic battle to adopt instead a strategy much like Wellington's in Iberia, relying on superior management of resources, both manpower and matériel to wear down the enemy and outlast him in a prolonged contest of attrition. The age of battles gave way to exchanges of casualties and resources in sustained combat on the pattern of the late campaigns of the American Civil War.[31]

Well, not if one wishes to describe the quick and decisive offensive campaigns of 1866 and 1870. The Russians at Plevna might have got bogged down in what can be described as an early form of trench warfare, but it was as part of a war (1877–78) in which they won a rapid victory. Furthermore, Plevna looked back, via Sevastopol to say Lille in 1708, the siege of which cost the besiegers 14,000 men, and Ostend in 1601–1604, as much as forward to World War One. Instead it is the specificity of conflict as much as its shaping into overarching theses that emerges from consideration of Weigley's conclusion. In the Peninsular War, Wellington sought to wear down the larger French forces, adopting a war-making technique that was closer to the Confederacy than to the Union; although, unlike the Confederacy, he benefited from naval power and was not defending his home base, both important reminders of specificity.

As far as attrition is concerned, Union strategy in 1864–65 has to be understood more widely than by a focus simply on the Virginia theatre. Union forces were more successful than the Allies in 1915–17 in finding a vulnerable opposing flank, although it was much easier, not least because there was much more space in which to operate in 1861–65. Sherman demonstrated the possibility and value of manoeuvre, just as Moltke was to do in 1870–71.

The Franco-Prussian War is a good point at which to probe changes in the culture of war. The focus on planning, and staff generalship and officers in the Prussian army and in those forces that were to be influenced by it marked a shift from an earlier practice of command that had placed less of an emphasis on sequential planning and prior organization and, instead, more of a stress on boldness, such as was the ethos of the *ancien régime* and of French Revolutionary and Napoleonic generalship. Although administrative aspects of command, such as recruitment and logistics, were known to be of great consequence, they did not determine the culture of warfare; just as the character of the domestic rule of kings was not decided by the financial issues that they knew to be important. Monarchs were expected to win glory through victory and conquest, priorities that were very much taken up by Napoleon. Napoleon III continued this tradition, and indeed was only dissuaded with great difficulty from going out to the Crimea. In the Franco-Prussian War, command positions were given to members of the Prussian royal family, but they were subordinated to a system.

There had also been an important shift in the character of international and domestic politics. Whereas, in the first half of the century, nationalism had largely been a liberal cause, this had ceased to be the case and, instead, in many states nationalism had become linked to state interest and conservative groups and tendencies. In international terms, this was related to a new legitimation of conflict in which a territorial aggrandizement was conceived and presented as of benefit to states rather than dynasties. In place of historic claims, the rationalism of expansionism focused on a logic of national identity and state interest.

CHAPTER EIGHT
Social and Political Contexts

Armies and navies were not forces "outside" society, but rather reflections of patterns of social control and influence, and the beliefs that gave cohesion to them. They have to be understood in this context. The most valuable and sustained attempt to develop a taxonomy and analysis of the development of military organizations, by John Lynn, locates the period in terms of a transition between three types of "army style": state-commission, popular-conscript, and mass-reserve. These are related to civilian-military relations and to the more general issues of state-building, and social change. Thus, the former characterized the *ancien régime* military, the second the French Revolutionary and Napoleonic period, and the third was particularly associated with Moltke's Prussian army and its emulators.[1]

This thesis has much to recommend it, but it suffers from the limitations of the paradigmatic approach and from the variety of military systems that co-existed. More specifically, it is necessary to consider the pressures that arose from asymmetrical as well as symmetrical warfare. Thus, for example, between 1830 and 1882, Britain, France and Russia all had to confront the operational and organizational problems posed by bitter resistance to the advancing frontiers of European control in, for example, India and South Africa, Algeria, and the Caucasus, Central Asia, and the Balkans respectively. Thus, far from the German army being paradigmatic, it was eccentric to the general pattern of colonizing states. The British, French and Russian armies had broader spectrum missions than that of Germany and required a correspondingly flexible, or at least differentiated, organization and ethos. These challenges were, in part, addressed by developing particular military practices and institutions that centred on the use of large numbers of native troops.

An abandonment of a paradigmatic approach suggests that it is more appropriate to focus on the particular needs of individual states and the manner in which these shaped military requirements. These needs can be seen in terms of political and social contexts. Thus, for example, to take an obvious point about the 1860s, the American army of the period was shaped by the sudden requirement to confront the secessionists in the Confederacy. This led to a total, albeit short-lived, reshaping of the military environment. Thus, conscription for the Confederacy was introduced in April 1862, and for the Union in March 1863; while generals had to respond at the same time to the problems of directing large bodies of men and to campaigning against an insurgency. Once war ceased, conscription was abandoned in the USA, while it was not practised in Britain throughout the period. Thus, the practice and ethos of recruitment varied, subverting any paradigmatic approach.

Given Britain's role as the world's leading power and the importance of the rise of the USA, it is surprising that more attention is not paid to their military cultures and practices. Although neither fitted into the Prussian paradigm, they were very different from each other, a reminder of the variety of the military history of the period that cannot be disguised by an emphasis on common developments in military technology. The Americans did not share the British emphasis on a navy nor the large colonial army, much of it recruited from subject and allied people, that the British had in India. Conversely, the British lacked the emphasis on militia that the Americans displayed in the War of 1812.[2] There were comparisons; the professionalism of Scott's army in Mexico in 1847 matched that of British regulars. However, the large forces deployed in the American Civil War were not matched in the British case until World War One, when, again, there was an emphasis on frontal assaults, in part because the tactic seemed most appropriate to large forces that had only limited training.

Recruitment

The importance of voluntary service varied considerably in the Western world but its existence reflected the appeal of the military life for many. It provided a career, and an escape from the burdens of civilian life, or the constraints of local society on young adult males. A valuable source of voluntary enlistment, matching what happened in many spheres of civilian life, was provided by the sons of soldiers and sailors.

The use of foreign soldiers was popular with many rulers, but decreasingly so in the nineteenth century. Foreign troops were felt to be more reliable politically, particularly in the event of domestic disorder. Encapsulating what could be the isolating effect of military life, their use avoided the problem of arming the population.

Yet, the willingness of governments to arm the people is more striking than their occasional hesitation. Training in the use of arms was given to what must have appeared the most unreliable members of the community. Many were from criminal backgrounds. For example, Russian peasants belonging to the patrimony of the crown were allowed to hand over migrants, landless labourers and other unwanted members of their villages to the army as a first stage in meeting their conscription quota. The willingness of governments to arm the poor and the marginal members of the community is an interesting indication of their confidence in the essential stability of the social order, as mirrored in the armed forces, and in the ability of discipline to direct action and attitudes. This was a view that was to be vindicated by the infrequency of army and naval mutinies.

Prior to the French Revolution, conscription systems were furthest developed in central and eastern Europe, possibly reflecting the greater indifference to personal liberties. To work effectively, these systems entailed considerable regulation of the population, which could only be achieved by means of the cooperation of the nobility, the local arm of the government across most of Europe. As the bulk of the officer corps was drawn from the same group, recruitment fitted into the same command structure. Governments regulated and benefited from this system and it was less dangerous for them than the older practice of nobles raising mercenary bands and directing them as they pleased.

The system also had hidden costs, leading to a degree of inflexibility and underlining the aristocratic control of the army. Behind the systems of conscription, and the militarist patina that they gave to society, with their passes, registers, annual inspections, musters, lists and numbers painted on houses, was the constant reality of aristocratic domination of society. The largest system of conscription was that in Russia, where serfdom lessened the scope of voluntary enlistment. Manpower was summoned by proportional levies on the male population liable for service. In contrast, French forces were raised voluntarily in the case of the regulars and by conscription in that of the militia.

Force and trickery were frequently employed in recruitment, which was not helped by the harshness of military life. The behaviour of soldiers, the attitude towards them of some officers, a group with whom they had little social affinity, the prevalence of desertion, and the need for drill led to discipline that was often savage. The limited effectiveness of the weaponry ensured that troops had to come close to the enemy, a frightening experience. The complicated loading drill for weapons required the conditioning of soldiers to repeat them under stress: the effect of weapon fire depended on the standard of fire discipline. Drill and discipline were therefore military necessities.

Recruitment, and the ability to mobilize resources for war in general, reflected the nature of society: the combination of a cash economy (which provided a basis for taxation), under-employment and governments that wielded great authority over the bulk of the population, although not the social élite, created the context for the major mobilization of manpower for war. The general assumption was that much of the male population would serve if required and on terms that they did not influence, and that their views on the purposes and methods of warfare would not be sought.

Conditions

In war, casualty rates were often high. Peacetime service was less dangerous, but the desire to prepare troops for future conflict was not always matched by care for them. Mutinies were rare, but desertion was far more common. It was a dangerous protest against often desperate conditions and was harshly punished. In general, training was harsh, discipline could be brutal and the conditions of service in terms of accommodation, food and pay were poor, although not always worse than those in civilian society. The slow spread of barracks, an expensive device, ensured that troops were often quartered among the civilian population. This policy made it harder to maintain discipline and train troops, and even harder to develop a distinctive military attitude. The use of barracks became more important in Austria, France and Prussia in the second half of the eighteenth century, but barracks were often unpleasant for the soldiers, frequently being gloomy, damp and insanitary. They contributed to what was often the boring character of peacetime life for soldiers.

The lack of interest in the views of soldiers and sailors did not mean that rulers, generals and admirals were oblivious to the condition of their troops and to casualties. They were well aware that poor food and accommodation could lead to debilitating diseases, although adequate provision was difficult to secure, especially on campaign. The military were a section of the community that governments needed and therefore cared for, albeit at a basic level. Although pay was generally low and was frequently delayed, troops were the largest group paid and provided for by governments.

Training seems to have created a bond, not only between soldiers but also between troops and their officers. Discipline was not always as savage in practice as it was in theory, a common feature of the law enforcement of the period, which was often tempered and episodic. In the Prussian army, only a relatively small number of hard cases received a disproportionate number of the most severe punishments. Frederick II used the death penalty very sparingly. Although even the most junior officer could inflict harsh penalties, the most vivid accounts of the horrors of Prussian discipline were misleading and selective. Experienced troops could be difficult to replace; new recruits were of limited value until blooded.

Although force played a role in the British navy, especially in recruitment, sailors were part of a trained unit, the crew of a warship, whose operational effectiveness reflected teamwork and high morale, rather than coercion. British sailors were paid far less in wartime than those in the merchant navy, desertion was a serious problem, and there was a major naval mutiny in 1797, but the food was of reasonably high quality, efforts were made to limit sickness and the ship was the essential unit of sailors' loyalty.

Medical services improved on sea and land during the period. During the War of American Independence, Admiral Rodney took great care of the health of his fleet in the West Indies. He supported the efforts of the fleet's doctor, Gilbert Blane, who emphasized the use of fresh fruit to deal with scurvy, and the importance of sanitation. Blane's recommendation of lemon juice as a weapon against scurvy led to its routine use in the British navy from 1796, and deaths due to the disease fell dramatically. Improvements in the health of seamen made it easier to maintain blockades.

On land, poor handling of the fevers that ravaged the 1809 Walcheren expedition led to the dismissal of all the members of the recently founded British Medical Board. However, James McGrigor, Surgeon General in the Peninsular War from 1811, presided over an impressive hospital system, and Dominique Larrey, who held the senior medical post in Napoleon's *Grande Armée*, designed the first purpose-built field ambulance, which contained equipment for field operations prior to the evacuation of the wounded, and he also improved the technique of amputations in order to reduce the risk of subsequent infection. Nevertheless, the Crimean War was to reveal serious deficiencies in the British, French and Russian armies, and to lead to pressure for improvements. This was taken further as a consequence of the plight of the wounded in the Franco-Austrian war of 1859. The Red Cross was founded. Nevertheless, disease still continued to be a serious problem, typhus, for example, killing many during the Franco-Prussian War of 1870–71.

The French Revolutionary/Napoleonic Period

Revolutionary France required a great number of troops to face an unprecedented range of foreign and domestic opponents. It swiftly became clear that volunteers alone would not suffice. By the start of 1793, there were too few troops left. The Revolutionary government's *levée en masse* ended the distinction between the volunteer professional army and the conscript militia. Such powers of conscription were not new in Europe, and, particularly as a result of draft avoidance and desertion, it proved difficult to raise the numbers that had been anticipated. Nevertheless, for France, land warfare was raised to a new level of scale. The mutual impact of warfare and growing national feeling were linked to the expansion of conscription. Yet desertion serves as a reminder of the degree to which the willingness to serve was contingent. Politics, in the widest sense, was as important as government in generating numbers.[3]

The spread of French control ensured that the impact of conscription widened. For example, conscription was introduced into the Austrian Netherlands and later the Kingdom of Holland when they were annexed, while France's ally Bavaria introduced it in 1804–1805, as did the client state of Naples in 1809. The army of the Kingdom of Italy grew from 23,000 in 1805 to 90,000 in 1813. The majority of those sent from it to fight in Spain, Russia and Germany died. The Grand Duchy of Warsaw had to man a 30,000-strong army, much of which died in Russia in 1812.[4]

The large numbers raised fed through into casualty figures. Over a million Frenchmen died as a result of the French Revolutionary and Napoleonic Wars. Partly as a consequence, France's population grew by less than 50 per cent in 1750–1850, while that of England nearly tripled. This contrast can in part be attributed to a fall in the French birth rate arising from the spread of birth control in the late eighteenth century, but repeated choices for war were also important.

A military ethos centred on the ideal of patriotic citizen-soldiers was not restricted to France. It also characterized the American War of Independence and the unsuccessful Polish uprising of 1794. In practice, most of the officers in these forces were men of property, but the developments of the Revolutionary period suggested that armies could serve to overthrow established social and political lineaments rather than to reflect and strengthen them. This toppling of much of the *ancien régime* was achieved by the armies of Revolutionary France, and in so doing they were certainly revolutionary. In addition, the French Revolution and the revolutionary ethos and purposes of the French army in the 1790s transformed the political context of military activity, freeing greater resources for warfare.

Established methods of waging war were challenged not only by the Revolutionary French, but also in countries where the government was overthrown, for example Spain in 1808,[5] or where there was a popular reaction against alien rule, as in Ireland in 1798 against the British and in Serbia in 1804 against the Turks. In these cases, the state monopoly on organized violence broke down. This helped ensure that Western warfare remained far from uniform. The Serbian rebels were able to defeat Turkish regulars at Ivankovac (1805) and Misar (1806) and then captured Belgrade. Cooperating with the Russians, the Serbs again won at Varvarin (1810), but the end of war between Russia and the Turks in 1812 permitted a concentration of Turkish forces and the rebels were beaten in 1813, although there was a fresh uprising in 1815 under Milos Obrenovic, which led to the Serbs gaining semi-autonomous status. The contrast between the fate of the 1804 Serbian revolt and those in the USA, and, later, Greece, indicated the importance of foreign intervention.

In 1775–1815, autonomous, mass patriotic action could thus be very important. It has been overshadowed by Napoleonic generalship, and it is true that "popular" warfare was on the whole suppressed, as in Ireland in

1798, or contained. Indeed, Revolutionary/Napoleonic France witnessed a major containment of the radical potential and practice of the Revolution, and a suppression of popular anti-Revolutionary forces, as in the suppression of the Federalist rising and of the Vendée. Within Napoleonic Europe, most areas did not rebel and most uprisings were suppressed, including those in Calabria in 1806–11 and in the Tyrol in 1809, although not in Spain. With Prussian support, the Russians suppressed opposition in Poland. Nevertheless, governments and armies had to develop counter-insurgency policies. In Calabria, the French eventually, in 1810–11, cut the guerrillas off from the peasantry and used flying columns to bring mobility and decisiveness to their hunt for the former.[6]

More generally, governmental control was reimposed on the organized use of force, in France, elsewhere in Europe, and in the USA, where, after 1783, the new state acted to suppress violent opposition. The process was to be repeated in Latin America after Spanish and Portuguese authority had been overthrown, but it proved difficult to end civil conflict and the habit of contesting government through violence.

After 1815

The latter was also increasingly an issue in post-Napoleonic Europe. Liberal and nationalist politicians challenged the authority of autocratic rulers and the anti-nationalist character of the territorial settlement decreed by the Congress of Vienna. This dissidence led to a number of uprisings in the 1820s, 1830s and 1840s, and challenged the practice of conscription. The Habsburg army responded by keeping an Austrian grip on its polyglot forces. The language of command was German and most of the officers were Austrian.

Furthermore, the generally peaceful nature of the years immediately after the defeat of Napoleon, in so far as large-scale international conflict was concerned, encouraged post-war demobilization. Some of those who were demobilized took service in the Latin American Wars of Independence. Fewer soldiers were required in Europe. In conjunction with the danger of mass forces revealed by the French Revolution, this encouraged a shift back towards long-service troops whose reliability was assured. In France, the restored Bourbons suspended conscription and cut the size of the army (although it rose again after the military edict of 1818). This was part of an ideological purge. The restored Bourbons also had Ney shot, removed 15,000 Napoleonic officers, added chaplains to every battalion, brought in foreign aristocrats as commanders, and sought to ensure a stability that critics interpreted as inertia. The French relied on volunteers supported by conscripts produced by a national lottery.

169

It was not until mid-century that the need for troops dramatically increased again. This was met by the use of large reserve armies. Conscripts served for two or three years and then entered the reserves, ensuring that substantial forces of trained men could be mobilized in the event of war, and that the state did not have to pay them in peace. This gave Germany numerical superiority over France, which continued to rely on long-service regulars, and had a smaller and less effective reserve than the Germans.[7] In 1870, the Germans could call on nearly a million troops.

Compulsory military service was underscored by the social politics of Europe, especially patterns of organized and obedient social behaviour. In particular, the social conservatism of the peasantry, and the widespread sway of nationalist sentiment helped foster a situation in which conscription worked, although it is important not to exaggerate willingness to serve. Opposition to the Italian government was so pronounced in 1866 that when 105,000 18-year-olds were conscripted to fight Austria, those from disaffected Naples, Sicily and Sardinia were excepted.[8] Whatever the means of raising troops, habits of deference were important for the tactics of the period. Deployment in massed formations that were vulnerable to infantry and artillery fire, and frontal assaults both entailed the risk of high casualties. Many factors explained why men were willing to do this, including comradeship and conviction.

At the same time, it is important not to exaggerate the willingness of all men to risk death. Many advances disintegrated as men saw comrades die, especially when the defensive situation seemed very forbidding. This helped to ensure that officers led from the front, seeking to encourage their men, and thus taking particularly heavy casualties. The very variable determination of units and forces was probably as crucial a factor in success as generalship or weaponry, and often more so. For example, after the defeat of the French Imperial forces, the Germans in 1870–71 benefited from the much lower morale of the French republican armies.[9]

Social conservatism was seen in reserve and militia units as well as in the regulars. A stress on the protection of order and property helped underwrite their use against domestic challenges. This was seen not only in Europe but also with the National Guard in the USA.[10]

At the same time, more than social conservatism was at stake. The idea of the citizen soldier was important in liberal circles, especially in France and Italy. More generally, there was a romanticization of military life and war throughout the West. It varied in its hold, was often more effective for the would-be or new soldier than for those with much experience, and did not prevent desertion. Nevertheless, military life and conflict were generally presented as manly and noble. They were applauded, praised and eulogized in popular song and church service, processions and celebrations, and print and on canvas. The uniforms presented military life as glamorous, even at the expense of utilitarian considerations.[11] This romanticism has been seen as sustaining morale in the bloody combat conditions of the American Civil War, although the role of religious conviction in this struggle should not be under-rated.[12] The same was probably true elsewhere, and not only in those conflicts that can be presented as having an ideological dimension, such as the Polish uprisings against Russia.

Aside from men, the military also demanded munitions and money. The per capita cost of soldiers remained an issue thanks to the large numbers under arms, but became more so, as weaponry specifications rose. In addition, the cost of artillery rose. Aside from cost, there was also a need to provide munitions that taxed the industrial capability of countries, but also stimulated economic growth and technological progress in the long run, especially as, after the Napoleonic Wars, muskets, cannon and warships were rapidly made redundant by a series of technical changes. This led to greater attention being devoted to the creation of effective national armaments industries, capable and willing to respond rapidly to demands for plentiful supplies of up-to-date weaponry. This need posed problems of industrial structure and investment availability. The funding and management of change became issues in military development and state oversight to an hitherto unprecedented extent. These overlapped with already existing control issues, such as the provision of sufficient gunpowder or horses. Alongside battles of hitherto unparalleled scale – Wagram (1809) with 341,000 troops and 1,022 cannon, and Leipzig (1813) with about 560,000 troops and about 2,070 cannon – there were also simultaneous deployments of large numbers, both in the same campaigning zone and across a full range of zones. This was not new – Philip II of Spain and Louis XIII, XIV, and XV of France had all deployed troops across a number of zones – but the scale from the 1790s was unprecedented.

Multiple-front wars placed a great emphasis on strategic skill, as it was necessary to decide how best to allocate resources between zones (fronts is generally not the appropriate term as it suggests a linear coherence that was commonly absent). This decision-making involved both political and military considerations and was a crucial example of the interaction of the two. In the case of alliances, military were generally subordinate to political considera-tions. The ability of Napoleon to ignore his allies helped give him a vital advantage in this sphere.

The military itself, on the whole, was under greater state control in the nineteenth century than it had been in many states prior to the French Revolutionary Wars. Aristocratic proprietorship of units had declined. In place of units being raised by military entrepreneurs, there was a system of state control, even conscription. This had consequences for command. Governments had more choice over whom to appoint, and thus in the disci-plining and promotion of officers. In 1784, having been angered by grave mistakes in tactics that he had observed during recent manoeuvres in Silesia, Frederick II had General von Erlach arrested and ordered officers to take a course to teach them how to train soldiers.[13]

The treatment of commanders and officers during the French Revolutionary and Napoleonic Wars witnessed a marked increase in governmental control. Political reliability became an important issue, interacting with the clientage and factionalism that were already present. This remained the case after 1815, especially in states prone to major and violent changes in regime, such as France and Spain. However, placing a premium on political reliability could lead to a compromising of military efficiency. There were numerous examples of this, both in Revolutionary forces, as in France in 1794, and in their conservative counterparts. Indeed, rather than suggesting that reliability might compromise efficiency, the issue could be reconceptualized to suggest that the issue of reliability took precedence and was seen as a prime definition of efficiency. Thus, the notion of a depoliticized command system defined and organized by talent emerged as an aspect, and construct, of the notion of an impersonal state that was important to the ideology of nineteenth-century government, but not a description of its reality.

Aside from individual reliability, there was also the question of the consequences of the definition of officership as a whole in terms of the prevailing social politics. This again could compromise efficiency. Thus in 1826 the Persians took the Russian army in Transcaucasia by surprise, because many of its officers were away on their estates, and, in addition, employing their troops as free labour.[14] Yet, this can also be looked at differently. Keeping troops on the land helped feed them, while allowing officers to spend time on their estates helped keep them willing to serve and loyal, the last an important point given the Decembrist rising of Russian officers in 1825. As the process of growing governmental control was, generally, one achieved through cooperation with social elites, and was greatly dependent on it, it was not surprising that the military shared in this process. Nearly 90 per cent of Spanish officers after 1776 were from the nobility. Napoleon created a new imperial aristocracy in which military service played a major role. Ney was made Duke of Elchingen in 1808 and Prince of Moscow in 1813, while Soult became Duke of Dalmatia in 1808 and Berthier Prince of Neuchatel in 1806. The Russian Commander in Chief during the Russo-Turkish war of 1877–78 was Grand Duke Nicholas, younger brother of Czar Alexander II.

The social politics of military organizations can be further located in terms of the competing currents of politics in the period. For the pre-Revolutionary period, it is appropriate to argue that whereas war was a forcing house of change, it was also designed to prevent it, both in terms of changes in territorial power and those in the prevailing political, social and ideological practices and norms. Armies suppressed rebellions and maintained or strengthened social and spatial patterns of control. In Europe, states had come to monopolize organized, large-scale violence, but with the cooperation of their social elites who monopolized command positions. The social elite was willing to cooperate with military change, including the organization of armies around a state-directed structure, and the downgrading of cavalry, processes that elites elsewhere were more reluctant to accept. Political-social revolutions, such as the English republic of 1649–60, were, in part, characterized by substantial changes in the composition and ethos of the officer corps and this helped to make them threatening forces. In general, however, armies did not act as revolutionary forces. Instead, it was the need to provide for them and to retain their capacity to resist territorial, political and social change that caused political pressures and governmental change.

This situation changed from the American Revolution, as some armies became the central force of revolution. This does not imply that they abandoned links with established structures and ethos of military activity, still less that troops and officers were motivated simply, or even, in many cases, partly, by enthusiasm and ideology. But, the nature of the conflict mattered, as, more generally, did the political alignment of armies. The social politics of the American Revolutionary army was very different to that of the *Mischianza* held by the British army in Philadelphia on 18 May 1778 with its mock tournament of knights.[15] French Revolutionary armies offer a prime example of radicalism, but there are many others. In the decades of reaction punctured by revolution that followed 1815, there are examples of radical garrisons leading the latter, as in Piedmont on 10 March 1821 when the garrison of Alessandria demanded liberty, to be followed two days latter by that of Turin. In Portugal, an unsuccessful liberal plot in 1817 was led by General Gomes Freire, and in 1820 the revolution was began by the Oporto garrison. In Spain, there were a series of military conspiracies and attempted coups after the expulsion of French forces, including in September 1814, September 1815, April 1817, July 1819 and early 1820. In Russia, elements in the army launched the unsuccessful Decembrist Revolt in 1825.

These uprisings are a reminder of the degree to which military power continued to pose a threat to governments. The extent to which this was the case was a product of political cultures rather than some particular stage on the trajectory of military development. Thus, it was especially true of Spain and Spanish America. Conversely, in the USA, the separatism that led to the American Civil War originated in political circles, not the military: political revolt led to military separatism, not vice versa.

Revolts from within the military were not the same as autonomous forces with a military character. The process by which these became far less common in the Western world continued. Power and organized violence were monopolized by states[16] and attempts to challenge this were overcome. Thus, the Republic of the Floridas, created by a multinational revolutionary force under Sir Gregor MacGregor on Amelia Island in 1817, defeated Spanish attempts to regain the island but was overcome that year by American forces who saw the republicans as pirates.[17]

Just as it was necessary to avoid a simplistic linear account of military development in terms of improved weaponry, so it is also important to avoid the equivalent account in terms of improved organization and professionalism.

173

Instead, it is necessary to address the multiple political and social roles of military power. Accepting that caveat, professionalism was important to military success in the nineteenth century; and was redefined in terms of more training and theory than hitherto; correspondingly social lineage and physical prowess alone became less important to professional success. A new emphasis on expertise in command led to a greater stress on formal education, offering a set of priorities that did not correspond directly to those of the social hierarchy. A warfare of scientific professionalism was implied by the formal education that was increasingly provided. Furthermore, this professionalism was linked to an institutionalization of war. Thus, in Russia in 1836, a War Ministry was established to give coherence to the military system, and in 1838 a codification of military law, the *Digest of Military Regulations*, was completed.[18]

Military education was most developed for artillery, engineering and naval officers, and less so for their infantry and cavalry counterparts. The American Military Academy at West Point, founded in 1802, initially focused on engineering and artillery officers. As with the impact on troops of the spread of national education systems, training helped encourage an identification with particular state structures. Furthermore, for officers, professionalization was linked to validation by state officer training schools. Officers were obliged to receive training in state institutions, although the level was often low, for example in Russia.[19] In France, Napoleon founded the École Militaire to train officers; some 4,000 officers were trained there between 1805 and 1815; and the École Militaire was moved to Saint-Cyr in 1808. Napoleon also reorganized the École Polytechnique in 1804 and the role of mathematics in military education increased. An emphasis on control and training enhanced the possibilities of planning war. This, in turn, led to a greater stress on publications about conflict and also on theoretical works about war.

There was also demand for accurate information. This can be seen in particular in a demand for more accurate maps, and thus a better ability to understand the absolute and relative location of units and to plan their moves. Indirect artillery fire depended on accurate maps: they were the basis for the accurate calculation of elevation, range and bearing. The ability to locate was linked to that to time, in order to provide another dimension to movements and planning. More accurate time pieces were important, but so also was a determination to think in a sequential fashion, to plan moves in a precise sequence and to ensure the effective implementation of these plans. This was the very antithesis of the tactics of repeated but generally poorly related assaults that had been so prevalent. These tactics had led to battles that were scarcely controlled and that could become shapeless mêlées.

The Prussians under Moltke represented the apogee of training in this period. Mobilization, deployment and logistics were all carefully calibrated and planned. Peacetime war games, staff rides and manoeuvres all ensured that plans were tested and capability enhanced. This process contributed greatly to the sense of armies as organizations that could be made to respond to central direction. Moltke's ability to use the organizational capability of the Prussian army ensured that innovations such as timed stages in mobilization were introduced successfully. In addition, planning did not take place in a vacuum, but rather with reference to the nature of potential opponents. An understanding of the dynamic nature of military change ensured that this planning had to be continually updated: armies and navies had to be receptive to changes elsewhere and to seek information.

The combination of professionalism and change in the conduct and character of operations helped to increase the importance and the pace of the action–reaction process in military development (in, not of, because there was no one linear process). This cut across any simple conservatism and could indeed in some contexts encourage a radicalism on the part of officers. This was particularly seen in Turkey in the early twentieth century. Irrespective of any political radicalism, military professionalism helped to create a sub-culture[20] that distinguished officers from other members of society to an extent that was more pronounced than in the eighteenth century.

The analysis of war

Theoretical discussion of the nature of war and of war-winning methods was characteristic of professionalism; it also provided material for use in training. Such discussion was not new. For example, Heinrich Dietrich von Bülow, a former Prussian officer, wrote a series of studies in which he sought to offer a comprehensive analysis and explanation of war. Interest in these works encouraged translation. His most important work, *Geist des neuern Kriegssystems* (1799), was published in London as *The Spirit of the Modern System of War* (1806).

Interest increased after the final defeat of Napoleon. The two most influential writers were Antoine-Henri de Jomini and Carl von Clausewitz. The Swiss-born Jomini (1779–1869) rose into French service through the army of the Helvetic Republic and became Chief of Staff to Marshal Ney. He subsequently served in the Russian army. Jomini's influential works, which included the *Traité des Grandes Opérations Militaires* (1804–11) and the *Précis de l'Art de la Guerre* (1838), sought to find logical principles at work in warfare, which was seen as having timeless essential characteristics, and, in particular, to explain Napoleon's success. Napoleon's generalship was the focus of much military discussion in the period, not only in France, but also in the institutions of the states that had overcome him, for example the Russian General Staff Academy.

For Jomini, the crucial military point was the choice of a line of operations that would permit a successful attack. Napoleonic operational art was

175

discussed in terms of envelopment – the use of exterior lines – and the selection of a central position that would permit the defeat in detail (separately) of opposing forces – or interior lines. This was an emphasis on battle-winning, rather than on the wider political mobilization that Napoleon had secured. Furthermore, Jomini failed to make sufficient allowance for changing aspects of war-making, not least the tactical and wider consequences of social, economic and technological change. He also offered little guidance on what was to be seen as "total war".

Jomini's influence was widespread. Thus, Edward Hamley, who in 1857 became the first Professor of Military History at the recently created Staff College and in 1866 published *The Operations of War*, owed much to Jomini. His influence was not restricted to Europe. He was much studied at West Point, and influenced many of its graduates, for example Henry Halleck, who served as Union Commander in Chief in 1862–64, and had earlier translated Jomini's *Vie Politique et Militaire de Napoléon*, and written his own *Elements of Military Art and Science* (1846).[21]

Clausewitz (1780–1831) was a Prussian officer who had also seen service in the Russian army, and, from 1818, was Director of the War Academy in Berlin. His *On War* (1832) was initially less influential than Jomini's works, in part because it was (and is) less accessible. In addition, he was not translated into English until 1873. A poor style was accompanied by philosophy, not an approach calculated to endear it to military readers. However, Clausewitz better understood the need to relate war and the socio-political context, and thus to assess military capability and skill in terms of political objectives. Furthermore, Clausewitz offered a more appropriate description of conflict. He emphasized uncertainty, and therefore risk, rather than Jomini's controllable environment, and thus the need for a continuous process of planning that could take account of the dynamic and unpredictable character of events, and the importance of an individual of genius as commander.

Clausewitz saw the French Revolution as having changed war. He regarded the direction of a national will, and the mobilization of a nation's resources that it made possible, as truly potent. Indeed, revolutionary sentiment and Napoleon had both transformed Clausewitz's world. He died of cholera (before finishing his book) after serving as Chief of State in a Prussian campaign directed against Polish revolutionaries in Posen, part of Poland that the Prussians had gained in the Partitions.[22]

Jomini and Clausewitz were not the sole writers on war. Others included the Prussian General von Willisen, whose *Theorie des grosses Krieges* appeared in 1840. More effort should be devoted to noting the impact of less theoretical writings. Alongside theoretical reflections, there was also much work on particular episodes of military history. Thus, the Prussian General Staff produced much military history and used it as an integral part of training. In addition, there was work designed for a commercial market, not least in Britain. The Peninsular War gave rise to works such as the *Atlas Militaire:*

Mémoires sur les opérations militaires des Français en Galice, en Portugal, et dans la Vallée du Tage en 1809 (Paris, no date), William Napier's *History of the War in the Peninsula* (1828–40), and James Wyld's *Maps and Plans, Showing the Principal Movements, Battles and Sieges, in which the British Army was Engaged during the War from 1808 to 1814 in the Spanish Peninsula* (1840). Napier's history was translated into French, Spanish, Italian and German. Several editions and abridgements appeared in English. Waterloo led to William Siborne's successful *History of the War in France and Belgium in 1815* (1844). Friedrich Wilhelm Benicken, a retired Prussian captain, published an edition of Polybius on war as well as his own *Die Elemente der Militär-Geographie von Europa* (Weimar, 1821). Freiherr von Kausler, a Major-General in the Württemberg army, produced an *Atlas des plus mémorables batailles, combats et sièges* (Dessau, 1847). This commercialization of war was an aspect of its public interest and normative status.

The analysis of war in a Western culture increasingly prone since the Enlightenment to put a premium on secular rationality served not to present war as unnecessary or as an aberration, but rather to present it as logical. Clausewitz's emphasis on the politicality of war – the belief that war should be dominated by political considerations and should be an instrument of policy – was not intended to present conflict as dynastic whim. Instead, scientifically analysed, war had to be prudent and rational. The traditional cultural bellicosity of the European landed elite was linked to a more "modern" planned and controlling warfulness. The more precise quantification of relative strengths and factors such as movement rates was linked to a rationalization of war. However, there was also an emphasis on will seen not only as a resource but, often, also as a force superior to resources. Intellectual and cultural interest in war, rather than peace, affected governments and led to the sense of conflict as normal.

Revolutionary movements shared with authoritarian regimes an emphasis on discipline. The individual was subservient to the unit, the people to the cause (or the dynast). As a consequence, alongside the change that stemmed from revolution, there was a basic continuity in the internal dynamics of the army and society and the nature of war. Military service was a disciplining process that was spread through conscription and the reserve system to a greater proportion of the active male population. This provided the essential enabler that permitted governments to derive benefit from demographic and economic resources, both of which increased during the period.

Armies were used to suppress discontent and to retain the state's monopoly of organized force. Thus, in May 1871, MacMahon commanded the suppression of the very radical Paris Commune, a striking example for other governments, and for the propertied as a whole, of the need for powerful armies. At a more mundane level, Hugh Rose, who was to achieve fame for his role in the suppression of the Indian Mutiny, first had independent command – in 1824 – in escorting an excise officer searching for illegal stills making liquor

177

in the west of Ireland. His Irish command also led him to suppress seditious meetings in 1832. In Australia, troops suppressed a convict rising at Vinegar Hill in 1804, and 50 years later helped the mounted police storm a stockade at Eureka manned by rebellious miners. British troops were deployed in 1812 to overawe the Luddites who destroyed new industrial machinery. In 1859, Robert E. Lee, then a colonel, suppressed John Brown's abortive anti-slavery insurrection at Harper's Ferry. Faced by widespread brigandage and a lack of local support that culminated in 1866 in a full-scale rebellion in Palermo, the new Italian state resorted in Sicily to military occupation and courts martial: military justice replaced a civilian system that, as a result of witness intimidation and other problems, was not trusted by the government.[23] In several states, the use of the army in order to maintain order became less important as police forces under central government were organized and strengthened. However, this process was not universal. The role of military forces in maintaining order has received insufficient attention in much of the literature on military history. This lack of attention is inappropriate for this period.

At the same time, states operated in an international system in which the peaceful resolution of disputes was weakened by the absence of effective practices, let alone institutions for, arbitration. Conflict was seen as the normal consequence of serious disputes, and cultural restraints on the decision to fight were minimal. The consent of the sovereign body was perceived as the sole requirement. The sense that international war was normal, combined with the monopolisation of the decision to fight and the control of organized force by governments, provided a basic continuity within the period and linked it with those on either side.

CHAPTER NINE
Conclusions: Revisiting Modernity

In large part, the importance of Western warfare in this period rests on its role in expanding Western imperial control over much of the world. The reasons for this, and the process itself, were not simply military in nature, although clearly the enhanced capability of Western military systems was crucial. It is less clear how helpful it is to draw on a direct linkage between conflict among, and within, the Western states and their power projection elsewhere. Although a causal relationship may seem logical, the links were less close than might appear to be the case. Different practices and doctrines were involved, and also, in part, different militaries: the Anglo-Indian army that dominated India was not coterminous with the British army which fought in the Napoleonic and Crimean Wars.

Nevertheless, it is pertinent to look for comparisons. Two, each of great importance, can readily be noted. First, Western militaries sought to operate in a planned fashion that entailed the analysis of goals and problems and a process of planned stages (and staged planning) designed to give effect to the resulting solution. Non-Western militaries also practised planning, but, although the empirical and methodological basis for any reliable comparison does not yet exist, there does appear to have been a more systematic process on the part of their Western counterparts. Secondly, on the whole, whether operating within or outside the West, Western militaries appear to have succeeded in freeing strategy from the pursuit of supplies. War was not a plundering exercise, although those who suffered from the Revolutionary French in the 1790s would have had a different view. Freeing strategy from the pursuit of supplies fostered planning. A warfare of pillage, as practised, for example, on many occasions by the Marathas in India, could be designed to achieve political objectives as a form of state conflict, but it also had its limitations as a means for waging war. When devastation was used by Western generals, for example Sherman in 1864, it served as part of a strategic plan.

There is a danger that such remarks suggest a smug assertion of Western superiority. That is not my intention. First, there is nothing inherently better about making the pursuit of victory more likely to result in success, or in killing more people more quickly. Secondly, Western military superiority on land was more conditional and less secure than is generally implied. Nevertheless, it was a case of Western troops in Beijing, Cairo and Delhi, not Chinese, Egyptians and Indians in London. When Washington was burned in 1814, or Paris occupied in 1815 and blockaded and bombarded in the winter of 1870–71, it was by Western troops, however barbarous they might appear. Western military capability was crucial to global history, and is a proper subject of academic study.

Any stress on the variety of conflicts in a period necessarily makes discussion in terms of modernity more complex if modernity is understood as a stage in military history. This is because the variety has to be understood not in terms of a differential "take up" of a given model of military organization, equipment and conduct, but, rather, as a response to very different circumstances and needs. In short, there was no paradigmatic trajectory that can then be scrutinized in a search for a turning point towards, or of (images vary), modernity.

The French Revolutionary and Napoleonic period left examples along the continuum from rapid and victorious offensives to slogging matches, a continuum that had also been true of *ancien régime* warfare, despite misleading subsequent attempts to present it as uniform and, also, as limited and indecisive. Napoleon's 1805 campaign, with its victories over the Austrians at Ulm and the Austrians and Russians at Austerlitz, leading to Austria's departure from the war, and his 1806 triumph over Prussia, served as models for subsequent commentators, but this underrated different lessons that could be learned from his 1808 invasion of Spain, the 1809 war with Austria, and the 1812 invasion of Russia. The first, indicated the limited value of battlefield victory if it did not lead to a surrender that prevented popular resistance. The second, at Wagram, highlighted the attritional possibilities of battle, and the campaign has been seen as prefiguring much in modern warfare. The third indicated the same at Borodino, but also the difficulty of forcing both battle and political settlement. The complex legacy of the Napoleonic wars was not, however, adequately teased out, not least because they were followed by over three decades without major conflict in Europe.

Change can certainly be discerned. The Revolutionary and Napoleonic Wars saw experiments with submarine warfare, the first use of the air for conflict (reconnaissance balloons for artillery spotting), and the first use in the West of rockets, although none of these made any real impact on the war, and investment in all of them combined was very small. It was not until the twentieth century that the dimensions of conflict expanded with air, submarine and rocket warfare on any scale. Furthermore, it was only then that the chemistry of war acquired the tool of gas.

These points cast into perspective the undoubted technical developments in battlefield capability and operations in the nineteenth century, and yet the latter were important. Land warfare was transformed by the continual incremental developments in firearms, from steps such as the introduction of the Minié ball rifle and, subsequently, of breech-loading cartridge rifles. The net effect for both hand-held firearms and artillery was of very substantial changes. In addition, there was greater and more predictable production of munitions from a more streamlined and systematized manufacturing process in the century after Napoleon's final defeat at Waterloo in 1815. The net result was a degree of change that was greater than that over the previous century.

This was even more the case if logistics, command and control, and naval warfare were considered. Steam power, the railway and the telegraph made a major difference for the Western powers both to nearby operations, for example the mid-century wars in Europe and the American Civil War, and to wars waged at a greater distance. The combination of the three made it possible to apply and direct greater resources, and in a more sustained fashion, than hitherto. This did not necessarily determine the course of conflict with those who lacked such technology, but it did make it far easier to organize war. A comparison, for example, of the British capture of Manila in 1762 with that of Alexandria in 1882 reveals very different military systems. So does the very limited French presence in Madagascar and South East Asia in the seventeenth and eighteenth centuries and their conquest of Madagascar and Indo-China in the late nineteenth. Nathanael Greene's description of the Revolutionary forces in the south was written from Charlotte in December 1780 as they recovered from defeat at Camden. Allowing for that, it still depicted very different circumstances to those in the Confederacy:

> Without tools we can do nothing and none are to be got in this country, not even a common felling axe. You will inquire of the Governor what steps have been taken by the Assembly to furnish the artificers and waggons required by me of the state, and press their immediate compliance. For without artificers we cannot aid the transportation.[1]

In the Western world, the potential to apply more resources was linked to their greater availability, thanks to demographic growth, industrialization and militarization, and the utilization of these through effective systems of recruitment, taxation and borrowing. It was less clear how best to employ these forces, and this helps to account for interest in military science and theory, as did the intellectualization of subjects in an age of increasingly self-conscious specialization and professionalization.

The pace of change in weaponry, on both land and sea, developed in the post-Napoleonic period at an hitherto unprecedented rate, as did the idea of change. Robert Fulton, a pioneer of submarine warfare, emphasized the ability of human ingenuity to surmount the apparently impossible:

> every year exhibits new combinations and effects: steam engines, cotton mills, telegraphs, balloons and submarine navigation and attack have all appeared almost within our memory: and only vulgar minds harbour the thought that a physical possibility is impracticable because it has not already been done.

Fulton also placed past, present, and future change in a continuum: "It does not require much depth of thought to trace that science by discovering gunpowder changed the whole art of war by land and sea; and by future combination may sweep military marines from the ocean".[2] Differences in weaponry were seen as crucial to operational effectiveness and success, and changing weaponry thus became the central issue in military capability. The notion that the rifle technology of the 1840s would no longer be at the cutting edge in 1870 (as with the Prussian needle gun) would have surprised military commentators a century earlier, as indeed would have rifles that were accurate, easy to load and readily maintainable.

The idea that tactics and formations should change markedly in response to the last war, as with the sequence of Franco-Austrian (1859), Austro-Prussian (1866) and Franco-Prussian (1870–71) wars, had not been seen with, say, the War of the Polish Succession (1733–35) and the War of the Austrian Succession (1740–48). This argument should not be overstated. In the Seven Years' War (1756–63), the Austrians successfully developed techniques to nullify Prussian tactics. Yet the pace of this process, both on land and at sea, was far greater by the mid-nineteenth century than hitherto. This encouraged a higher degree of built in responsiveness to the possibility of change and "progress" within the military system, and close attention to developments in other militaries. In such a context it was possible for the Prussian army of Moltke to become a paradigm of military organization and planning to a greater extent than, say, the Austrian and French armies of the 1840s and 1850s.

A sense of change did not preclude interest in the past. Indeed campaigns and victories in history were scrutinized for apparent laws, or at least lessons, of military success. Napoleon thus served his successors, just as he had scrutinized his predecessors,[3] but many of the examples were of much older vintage. The Prussians were interested in Hannibal's use of envelopment against the Romans in the Second Punic War (218–201 BCE), especially at Cannae (216 BCE).

The Second Punic War was also a good instance of the fallacy that only "modern" wars showed a total mobilization of the resources of a society in order to achieve total victory. That said, the possibilities of state direction of a sophisticated and industrially advanced economy were greater by the age of rail and steamship than they had been hitherto. That did not mean that the more advanced economy was necessarily more subject to direction. In the Crimean War, Britain and France experienced far less direction (and disruption) than the Confederacy in the American Civil War. Again, in part, this was a matter of military objectives, which were framed by political goals. In 1854, the British set out to defeat, not conquer, Russia; in 1861, in contrast, the Union sought to end the Confederacy.

If the concept of modernity has to extend to war goals then judgements are necessarily subjective. It can be asked if conquest itself is an anachronistic concept, a view that might have seemed absurd in 1900, but far less so in 2000. This reminds us that modernity recedes from the past with the passage of time.

As a working definition for the present, Western military modernity relates to approximations to the age of war in 1914–45, one that was very much dominated by Western warfare; although the Chinese and Japanese were keener to borrow weapons than concepts. From that perspective, the rapid victories of the Wars of German Unification corresponded to the ideal of German aggressors in the two world wars, and the high-tempo attritional conflict in Virginia in 1864–65 to much that was to follow. There was no comparable prefigurement in naval warfare; the Confederacy lacked a long-range submarine force, and in 1870–71 France and Germany did not clash at sea. As an example of what was to come, the Prussians deployed 122 rifled cannon at the siege of Dybbol in Denmark in 1862. By the close of the siege, they were firing at least 4,000 shells and maybe twice as much per day. These shells were brought by train and wagon. Each Prussian battery was given a particular target at which to fire. The heavy damage caused by the bombardment prepared the way for a successful storming.[4]

It is also possible to look back in order to ask whether Prussia's far greater success in the invasion of Bohemia in 1866 compared to earlier Prussian invasions in 1744, 1757 and 1778–79, and its triumph over France in 1870–71 compared to the failures of eighteenth-century German attacks on France, such as those in 1744 and 1792, reflected a change in warfare. In 1744, 1778 and 1779, Frederick II had taken the initiative in Bohemia, but failed to bring his opponents to battle. In 1744, Frederick captured Prague after a short siege, but failed to consolidate this success. He could not bring the Austrians to a decisive battle: their position near Beneschau was too strong to attack, while Frederick's army was being harassed by light Austrian forces that attacked his supply lines and foragers. At the end of the campaign, Frederick retreated, having suffered heavy losses. In 1778, he did not break through to Prague. Frederick advanced to the Austrian positions near Jaromiersch, but decided that their lines, composed of batteries, palisades and *abatis* (ramparts constructed of felled trees) supported by Field-Marshal Lacy's 100,000-strong Elbe Army, were too strong. When Frederick subsequently crossed the river at Hohenelbe, a rapid Austrian response blocked his advance. The advance by his brother, Prince Henry, was affected by supply problems and a crisis of confidence. In contrast, in 1757, there were major battles; victory for Frederick at Prague followed defeat at Kolin.

Comparing these campaigns with that in 1866 can be seen as providing evidence of modernization. The pace of campaigning in that Austro-Prussian conflict was faster and the number of troops involved was greater; while supply structures had become better. Similar comments can be made by comparing the American Civil War with the War of Independence. As with any comparison, the conflicts were dissimilar, but certainly factors of scale and tempo were different. Greater numbers also required more effective systems of transport, supply, and command and control.

Yet caveats can be entered, both in the case of particular comparisons and, more generally, with regard to the modernity of some aspects of late-nineteenth-century conflict. For example, Moltke's greater success in 1866 and 1870 than that of Austrian attacks on France in, say, 1706 and 1709, can be attributed to a range of factors, some of which cannot be so securely located in a debate over modernization. Had Benedek displayed the skill in defence showed by Lacy in 1778, and vice versa, then the wars might well have had different results. The idea that success in attack demonstrates modernity, more particularly a successful overcoming of traditional limitations on victory, is misleading. The relationship between attack and defence, both in particular cases and in general, cannot be simply located in, and used to demonstrate, a narrative of modernization.

A continued emphasis on the offensive can be seen throughout the period. This is unsurprising, as the best way to achieve political objectives was generally that of taking the war to the enemy, not least by seizing territory that might be in dispute. Nevertheless, there was also a continued conviction of the military value of taking the offensive. This was repeatedly seen as the way to gain and then use the initiative and thus as providing what would today be described as an operational basis for victory. In part, this reflected the legacy of Napoleon, who had done much to revive confidence in the ability to achieve sweeping success. This legacy was particularly powerful in the half century after his final defeat. In part, this rested on a relative neglect of the tactical strength of defensive fire-power thanks to which the British had defeated French armies in Spain and at Waterloo and thanks to which Napoleon had suffered heavy battlefield casualties in 1809 and 1812. However, such fire-power appeared to have little to offer at the operational level, and there was a conviction that it could be overcome by manoeuvre before and during the battle and by the élan of a shock attack.

Moltke was to seek to fuse the two traditions by combining the operational offensive and the tactical defensive, forcing the Austrians and the French to advance into Prussian fire-power, but this seemed less necessary to his predecessors. Instead, in the warfare of the 1820s–50s, there was a determination to fix and then overcome opponents. The desire for a speedy victory and, in the "wars of liberation", the importance of defeating rebels, provided a rationale for this, but, in addition, the value of well directed shock assault was seen as a major legacy of the French Revolutionary and Napoleonic Wars. The Austrians relied on shock columns in the 1820s, 1830s and 1840s, responding to a more general shift from line tactics. In 1852, Napoleon III asked Jomini about the likely impact of modern firearms on tactics, only to be told to continue the tactics of attack: bayonet assaults by mobile columns.[5] The Wars of German Unification were won by the power that took the offensive, but that owed much to a more skilful Prussia response to modern firearms, not least in the development of open-order deployment and small-unit fire tactics. As throughout the period, infantry was the dominant arm.

Alongside signs of major change in the technological context of warfare, it is also important to point to continued limitations. Railways had improved transport to the battlefield but not on it. Instead, marching remained crucial on campaign and in battle. This restricted opportunities for breakthroughs and pursuits. There was to be no major change in this regard until the internal combustion engine. Similarly, the command and control possibilities provided by the telegraph were not matched on the battlefield. Field communications continued to be more reliant on traditional means of conveying information and instructions. In battle, the increased effectiveness of both artillery and infantry was not matched by cooperation between the two, certainly not to the standards that were to be shown in 1917–18.[6]

The first century of air power had proved a disappointment. Balloons were used for reconnaissance from 1793, but they were found to be of limited utility, and this was as true in the American Civil War as it had been in the French Revolutionary Wars. They took time to operate and were affected by the weather and by night-time, while there were delays in the transmission of messages to the ground. Hot air balloons were used by the French in 1793. The following year, a balloon company was formed by the French. Its hydrogen-filled silk balloon was first used on the battlefield at Fleurus in 1794. A second company was formed after the battle, but the balloon companies were disbanded by Napoleon because he doubted their value. During the Peninsular Campaign in 1862, McClellan's army used gas-filled observer balloons, but they proved of little value in practice. The use of rigid balloons for bombardment developed during World War One, when German zeppelins (airships) travelled great distances, taking part in the bombing of London. More generally, air power was of limited value prior to the 1910s.

At the close of our period, air power was anticipated by futurologists rather than general staffs. On 27 October 1883, Albert Robida (1848–1926) published in *La Caricature* an anticipation of warfare in the twentieth century that included cannon-firing streamlined balloons, as well as electric-powered, armoured trains firing cannon and machine guns. The caption announced:

La Guerre de Railway. Prise d'une bifurcation importante par les troupes de railway d'avant-garde.

Les locomotives-forteresses blindées [armoured] des Australiens, lancées avec toute la vitesse que les capitaines-ingénieurs ont pu obtenir de leurs propulseurs électriques, ont surpris et bousculé les premiers blockhaus roulants recontrés après la frontiére, et, soutenues par une division aérienne, se sont emparées des lignes, malgré les efforts désespérés d'une division de railway mozambiquoise et de quelques ballonnets blindés.

If air and tanks are seen as signs of modernity, then it is difficult to feel confident that even the early years of World War One can be located in terms of modern warfare. Instead, it was developments during the war, many of which were not fully realized until the following world war, that can be seen as crucial to changes in battle. Early visions of submarine warfare were also unfulfilled.[7]

However, a machinization of aspects of conflict was already well advanced at sea by the close of our period. The replacement of wooden ships by ironclads was invested with significance as a triumph for modernity. Thus, the *Monitor* symbolized the power of the machine.[8] So, more mundanely, did the assessment of the respective merits of new types of weapon and ammunition, as these trials were based on the notion that these types could be accurately reproduced in large quantities. For example, in 1848–49 officers commanding regiments in the British army in India that contained rifle companies reported to the Secretary of the Military Board about the best type of rifle ammunition.[9]

The concern with machines was not new. Indeed, efforts to move beyond craft ethos in arms production had affected military procurement in the eighteenth century, especially in the French naval dockyards. Interest in rational systems also affected French production of weapons for the army in this period.[10] A sense of the potency of the new can be glimpsed in Major-General Thomas Grosvenor's account of the bombardment of Copenhagen in September 1807. On 2 September, he wrote:

Began the bombardment of Copenhagen at sunset, 3 mortar batteries of twelve each all opened at the same time . . . The Congreve arrows [rockets] made a very singular appearance in the air. Six or seven comet-like appearances racing together. They seemed to move very slow. The town was set on fire.

Three days later he added, "the Great Church was on fire to the very pinnacle of the steeples. The appearance was horrifyingly grand".[11]

Although the past provided models of heroism, as in the names of some of the steam warships the British took to the Baltic in 1854 – *Ajax, Blenheim,*

Hogue, Russell – there was a strong awareness, in at least some military and, more commonly, naval circles, of the need to plan not only for the new but also for the future.

Yet, as already suggested, in large part the importance of Western warfare in this period rests on its role in expanding Western imperial control. Here the situation had radically changed by 1882. This was true both at the point of delivery of force and of the wider currents of activity that military force arose from and fostered. The successes achieved in Egypt in 1798 and in Algeria in the 1830s and, more particularly, the 1840s were repeated more widely and at a greater pace. At the close of our period, the French seized Tunisia (1881) and the British Egypt (1882). More and more of the world's people and territory were affected by Western power, and Western states and their agents were able to plan expansionism with a high predictability of success. This was different to the more faltering Western expansionism (certainly in Africa and most of South and East Asia) in the seventeenth and early eighteenth centuries.

Deploying forces to the interior of southern Africa to shoot down Zulus in 1879 does not today seem attractive or even defensible, as it would indeed have struck many contemporaries. Yet there is no denying the importance of this projection of power for the history of much of the world.

Conflict in 1914–45 does not define modern war. It is also necessary to look to the insurrectionary and counter-insurgency warfare that followed 1945, especially the anti-colonial struggles, and to the ideological conflicts of the Cold War, many of which were civil wars. This also can be prefigured in 1775–1882, especially with the Latin American Wars of Liberation, and with the interventionist episodes of the 1790s, 1820s, 1830s and 1840s. As yet, parallels and links between these conflicts, and also between them and more recent struggles, have not been probed to anything like the extent of the trajectory from Wars of German Unification and American Civil War to the two World Wars, already mentioned. That is a fruitful task that awaits. An understanding of the multiplicity and variety of conflict in 1775–1882 opens our eyes to the very varied character of military modernity and to the diverse nature of the military history of more recent times.

Notes

Introduction

1. H. Rosinski, "Scharnhorst to Schlieffen: The Rise and Decline of German Military Thought", *Naval War College Review* **29** (1976), pp. 83–103.

Chapter 1: Western Warfare in its Global Context, 1775–1815

1. J. M. Black, *Britain as a Military Power, 1688–1815* (1999).
2. S. Gordon, *Marathas, Marauders and State Formation in Eighteenth-Century India* (Delhi, 1994).
3. R. G. S. Cooper and N. K. Waple, "Maratha Artillery: From Dalhoi to Assaye", *Journal of the Ordnance Society* **7** (1995); J. Weller, *Wellington in India* (1972), p. 192.
4. P. Griffith, "The Myth of the Thin Red Line – Wellington's Tactics", in *Wellington Commander: The Iron Duke's Generalship*, P. Griffith (ed.) (Chichester, 1985), p. 149.
5. R. G. S. Cooper, "Wellington and the Marathas in 1803", *International History Review* **11** (1989), pp. 36–8. See also, J. Pemble, "Resources and Techniques in the Second Maratha War", *Historical Journal* **19** (1976), pp. 375–404.
6. A. S. Bennell, "Factors in Marquis Wellesley's Failure Against Holkar, 1804", *Bulletin of the School of Oriental and African Studies* **28** (1965), pp. 553–81.
7. R. G. S. Cooper, "Cross-Cultural Conflict Analysis: The 'Reality' of British Victory in the Second Anglo-Maratha War, 1803–5", PhD thesis (University of Cambridge, 1992).
8. J. M. Lafont, *Indika: Essays in Indo-French Relations, 1630–1976* (New Delhi, 2000), pp. 177–204.
9. P. Carey (ed.), *The British in Java, 1811–1816: A Javanese Account* (Oxford, 1992).
10. D. H. A. Kolff, *Naukar, Rajput and Sepoy: The Ethnohistory of the Military Labour Market in Hindustan, 1450–1850* (Cambridge, 1990).
11. J. Pemble, *The Invasion of Nepal: John Company at War* (Oxford, 1971), p. 356.
12. D. H. A. Kolff, "The End of an *Ancien Régime*: Colonial War in India, 1798–1818", in *Imperialism and War: Essays on Colonial Wars in Asia and Africa*, J. A. de Moor and H. L. Wesseling (eds) (Leiden, 1989), pp. 22–49.
13. J. R. Fischer, *A Well-Executed Failure: The Sullivan Campaign Against the Iroquois, July–September 1779* (Columbia, South Carolina, 1997); M. Mintz, *Seeds of Empire: The American Revolu-*

tionary Conquest of the Iroquois (New York, 1999).

14. W. Sword, *President Washington's Indian War: The Struggle for the Old Northwest, 1790–1795* (Norman, Oklahoma, 1985).
15. S. Antal, *A Wampum Denied: Procter's War of 1812* (Ottawa, 1997).
16. D. Sweet, "Native Resistance in Eighteenth-Century Amazonia: The 'Abominable Muras' in War and Peace", *Radical History Review* 53 (1992), pp. 49–82.
17. J. R. Fisher, A. J. Kuethe and A. McFarlane (eds), *Reform and Insurrection in Bourbon New Granada and Peru* (Baton Rouge, 1990).
18. C. L. R. James, *The Black Jacobins: Toussaint L'Ouverture and the San Domingo Revolution* (1980); D. P. Geggus, "The Haitian Revolution", in *The Modern Caribbean*, F. W. Knight and C. A. Palmer (eds) (Chapel Hill, North Carolina, 1989), pp. 21–50.
19. R. L. Tignor (ed.), *Napoleon in Egypt: Al-Jabarti's Chronicle of the French Occupation, 1798* (Princeton, New Jersey, 1993), pp. 37.
20. N. Schur, *Napoleon in the Holy Land* (Mechanicsburg, Pennsylvania, 1999).
21. Tignor, *Napoleon in Egypt*, pp. 154, 160–61.
22. T. Porterfield, *The Allure of Empire: Art in the Service of French Imperialism, 1798–1836* (Princeton, New Jersey, 1998).
23. A. Palluel-Guillard, "Napoléon et les Indes", in *L'Inde, la France, la Savoie: Le Général de Boigne* (Chambéry, 1997), pp. 87–108.
24. R. L. Stein, *The French Slave Trade in the Eighteenth Century: An Old Regime Business* (Madison, Wisconsin, 1979); W. B. Cohen, *The French Encounter with Africans: White Response to Blacks, 1530–1580* (Bloomington, Indiana, 1980).

Chapter 2: Two Episodes of Modernity? The American War of Independence and the French Revolutionary Wars

1. Gage to Barrington, Secretary at War, 26 June 1775, British Library [BL] Add. 73550.
2. S. Conway, *The War of American Independence 1775–1783* (1995), pp. x, 247.
3. H. Ward, *The War for Independence and the Transformation of American Society* (1999); and, less successfully, C. P. Niemeyer, *America Goes to War: A Social History of the Continental Army* (New York, 1996).
4. Evelyn to Sir Frederick Evelyn, 23 April, 19 August, 1775, BL Evelyn papers LEI.
5. Congreve to Reverend Richard Congreve, 4 September 1776, Stafford, County Record Office D1057/M/F/30.
6. Gage to Barrington, 3 October 1774, BL Add. 73550.
7. P. Mackesy, *The War for America 1775–1783* (2nd edn, Lincoln, Nebraska, 1993).
8. D. Twohig (ed.), *The Papers of George Washington: Revolutionary War Series*, VIII (Charlottesville, 1998), pp. 182, 238; Twohig, *Papers of George Washington* IX (Charlottesville, 1999), pp. 317, 561.
9. Twohig, *Papers of George Washington*, VIII, p. 454.
10. C. J. Duffy, *The Army of Frederick the Great* (1974); D. E. Showalter, "Tactics and Recruitment in Eighteenth-Century Prussia", *Studies in History and Politics* 3 (1984), pp. 15–41.
11. R. S. Quimby, *Background of Napoleonic Warfare: The Theory of Military Tactics in Eighteenth Century France* (New York, 1957); S. Ross, "Development of the Combat Division in Eighteenth Century French Armies", *French Historical Studies* 1 (1965), pp. 84–94; C. J. Duffy, *The Fortress in the Age of Vauban and Frederick the Great, 1660–1789* (1985), pp. 153–63.
12. S. F. Scott, *Response of the Royal Army to the French Revolution: The Role and Development of the Line Army, 1787–1793* (Oxford, 1978); S. F. Scott, *From Yorktown to Valmy* (Niwot, Colorado, 1999); J. Luvaas (ed.), *Napoleon on the Art of War* (New York, 1999), p. 73.
13. D. Reichel, "Les Guerres de la Révolution", in *Atlas de la Révolution Française. III. L'Armée et la Guerre*, J. P. Bertaud and D. Reichel (eds) (Paris, 1989), p. 53.

14. H. G. Brown, *War, Revolution, and the Bureaucratic State: Politics and Army Administration in France, 1791–1799* (Oxford, 1995); R. Blaufarb, "The Politics of the Amalgame", *The Consortium on Revolutionary Europe, 1750–1850, Selected Papers* (1998), pp. 106–13.

15. P. Wetzler, *War and Subsistence: The Sambre and Meuse Army in 1794* (New York, 1985); J. P. Bertaud, *The Army of the French Revolution* (Cambridge, 1988); J. Lynn, *The Bayonets of the Republic. Motivation and Tactics in the Army of Revolutionary France, 1791–94* (2nd edn, Boulder, Colorado, 1996). On its subject, S. T. Ross, *Quest for Victory, French Military Strategy 1792–1799* (New York, 1973).

16. G. Rothenburg, *Napoleon's Great Adversaries: The Archduke Charles and the Austrian Army, 1792–1814* (1982).

17. T. C. W. Blanning, *The French Revolution in Germany: Occupation and Resistance in the Rhineland, 1792–1802* (Oxford, 1983); T. C. W. Blanning, *The French Revolutionary Wars 1787–1802* (1996), pp. 158–69.

18. S. Wilkinson, *The Rise of General Bonaparte* (Oxford, 1930); G. Ferrero, *The Gamble: Bonaparte in Italy 1796–1797* (1939); W. G. F. Jackson, *Attack in the West: Napoleon's First Campaign Re-Read Today* (1953).

19. J. Lukowski, *The Partitions of Poland 1772, 1793, 1795* (Harlow, 1999), pp. 163–74.

20. P. Longworth, *The Art of Victory: The Life and Achievements of Generalissimo Suvorov, 1729–1800* (1965).

21. A. B. Rodger, *The War of the Second Coalition 1798 to 1801: A Strategic Commentary* (Oxford, 1964); P. Mackesy, *Statesmen at War. The Strategy of Overthrow 1798–1799* (1974).

Chapter 3: Napoleon and His Opponents

1. C. Prendergast, *Napoleon and History Painting: Antoine-Jean Gros's "La Bataille d'Eylau"* (Oxford, 1997).

2. G. Rowlands, "Louis XIV, Aristocratic Power and the Elite Units of the French Army", *French History* 13 (1999), pp. 303–31.

3. A. Forrest, *Conscripts and Deserters: The Army and French Society during the Revolution and Empire* (Oxford, 1989); and A. Forrest, *Soldiers of the French Revolution* (Durham, North Carolina, 1990).

4. J. M. Keefe, "Failure in Independent Tactical Command: Napoleon's Marshals in 1813", *The Consortium on Revolutionary Europe, 1750–1850, Selected Papers* (1997), pp. 420–32.

5. D. Chandler, *The Campaigns of Napoleon* (1966); G. Rothenburg, *The Art of Warfare in the Age of Napoleon* (1978); J. R. Elting, *Swords Around a Throne: Napoleon's Grande Armée* (New York, 1988); B. Nosworthy, *Battle Tactics of Napoleon and his Enemies* (1995); D. Gates, *The Napoleonic Wars 1803–1815* (1997).

6. R. Muir, *Tactics and the Experience of Battle in the Age of Napoleon* (1998). Nosworthy is more concerned with tactical doctrine, Muir with tactics on the battlefield and the role of attitudes and feelings.

7. O. Connelly, *Blundering to Glory: Napoleon's Military Campaigns* (2nd edn, Wilmington, Delaware, 1999).

8. P. Griffith, *The Art of War of Revolutionary France 1789–1802* (1998), p. 11.

9. R. Epstein, *Napoleon's Last Victory and the Emergence of Modern War* (Lawrence, Kansas, 1994), p. 182.

10. A. Forrest, "The French Abroad: The Soldiers' View of the Napoleonic Campaign", in *L'Europa Scopre Napoleone 1793–1804*, V. S. Douglas (ed.) (1999), pp. 382–3.

11. F. N. Maude, *The Ulm Campaign 1805* (1912).

12. C. Duffy, *Austerlitz 1805* (1977); S. Bowden, *Napoleon and Austerlitz* (Chicago, 1997).

13. F. N. Maude, *The Jena Campaign 1806* (1909).

14. F. L. Petre, *Napoleon's Campaign in Poland, 1806–7* (1901).

15. D. Gates, *The Spanish Ulcer. A History of the Peninsular War* (1986).

16. J. R. Arnold, *Crisis on the Danube: Napoleon's Austrian Campaign of 1809* (1990).
17. Epstein, *Napoleon's Last Victory*, esp. p. 171; J. R. Arnold, *Napoleon Conquers Austria: The 1809 Campaign for Vienna* (Westport, Conn., 1995), p. 197.
18. C. Duffy, *Borodino and the War of 1812* (1972).
19. A. W. Palmer, *Napoleon in Russia* (New York, 1967); G. Nafziger, *Napoleon's Invasion of Russia* (Novato, 1988).
20. S. Bowden, *Napoleon's Grande Armée of 1813* (Chicago, 1990), p. 19
21. G. Craig, "Problems of Coalition Warfare: The Military Alliance Against Napoleon, 1813–14", in G. Craig, *War, Politics and Diplomacy: Selected Essays* (New York, 1966), pp. 22–45.
22. Chandler, *Campaigns of Napoleon*, p. 950.
23. J. P. Lawford, *Napoleon: The Last Campaigns, 1813–1815* (New York, 1977).
24. N. Gash, "Wellington and the Waterloo Campaign", *Wellington Studies* 2 (1999), pp. 214–38; A. S. Uffindell, *The Eagle's Last Triumph: Napoleon's Victory at Ligny, June 1815* (1994); E. Owen (ed.), *The Waterloo Papers: 1815 and Beyond* (Tavistock, 1997); P. Hofschroer, *1815: The Waterloo Campaign* (1998).
25. W. Shanahan, *Prussian Military Reforms, 1788–1813* (New York, 1945); P. Paret, *Yorck and the Era of Prussia Reform, 1807–1815* (Princeton, 1966); D. E. Showalter, "Manifestation of Reform: The Rearmament of the Prussian Infantry, 1806–1813", *Journal of Modern History* **44** (1972), pp. 364–80.
26. P. Paret, *Clausewitz and the State* (New York, 1984).
27. C. E. White, "Organization and Intellect: The Prussian Staff System During the Leipzig Campaign", *The Consortium on Revolutionary Europe, 1750–1850, Selected Papers* (1998), pp. 540–8.

Chapter 4: Naval Power and Warfare

1. P. D. Chase (ed.), *The Papers of George Washington: Revolutionary War Series,* vol. 10 (Charlottesville, 2000), p. 507. For naval strategy see in particular N. A. M. Rodger, *The Insatiable Earl: A Life of John Montagu, Fourth Earl of Sandwich* (1993), pp. 266–300. On the economic consequences, see R. Buel Jr., *In Irons: Britain's Naval Supremacy and the American Revolutionary Economy* (New Haven, 1999).
2. J. Glete, *Navies and Nations: Warships, Navies and State Building in Europe and America, 1500–1860* (Stockholm, 1993), e.g. pp. 286, 308–9.
3. J. E. Talbot, *The Pen and Ink Sailor: Charles Middleton and the King's Navy, 1778–1813* (1998).
4. S. C. Tucker, *The Jeffersonian Gunboat Navy* (Columbia, South Carolina, 1993).
5. H. Legoherel, *Les Trésoriers Généraux de la Marine, 1517–1788* (Paris, 1963), pp. 351–5; W. S. Cormack, *Revolutionary and Political Conflict in the French Navy, 1789–1794* (Cambridge, 1995); and W. S. Cormack, "Legitimate Authority in Revolution and War: The French Navy in the West Indies, 1787–1793", *International History Review* 18 (1996), pp. 1–27.
6. The massive literature on this subject can be approached through B. Lavery, *Nelson's Navy: The Ships, Men and Organisation, 1793–1815* (1989).
7. See, most recently, P. Krajeski, *In the Shadow of Nelson: The Naval Leadership of Admiral Sir Charles Cotton, 1753–1812* (Westport, Conn., 2000).
8. L. Maloney, "The War of 1812: What Role for Sea Power?", in *This People's Navy: The Making of American Sea Power*, K. J. Hagan (ed.) (New York, 1991), pp. 46–62.
9. R. Morris, *The Royal Dockyards During the Revolutionary and Napoleonic Wars* (Leicester, 1983).
10. The best book on this period is L. Sondhaus, *Naval Warfare 1815–1914* (2001). See also S. C. Tucker, *Handbook of 19th Century Naval Warfare* (Stroud, 2000).
11. Cockburn memorandum, 9 June 1845, BL Add. 40458 fo. 57; M. S. Partridge, *Military Planning for the Defense of the United Kingdom, 1814–1870* (Westport, Conn., 1989); A. T. Patterson, *Palmerston's Folly: The Portsdown and Spithead Forts* (Portsmouth, 1985).

12. P. Hore, "Lord Melville, The Admiralty and the Coming of Steam Navigation", *Mariner's Mirror* 86 (2000), pp. 157–72.
13. C. I. Hamilton, *Anglo-French Naval Rivalry, 1849–1870* (Oxford, 1993).
14. A. Lambert, *Battleships in Transition: The Creation of the Steam Battlefleet, 1815–1860* (1984); D. K. Brown, *Before the Ironclad: Development of Ship Design, Propulsion and Armament in the Royal Navy, 1815–1860* (1990); A. Lambert, *The Last Sailing Battlefleet: Maintaining Naval Mastery 1815–1850* (1991); A. Lambert, *Steam, Steel and Shellfire: The Nineteenth Century Naval Technical Revolution* (1992).
15. R. Luraghi, *A History of the Confederate Navy* (1996).
16. R. M. Browning, *From Cape Charles to Cape Fear: The North Atlantic Blockading Squadron during the Civil War* (Tuscaloosa, Alabama, 1993).
17. J. F. Beeler, *British Naval Policy in the Gladstone-Disraeli Era 1866–1880* (Stanford, California, 1997), pp. 199–200.
18. J. Greene and A. Massigani, *Ironclads at War: The Origin and Development of the Armored Warship, 1854–1891* (Conshohocken, Pennsylvania, 1998), pp. 311–15.
19. Cockburn memorandum, 9 June 1845, BL Add. 40458 fos. 63–4.
20. P. B. Wiley, *Yankees in the Land of the Gods: Commodore Perry and the Opening of Japan* (New York, 1990).
21. L. Sondhaus, *Preparing for Weltpolitik: German Sea Power Before the Tirpitz Era* (Annapolis, 1997).

Chapter 5: The Global Context, 1815–82

1. Pierce's journal, 27 Jan. 1846, BL IO MSS Eur. A 108, fo. 14.
2. Letter by unidentified officer of Bengal 30th Native Infantry, 26 Jan. 1849, BL IO MSS Eur. C 605, fos. 1–2.
3. B.S. Nijjar, *Anglo-Sikh Wars, 1845–1849* (New Delhi, 1976).
4. A. T. Sullivan, *Thomas-Robert Bugeaud, France and Algeria, 1784–1849: Power, Politics and the Good Society* (Hamden, Conn., 1983).
5. M. C. Ricklefs, *A History of Modern Indonesia since c. 1300* (2nd edn, Basingstoke, 1993), pp. 140–42, 116–17.
6. W. E. D. Allen and P. Maratoff, *Caucasian Battlefields: A History of the Wars on the Turco-Caucasian Border, 1828–1921* (Cambridge, 1953), pp. 23–45.
7. M. Gammer, "Russian Strategies in the Conquest of Chechnia and Daghestan, 1825–1859", in *The North Caucasus Barrier: The Russian Advance Towards the Muslim World*, M. B. Broxup (ed.) (1992), p. 58; and M. Gammer, *Muslim Resistance to the Tsar: Shamil and the Conquest of Chechnia and Daghestan* (1994).
8. I. Stebelsky, "The Frontier in Central Asia", in *Russian Historical Geography I*, J. A. Bates and R. A. French (eds) (1983), pp. 154–5.
9. J. K. Mahon, *History of the Second Seminole War* (Gainesville, Florida, 1967).
10. R. M. Utley, *Frontiersmen in Blue: The United States Army and the Indian, 1848–1865* (1967).
11. Napier to Governor General of India, Lord Dalhousie, 22 May 1850, BL Add. 49016, fos. 107–8; J. A. B. Palmer, *The Mutiny Outbreak at Meerut in 1857* (Cambridge, 1966); D. Domin, *India in 1857–58: A Study of the Sikhs in the People's Uprising* (Berlin, 1977); J. Pemble, *The Raj, the Indian Mutiny and the Kingdom of Oudh 1801–1858* (Hassocks, 1977); R. Mukherjee, *Awadh in Revolt 1857–1858* (Delhi, 1984).
12. Pearson to his parents, 19 July, 1 Aug. 1857, 14 May 1858, BL IO MSS Eur. C 231, pp. 51, 54, 56, 161.
13. T. R. Moreman, *The Army in India and the Development of Frontier Warfare, 1849–1947* (1998), pp. 16–21.
14. H. Reynolds, *The Other Side of the Frontier: Aboriginal Resistance to the European Invasion of Australia* (Ringwood, 1982); N. Loos, *Invasion and Resistance: Aboriginal-European Relations*

on the North Queensland Frontier, 1861–1897 (Canberra, 1982); J. Grey, *A Military History of Australia* (2nd edn, Cambridge, 1999), pp. 25–37.

15. P. Adams, *Fatal Necessity: British Intervention in New Zealand 1830–1847* (Auckland, 1977); J. Belich, *The New Zealand Wars and the Victorian Interpretation of Racial Conflict* (Auckland, 1986); J. Cowan, *The New Zealand Wars: A History of the Maori Campaigns and the Pioneering Period* (Wellington, 1983).

16. B. Keegan, "The Ashanti Campaign 1873–4", in *Victorian Military Campaigns*, B. Bond (ed.) (1967), pp. 163–9; D. Killingray, "The British and Asante 1870–1914", in *Imperialism and War: Essays on Colonial Wars in Asia and Africa*, J. A. de Moor and H. L. Wesseling (eds) (Leiden, 1989), pp. 158–67; I. Wilks, *Asante in the Nineteenth Century* (Cambridge, 1975).

17. G. Hardy, *Faidherbe* (Paris, 1947); A. S. Kanya-Forstner, *The Conquest of the Western Sudan: A Study in French Military Imperialism* (Cambridge, 1969).

18. J. A. de Moor, "Warmakers in the Archipelago: Dutch Expeditions in Nineteenth Century Indonesia", in de Moor and Wesseling (eds), *Imperialism and War*, pp. 50–71, esp. 70–71; M. Brossenbroek, "The Living Tools of Empire: The Recruitment of European Soldiers for the Dutch Colonial Army, 1814–1909", *Journal of Imperial and Commonwealth History* **23** (1995).

19. W. H. Leckie, *The Military Conquest of the South Plains* (Norman, Oklahoma, 1963); S. L. A. Marshall, *Crimsoned Prairie: The Wars Between the United States and the Plains Indians During the Winning of the West* (New York, 1972); R. M. Utley, *Frontier Regulars: The United States Army and the Indian, 1866–1891* (New York, 1973); P. A. Hutton, *Phil Sheridan and His Army* (Lincoln, Nebraska, 1985); J. A. Greene, *Yellowstone Command: Colonel Nelson A. Miles and the Great Sioux War, 1876–1877* (Lincoln, Nebraska, 1991); R. Wooster, *Nelson A. Miles and the Twilight of the Frontier Army* (Lincoln, Nebraska, 1993); P. R. DeMontravel, *A Hero to His Fighting Men: Nelson A. Miles, 1839–1925* (Kent, Ohio, 1998).

20. J. P. C. Laband and P. S. Thompson, *Field Guide to the War in Zululand and the Defence of Natal, 1879* (Pietermaritzburg, 1983), pp. 54–7; J. P. C. Laband, *Kingdom in Crisis: The Zulu Response to the British Invasion of 1879* (Manchester, 1992). For a warning against an exaggeration of the role of firearms, see J. J. Guy, "A Note on Firearms in the Zulu Kingdom with Special Reference to the Anglo-Zulu War, 1879", *Journal of African History* **12** (1971), pp. 557–70.

21. B. Robson (ed.), "The Kandahar Letters of the Reverend Alfred Cane", *Journal of the Society for Army Historical Research* **69** (1991), pp. 206, 211–12.

22. D. G. Chandler, "The Expedition to Abyssinia", in Bond (ed.), *Victorian Military Campaigns*, pp. 105–59; D. Bates, *The Abyssinian Difficulty* (Oxford, 1979).

23. W. McElwee, *The Art of War from Waterloo to Mons* (Bloomington, Indiana, 1974), pp. 189–91.

24. Warren, Reminiscences, BL IO MSS Eur. C 607, pp. 188–91.

25. B. W. Menning, *Bayonets Before Bullets: The Imperial Russian Army, 1861–1914* (Bloomington, Indiana, 1992), p. 64.

26. Lister to Secretary to Governor of Bengal, 2 Feb. 1850, BL Add. 49016, fo. 88.

Chapter 6: After Waterloo: Conflict Within the West, 1815–60

1. J. E. Rodríguez O., "The Emancipation of America", *American Historical Review* **105** (2000), p. 145.

2. Amid the massive literature on the subject, it is worth noting S. Clissold, *Benjamin O'Higgins and the Independence of Chile* (1968); J. Lynch, *The Spanish American Revolutions, 1808–1826* (New York, 1986); S. P. Mackenzie, *Revolutionary Armies in the Modern Era: A Revisionist Approach* (1997), pp. 51–67.

3. M. P. Costeloe, *Response to Revolution: Imperial Spain and the Spanish American Revolutions, 1810–1840* (Cambridge, 1986).

4. M. L. Woodward, "The Spanish Army and the Loss of America, 1810–1824", *Hispanic American Historical Review* **48** (1968), pp. 586–607.

5. M. T. Ducey, "Village, Nation, and Constitution: Insurgent Politics in Papantla, Veracruz, 1810–1821", *Hispanic American Historical Review* 79 (1999), pp. 471–2, 476.
6. C. I. Archer, "The Army of New Spain and the Wars of Independence, 1790–1821", *Hispanic American Historical Review* 61 (1981), pp. 705–14; C. I. Archer, "Insurrection-Reaction-Revolution-Fragmentation: Reconstructing the Choreography of Meltdown in New Spain during the Independence Era", *Mexican Studies* 10 (1994), pp. 63–98; B. Hamnett, "Royalist Counterinsurgency and the Continuity of Rebellion: Guanajuato and Michoacán, 1813–1820", *Hispanic American Historical Review* 62 (1982); V. Guedea, "The Process of Mexican Independence", *American Historical Review* 105 (2000), pp. 119–20.
7. T. Anna, *The Fall of the Royal Government in Mexico City* (Lincoln, Nebraska, 1978); Rodríguez O. (ed.), *Mexico in the Age of Democratic Revolutions* (Boulder, Colorado), pp. 97–132.
8. B. Vale, *Independence or Death! British Sailors and Brazilian Independence, 1822–1825* (1996).
9. D. E. Dumond, *The Machete and the Cross: Campesino Rebellion in Yucatán* (Lincoln, Nebraska, 1997).
10. S. C. Green, *The Mexican Republic: The First Decade, 1823–1832* (Pittsburgh, 1987); M. P. Costeloe, *The Central Republic in Mexico, 1835–1846: Hombres de Bien in the Age of Santa Anna* (Cambridge, 1993); T. Anna, *Forging Mexico, 1821–1835* (Lincoln, Nebraska, 1998).
11. J. Lynch, *Caudillos in Spanish America, 1800–1850* (Oxford, 1992).
12. O. P. Singletary, *The Mexican War* (Chicago, 1960); K. J. Bauer, *The Mexican War, 1846–1848* (New York, 1974); J. E. Weems, *To Conquer a Peace: The War Between the United States and Mexico* (New York, 1974); J. S. D. Eisenhower, *So Far from God: The US War with Mexico, 1846–1848* (New York, 1989); J. S. D. Eisenhower, *Agent of Destiny: The Life and Times of General Winfield Scott* (New York, 1997); J. A. Meyer, "'He is the Greatest Living Soldier': Wellington and Winfield Scott Compared", *The Consortium on Revolutionary Europe 1750–1850, Selected Papers* (1998), pp. 240–7; W. A. DePalo, *The Mexican National Army, 1822–1852* (College Station, Texas, 1997).
13. D. F. Stevens, *Origins of Instability in Early Republican Mexico* (Durham, North Carolina, 1991); P. Santoni, "A Fear of the People: The Civic Militia of Mexico in 1845", *Hispanic American Historical Review* 68 (1988), pp. 269–88; P. Santoni, "The Failure of Mobilization: The Civic Militia of Mexico in 1846", *Mexican Studies* 12 (1996), pp. 169–94.
14. E. Christiansen, *The Origins of Military Power in Spain, 1800–1854* (1967); E. Holt, *The Carlist Wars in Spain* (1967); J. F. Coverdale, *The Basque Phase of Spain's First Carlist War* (Princeton, New Jersey, 1984).
15. P. W. Schroeder, *The Transformation of European Politics, 1763–1848* (Oxford, 1994), e.g. p. 581.
16. D. Porch, *Army and Revolution: France 1815–1848* (1974), pp. 26–37.
17. J. S. Fishman, *Diplomacy and Revolution: The London Conference of 1830 and the Belgian Revolt* (Amsterdam, 1988); C. Duffy, *Fire and Stone: The Science of Fortress Warfare, 1660–1860* (2nd edn, 1996).
18. C. H. Church, *Revolution in 1830: Revolution and Political Change* (1983).
19. J. Schull, *Rebellion: The Rising in French Canada – 1838* (Toronto, 1971); C. Read and R. J. Stagg (eds), *The Rebellion of 1837 in Upper Canada* (Ottawa, 1985).
20. J. Remak, *A Very Civil War: The Swiss Sonderbund War of 1847* (Boulder, Colorado, 1993).
21. A. Sked, *The Survival of the Habsburg Empire: Radetzky, the Imperial Army and the Class War, 1848* (1979).
22. R. Price, *The Revolutions of 1848* (1988).
23. O. Chadwick, *A History of the Popes, 1830–1914* (Oxford, 1998).
24. For another dimension, see D. Showalter, "Weapons, Technology and the Military in Metternich's Germany: A Study in Stagnation?", *Australian Journal of Politics and History* 25 (1978), pp. 227–38.
25. J. Sweetman, *Raglan: From the Peninsula to the Crimea* (1993).
26. P. Griffith, *Military Thought in the French Army 1815–1851* (Manchester, 1989); G. P. Cox, *The Halt in the Mud: French Strategic Planning from Waterloo to Sedan* (Boulder, Colorado, 1994).

27. Napier to Lord Dalhousie, 27 June 1849, BL Add. 49106, fos. 1–4.
28. S. T. Ross, *From Flintlock to Rifle: Infantry Tactics, 1740–1866* (2nd edn, 1996), pp. 161–4; D. Showalter, "Weapons and Ideas in the Prussian Army from Frederick the Great to Moltke the Elder", in *Tools of War: Instruments, Ideas, and Institutions of Warfare, 1445–1871*, J. A. Lynn (ed.) (Urbana, 1990), pp. 193–8.
29. D. M. Goldfrank, *The Origins of the Crimean War* (1993).
30. H. Strachan, "The British Army and 'Modern' War: The Experience of the Peninsula and of the Crimea", in *Tools of War*, Lynn (ed.), pp. 215–17.
31. C. Hibbert, *The Destruction of Lord Raglan* (1961).
32. B. D. Gooch, *The New Bonapartist Generals in the Crimean War* (The Hague, 1959).
33. A. Lambert, *The Crimean War: British Grand Strategy Against Russia* (Manchester, 1990).
34. A. Blumberg, *A Carefully Planned Accident: The Italian War of 1859* (1990).
35. B. H. Reid, *The American Civil War and the Wars of the Industrial Revolution* (1999), p. 41.
36. W. J. Wood (ed.), *Civil War Generalship: The Art of Command* (Westport, Conn., 1996); G. W. Gallagher (ed.), *Three Days at Gettysburg: Essays on the Confederate and Union Leadership* (Kent, Ohio, 1999); S. E. Woodworth, *Six Armies in Tennessee: The Chickamauga and Chattanooga Campaigns* (Lincoln, Nebraska, 1998); S. E. Woodworth, *No Band of Brothers: Problems of the Rebel High Command* (Columbia, Missouri, 1999).
37. Ross, *Flintlock to Rifle*, pp. 164–6.
38. P. Griffith, *Battle Tactics of the Civil War* (New Haven, 1987).
39. J. Black, *War: Past, Present and Future* (Stroud, 2000).

Chapter 7: Conflict Within the West, 1861–82

1. G. Wawro, *The Austro-Prussian War: Austria's War with Prussia and Italy in 1866* (Cambridge, 1996).
2. C. J. J. J. Ardant du Picq, *Études sur le Combat: Combat Antique et Moderne*, J. M. Greeley and R. C. Cotton (trans.) (New York, 1921 [Paris, 1942]; partial version, Paris, 1880).
3. D. Showalter, "Soldiers into Postmasters: The Electric Telegraph as an Instrument of Command in the Prussian Army", *Military Affairs* 37 (1973), pp. 48–52.
4. D. D. Irvine, "The Origin of Capital Staffs", *Journal of Modern History* 10 (1938), pp. 161–79.
5. P. D. Jamieson, *Crossing the Deadly Ground: United States Army Tactics, 1865–1899* (Tuscaloosa, Alabama, 1994); T. R. Brereton, *Educating the US Army: Arthur L. Wagner and Reform, 1875–1905* (Lincoln, Nebraska, 2000).
6. D. Showalter, "From Deterrence to Doomsday Machine: The German Way of War, 1890–1914", *Journal of Military History* 64 (2000), p. 682; M. Howard, *The Franco-Prussian War* (1961); D. Showalter, *Railroads and Rifles: Soldiers, Technology and the Unification of Germany* (Hamden, Connecticut, 1975); A. Bucholz, *Moltke, Schlieffen, and Prussian War Planning* (1991); A. Bucholz, *Moltke and the German Wars, 1864–1871* (2001); D. J. Hughes (ed.), *Moltke on the Art of War* (Novato, California, 1993).
7. B. H. Reid, *The Origins of the American Civil War* (1996).
8. P. Griffith, *Battle Tactics of the Civil War* (New Haven, 1987); B. H. Reid, *Civil War in the United States 1861–1865* (2000).
9. E. Hagerman, *The American Civil War and the Origins of Modern Warfare* (Bloomington, Indiana, 1988).
10. R. Pickenpaugh, *Rescue By Rail: Troop Transfer and the Civil War in the West* (Lincoln, Nebraska, 1998).
11. D. Evans, *Sherman's Horsemen: Union Cavalry Operations in the Atlanta Campaign* (Bloomington, Indiana, 1996).
12. P. Maslowski, "To the Edge of Greatness: The United States, 1783–1865", in *The Making of Strategy. Rulers, States, and War*, W. Murray, M. Knox and A. Bernstein (eds) (Cambridge, 1994), p. 236.
13. J. R. Arnold, *Grant Wins the War* (New York, 1997).

14. S. W. Sears, *To the Gates of Richmond: The Peninsula Campaign* (New York, 1992); S. H. Newton, *Joseph E. Johnston and the Defense of Richmond* (Lawrence, Kansas, 1999).

15. B. H. Reid, "Rationality and Irrationality in Union Strategy, April 1861–March 1862", *War in History* 1 (1994), p. 38.

16. A. Castel, *Decision in the West: The Atlanta Campaign of 1864* (Lawrence, Kansas, 1994); G. C. Rhea, *The Battle of the Wilderness, May 5–6, 1864* (Baton Rouge, Louisiana, 1994); M. A. Palmer, *Lee Moves North: Robert E. Lee on the Offensive* (New York, 1998).

17. R. W. Maney, *Marching to Cold Harbor: Victory and Failure, 1864* (Shippensburg, Pennsylvania, 1995).

18. G. W. Gallagher, *The Confederate War. How Popular Will, Nationalism, and Military Strategy Could Not Stave Off Defeat* (Cambridge, Mass., 1997), pp. 58–9, 115.

19. V. D. Hanson, *The Soul of Battle: From Ancient Times to the Present Day. How Three Great Liberators Vanquished Tyranny* (New York, 1999).

20. J. T. Glatthaar, *The March to the Seas and Beyond: Sherman's Troops in the Savannah and Carolinas Campaigns* (Baton Rouge, Louisiana, 1995).

21. G. W. Gallagher (ed.), *Fighting for the Confederacy. The Personal Recollections of General Edward Porter Alexander* (Chapel Hill, North Carolina, 1989), p. 436.

22. M. R. Grandstaff, "Preserving the 'Habits and Usages of War': William Tecumseh Sherman, Professional Reform, and the US Army Officer Corps, 1865–1881, Revisited", *Journal of Military History* 62 (1988), pp. 521–45.

23. J. L. Tone, "The Machete and the Liberation of Cuba", *Journal of Military History* 62 (1998), pp. 14–15

24. A. Ferrer, *Insurgent Cuba: Race, Nation, and Revolution, 1868–1898* (Chapel Hill, North Carolina, 1999).

25. J. A. Dabbs, *The French Army in Mexico, 1861–1867* (The Hague, 1963).

26. S. M. O'Brien, *Mountain Partisans: Guerrilla Warfare in the Southern Appalachians, 1861–1865* (Westport, Connecticut, 1999).

27. H. G. Warren, *Paraguay and the Triple Alliance: The Postwar Decade, 1869–1878* (Austin, Texas, 1978), pp. 8–26.

28. W. F. Sater, "Chile During the First Months of the War of the Pacific", *Journal of Latin American Studies* 5 (1973), pp. 133–58.

29. W. F. Sater, *Chile and the War of the Pacific* (Lincoln, Nebraska, 1986).

30. G. V. Rauch, *Conflict in the Southern Cone: The Argentine Military and the Boundary Dispute with Chile, 1870–1902* (Westport, Connecticut, 1999).

31. R. Weigley, *The Age of Battles: The Quest for Decisive Warfare from Breitenfeld to Waterloo* (Bloomington, Indiana, 1991), p. 538. For emphasis on attrition see also R. Epstein, "Patterns of Change and Continuity in Nineteenth-Century Warfare", *Journal of Military History* 56 (1992), pp. 375–88.

Chapter 8: Social and Political Contexts

1. J. A. Lynn, "The Evolution of Army Style in the Modern West, 800–2000", *International History Review* 18 (1996), pp. 505–45.

2. R. Kohn, *Eagle and Sword: The Beginnings of the Military Establishment in America* (New York, 1975); M. D. Pearlman, *Warmaking and American Democracy: The Struggle over Military Strategy 1700 to the Present* (Lawrence, Kansas, 1999).

3. A. Forrest, *Conscripts and Deserters: the Army and French Society during the Revolution and Empire* (Oxford, 1989); J. E. Cookson, *The British Armed Nation, 1793–1815* (Oxford, 1997). For desertion from the army of the Napoleonic Kingdom of Italy, see F. C. Schneid, *Soldiers of Napoleon's Kingdom of Italy. Army, State, and Society, 1800–1815* (Boulder, Colorado, 1995), pp. 90–103.

4. O. Connelly, *Napoleon's Satellite Kingdoms* (New York, 1966); S. Woolf, *Napoleon's Integration*

of Europe (1991).

5. J. R. Aymes, *La Guerre d'Indépendence Espagnole, 1808–1814* (Paris, 1973).

6. M. Finley, *The Most Monstrous of Wars: The Napoleonic Guerrilla War in Southern Italy, 1806–1811* (Columbia, South Carolina, 1994); G. Eyck, *Loyal Rebels: Andreas Hofer and the Tyrolean Uprising of 1809* (Lanham, Maryland, 1986); D. W. Alexander, *Rod of Iron: French Counterinsurgency Policy in Aragon during the Peninsular War* (Wilmington, Delaware, 1985); J. L. Tone, *The Fatal Knot: The Guerrilla War in Navarre and the Defeat of Napoleon in Spain* (Chapel Hill, 1994).

7. J. A. Lynn, "The Pattern of Army Growth, 1445–1945", in *Tools of War. Instruments, Ideas and Institutions of Warfare, 1445–1871*, J. A. Lynn (ed.) (Urbana, Illinois, 1990), pp. 4–5, 9.

8. G. Wawro, *The Austro–Prussian War: Austria's War with Prussia and Italy in 1866* (Cambridge, 1996), pp. 83–7.

9. S. Förster and J. Nagler (eds.), *On the Road to Total War: the American Civil War and the German Wars of Unification, 1861–71* (Cambridge, 1997), pp. 393–411.

10. W. H. Riker, *Soldiers of the States: The Role of the National Guard in American Democracy* (Washington, 1957); R. M. Fogelson, *America's Armories: Architecture, Society, and Public Order* (Cambridge, Mass., 1989).

11. S. H. Myerly, *British Military Spectacle from the Napoleonic Wars through the Crimea* (Cambridge, Mass., 1996).

12. E. J. Hess, *The Union Soldier in Battle: Enduring the Ordeal of Combat* (1997); S. J. Watson, "Religion and Combat Motivation in the Confederate Armies", *Journal of Military History* 58 (1994), pp. 29–56; J. M. McPherson, *For Cause and Comrades: Why Men Fought in the Civil War* (New York, 1997); J. A. Frank, *With Ballot and Bayonet: The Political Socialization of American Civil War Soldiers* (Athens, Georgia, 1998).

13. Frederick II to General von Tauentzien, 2 Sept. 1784, Christie's catalogue for auction on 29 May 1985, p. 20.

14. E. Ingram, "Great Britain and Russia", in *Great Power Rivalries*, W. R. Thompson (ed.) (Columbia, South Carolina, 1999), p. 294.

15. H. M. Ward, *The War for Independence and the Transformation of American Society* (1999), p. 93

16. J. E. Thomson, *Mercenaries, Pirates, and Sovereigns: State-building and Extraterritorial Violence in Early Modern Europe* (Princeton, 1994).

17. D. J. Weber, *The Spanish Frontier in North America* (New Haven, 1992), p. 198.

18. F. W. Kagan, *The Military Reforms of Nicholas I: The Origins of the Modern Russian Army* (1999).

19. C. Van Dyke, *Russian Imperial Military Doctrine and Education, 1832–1914* (New York, 1990).

20. W. B. Skelton, *An American Profession of Arms: The Army Officer Corps, 1784–1861* (Lawrence, Kansas, 1992).

21. J. L. Morrison, *The Best School in the World: West Point, the Pre-Civil War Years 1833–1866* (Kent, Ohio, 1986).

22. C. von Clausewitz, *On War*, M. Howard and P. Paret (eds) (Princeton, New Jersey, 1976); P. Paret, *Clausewitz and the State* (Oxford, 1976); A. Gat, *The Origins of Military Thought from the Enlightenment to Clausewitz* (Oxford, 1989); *Carl von Clausewitz: Historical and Political Writings*, P. Paret and D. Moran (eds) (Princeton, 1992).

23. L. Riall, *Sicily and the Unification of Italy: Liberal Policy and Local Power, 1859–1866* (Oxford, 1998).

Chapter 9: Conclusions: Revisiting Modernity

1. Greene to Colonel Edward Carrington, 4 Dec. 1780, in R. K. Showman (ed.), *The Papers of General Nathanael Greene*, vol. VI (Chapel Hill, 1991), p. 517.

2. Fulton to Lord Grenville, British Foreign Secretary, 2 Sept. 1806, BL Add. 71593, fo. 134.

3. S. Wilkinson, *The Rise of General Bonaparte* (Oxford, 1930), pp. 149–50.

4. A. Bucholz, *Moltke and the German Wars, 1864–1871* (2001).

5. G. Wawro, "An 'Army of Pigs': The Technical, Social, and Political Bases of Austrian Shock Tactics, 1859–1866", *Journal of Military History* 59 (1995), pp. 410–13.

6. J. Bailey, *The First World War and the Birth of Modern Warfare* (Camberley, 1996).

7. A. Roland, *Underwater Warfare in the Age of Sail* (Bloomington, Indiana, 1978).

8. D. A. Mindell, *War, Technology, and Experience aboard the USS "Monitor"* (Baltimore, 2000), e.g. p. 15.

9. BL Add. 49016, fos. 7–26.

10. K. Alder, *Engineering the Revolution: Arms and Enlightenment in France, 1763–1815* (Princeton, 1997).

11. BL Add. 49059, fos. 27, 30.

Selected Bibliography

For reasons of space, there is an emphasis on recent works. Earlier and other scholarship can be pursued through their bibliographies and footnotes. It is very useful to consult two relevant journals, the *Journal of Military History* and *War in History*, as well as a yearbook, *The Consortium on Revolutionary Europe 1750–1850, Selected Papers*.

General works

G. Best, *War and Society in Revolutionary Europe, 1770–1870* (1982).
J. M. Black, *War and the World 1450–2000* (New Haven, 1998).
J. M. Black, *War: Past, Present and Future* (Stroud, 2000).
B. Bond, *The Pursuit of Victory: From Napoleon to Saddam Hussein* (Oxford, 1996).
M. Howard, *The Invention of Peace: Reflections on War and International Order* (2000).
W. H. McNeill, *The Pursuit of Power: Technology, Armed Force, and Society since A.D. 1000* (Oxford, 1982).

Chapter 1. Western Warfare in its Global Context 1775–1815

C. A. Bayly, *Imperial Meridian: The British Empire and the World 1780–1830* (Harlow, 1989).
J. A. de Moor and H. L.Wesseling (eds), *Imperialism and War: Essays on Colonial Wars in Asia and Africa* (Leiden, 1989).
A. Starkey, *European and Native American Warfare in North America 1675–1795* (1998).

Chapter 2. Two Episodes of Modernity? The American War of Independence and the French Revolutionary War

J.-P. Bertaud, *The Army of the French Revolution* (Princeton, 1988).
J. M. Black, *European Warfare, 1660–1815* (1994).

C. Duffy, *The Military Experience in the Age of Reason* (2nd edn, 1998).
J. Lynn, *The Bayonets of the Republic: Motivation and Tactics in the Army of Revolutionary France, 1791–94* (2nd edn, Boulder, Colorado, 1996).
R. S. Quimby, *The Background of Napoleonic Warfare. The Theory of Military Tactics in Eighteenth-Century France* (New York, 1957).
H. M. Ward, *The War for Independence and the Transformation of American Society: War and Society in The United States 1775–83* (1999).
P. Wilson, *German Armies: War and German Society, 1648–1806* (1997).

Chapter 3. Napoleon and His Opponents

D. Alexander, *Rod of Iron: French Counterinsurgency Policy in Aragon during the Peninsular War* (Wilmington, 1985).
D. G. Chandler, *The Campaigns of Napoleon* (1966).
O. Connelly, *Blundering to Glory: Napoleon's Military Campaigns* (2nd edn, 1998).
R. M. Epstein, *Napoleon's Last Victory and the Emergence of Modern War* (Lawrence, 1994).
C. J. Esdaile, *The Wars of Napoleon* (1995).
R. Muir, *Tactics and the Experience of Battle in the Age of Napoleon* (New Haven, 1998).
G. E. Rothenberg, *The Art of Warfare in the Age of Napoleon* (Bloomington, Indiana, 1978).

Chapter 4. Naval Power and Warfare

J. F. Beeler, *British Naval Policy in the Gladstone-Disraeli Era, 1866–1880* (Cambridge, 1997).
D. K. Brown, *Before the Ironclad: Development of Ship Design, Propulsion and Armament in the Royal Navy, 1815–1860* (1990).
J. Glete, *Navies and Nations: Warships, Navies and State Building in Europe and America, 1500–1860* (Stockholm, 1993).
C. I. Hamilton, *Anglo-French Naval Rivalry, 1840–1870* (Oxford, 1994).
R. Harding, *Seapower and Naval Warfare 1650–1830* (1999).
A. Lambert, *Battleships in Transition: The Creation of the Steam Battlefleet, 1815–1860* (1984).
D. A. Mindell, *War, Technology and Experience Abroad the USS "Monitor"* (Baltimore, 2000).
T. Ropp, *The Development of a Modern Navy: French Naval Policy, 1871–1904* (1987).
L. Sondhaus, *Naval Warfare 1815–1914* (2000).

Chapter 5. The Global Context, 1815–1882

J. Belich, *The New Zealand Wars and the Victorian Interpretation of Racial Conflict* (Auckland, 1986).
D. Headrick, *The Tentacles of Progress: Technology Transfer in the Age of Imperialism* (Oxford, 1988).
V. G. Kiernan, *From Conquest to Collapse: European Empires from 1815 to 1960* (New York, 1982).
A. T. Sullivan, *Thomas-Robert Bugeaud, France and Algeria, 1784–1849: Power, Politics, and the Good Society* (Hamden, 1983).
B. Vandervort, *Wars of Imperial Conquest in Africa, 1830–1914* (1998).

Chapter 6. After Waterloo: Conflict Within the West, 1815–60

F. Coppa, *The Origins of the Italian Wars of Independence* (1992).
G. Cox, *The Halt in the Mud: French Strategic Planning from Waterloo to Sedan* (Boulder, 1994).
J. S. Curtiss, *Russia's Crimean War* (Durham, North Carolina, 1979).

P. Griffith, *Military Thought in the French Army, 1815–51* (Manchester, 1989).

A. Lambert, *The Crimean War: British Grand Strategy Against Russia* (Manchester, 1990).

H. Strachan, *Wellington's Legacy: The Reform of the British Army, 1830–54* (Manchester, 1984).

H. Strachan, *From Waterloo to Balaclava: Tactics, Technology, and the British Army, 1815–54* (Cambridge, 1985).

G. Wawro, *Warfare and Society in Europe 1792–1914* (2000).

J. R. White, *The Prussian Army, 1640–1871* (Lanham, 1996).

Chapter 7. Conflict Within the West, 1861–82

A. Bucholz, *Moltke, Schlieffen and Prussian War Planning* (New York, 1991).

G. Craig, *The Battle of Königgrätz* (Philadelphia, 1964).

S. Förster and J. Nagler (eds.), *On the Road to Total War: the American Civil War and the German Wars of Unification, 1861–71* (Cambridge, 1997).

H. Hattaway and A. Jones, *How the North Won* (Urbana, Illinois, 1984).

R. Holmes, *The Road to Sedan: The French Army, 1866–70* (1984).

M. Howard, *The Franco–Prussian War* (1961).

D. Hughes (ed.), *Moltke on the Art of War: Selected Writings* (Novato, California, 1993).

B. W. Menning, *Bayonets before Bullets: The Imperial Russian Army, 1861–1914* (Bloomington, Indiana, 1992).

A. Sked, *The Survival of the Habsburg Empire: Radetzky, the Imperial Army and the Class War, 1848* (1979).

G. E. Rothenberg, *The Army of Francis Joseph* (West Lafayette, Indiana, 1976).

D. E. Showalter, *Railroads and Rifles: Soldiers, Technology, and the Unification of Germany* (Hamden, Conn., 1975).

G. Wawro, *The Austro–Prussian War: Austria's War with Prussia and Italy in 1866* (Cambridge, 1996).

Chapter 8. Social and Political Contexts

G. Craig, *The Politics of the Prussian Army, 1640–1945* (Oxford, 1955).

A. Gat, *The Development of Military Thought: The Nineteenth Century* (Oxford, 1992).

M. Howard, *Clausewitz* (Oxford, 1983).

S. H. Myerly, *British Military Spectacle: From the Napoleonic Wars through the Crimea* (Cambridge, Massachusetts, 1996).

D. Porch, *Army and Revolution: France, 1815–48* (1974).

L. Sondhaus, *In the Service of the Emperor: Italians in the Austrian Armed Forces, 1814–1918* (Boulder, 1990).

E. Weber, *Peasants into Frenchmen* (Stanford, 1976).

Index